(P)RESCRIPTION NARRATIVES

Interventions in Nineteenth-Century American Literature and Culture
Series Editors: Christopher Hanlon, Sarah R. Robbins, Andrew Taylor

Available
Liminal Whiteness in Early US Fiction
Hannah Lauren Murray

Carlyle, Emerson and the Transatlantic Uses of Authority: Literature, Print, Performance
Tim Sommer

Crossings in Nineteenth-Century American Culture: Junctures of Time, Space, Self and Politics
Edward Sugden

(P)rescription Narratives: Feminist Medical Fiction and the Failure of American Censorship
Stephanie Peebles Tavera

Forthcoming
Melville's Americas: Hemispheric Sympathies, Transatlantic Contagion
Nicholas Spengler

The Aesthetics of History and Slave Revolution in Antebellum America
Kevin Modestino

New Perspectives on Mary E. Wilkins Freeman: Reading with and against the Grain
Stephanie Palmer, Myrto Drizou and Cécile Roudeau

www.edinburghuniversitypress.com/series/incal

(P)RESCRIPTION NARRATIVES

Feminist Medical Fiction and the Failure of American Censorship

Stephanie Peebles Tavera

EDINBURGH
University Press

Edinburgh University Press is one of the leading university presses in the UK. We publish academic books and journals in our selected subject areas across the humanities and social sciences, combining cutting-edge scholarship with high editorial and production values to produce academic works of lasting importance. For more information visit our website: edinburghuniversitypress.com

© Stephanie Peebles Tavera 2022

Edinburgh University Press Ltd
The Tun—Holyrood Road
12(2f) Jackson's Entry
Edinburgh EH8 8PJ

First published in hardback by Edinburgh University Press 2022

Typeset in 10/12.5 Adobe Sabon by
IDSUK (DataConnection) Ltd

A CIP record for this book is available from the British Library

ISBN 978 1 4744 9319 2 (hardback)
ISBN 978 1 4744 9320 8 (paperback)
ISBN 978 1 4744 9321 5 (webready PDF)
ISBN 978 1 4744 9322 2 (epub)

The right of Stephanie Peebles Tavera to be identified as the author of this work has been asserted in accordance with the Copyright, Designs and Patents Act 1988, and the Copyright and Related Rights Regulations 2003 (SI No. 2498).

CONTENTS

List of Figures	vi
Acknowledgments	vii
Introduction	1
R_x 1 Crip Medicine: Environmental Health and the Matter of Hysteria	29
R_x 2 Listen for the New Man: From Narrative Prosthesis to Narrative Medicine	68
R_x 3 Kinetic Medicine: Superposition of Black Female Subjectivity before the Law	102
R_x 4 Affective Fear: Vulnerability and Risk in Anti-VD Campaign Counternarratives	141
Conclusion: Medical Theater—The Birth of Anti-Lynching Plays and Reproductive Justice	178
Bibliography	197
Index	210

FIGURES

3.1 *Practical Amalgamation* series, title unknown (1839). Lithograph print by Edward William Clay. Courtesy of the American Antiquarian Society. 104
3.2 *Practical Amalgamation* series, "The Wedding" (1839). Lithograph print by Edward William Clay. Courtesy of the American Antiquarian Society. 104
4.1 Herald for *Damaged Goods* (1914), an American silent film starring Richard Bennett. The herald boasts the original Broadway cast. 148
4.2 Herald for *Damaged Goods* (1914), featuring Richard Bennett in the starring role of George Dupont, who originated the role in the Broadway play. This herald contains the full cast listing. 149

ACKNOWLEDGMENTS

(P)rescription Narratives was a completely different book prior to the COVID-19 pandemic. Teaching from home, while parenting children (and recovering from giving birth just one day before quarantine began), as well as navigating the anxiety of an unknown future, taught me how to express compassion for myself and others. I've learned to slow down and be patient with myself, my students, and my children. Importantly, I no longer ascribe to the cultural belief that (hyper)productivity is a marker of success. I write on my own terms. My experience of the pandemic also taught me to read differently, not least because I read for expressions of compassion and empathy in the text. I have become acutely aware of how the cultural milieu in which I live shapes my reading, thinking, and writing. My life is woven throughout this book. I could not have written it any other way. Not after the summer of 2020, when we were in lockdown in Texas with a newborn babe, a stir-crazy ten-year-old, and two very confused canines whose owners rarely left the house anymore. Although the research for this book project began during my doctorate and evolved out of my dissertation at the University of Texas at Arlington, *(P)rescription Narratives* is my "pandemic baby." It was inexorably affected—impressed—by the pandemic, and that context shaped my thinking.

I have dedicated this book to my boys, Aidan and Micah. It is my sincerest hope that when you are old enough to read it, you not only glean some understanding of who I am—who your mother is and was at this moment in her life—but also that you recognize this book as a symbol of what is possible

ACKNOWLEDGMENTS

with hard work and determination. I love you both deeply. To be your mother is the greatest pleasure of my life. To my husband, my love, and my partner, Esteban Tavera Morales: How do I begin to thank you for your unwavering perseverance, partnership, and love through this impossible career of mine? Thank you for your generosity, for allowing me to disappear and write without distractions when I need to meet a deadline. And of course, for being a sounding board and listening to me work out the specifics of my claims, the frustrations of the writing process, and my own self-doubt. Thank you also for resisting the urge to fix my frustrations. You are the best friend and partner this gal could have.

I have had the extraordinary privilege of working and thinking alongside exceptional people throughout my doctoral studies and early career. I must first and foremost thank my doctoral cohort, my accountibili-buddies, and *the original* writing group: Mimi Rowntree, Sarah Shelton, and Joul Smith. Once, many years ago during our first semester of doctoral studies, Joul prophesied that "one of us" would "make it big" with the tenure job, the book publication, the recognizability. And he would be proud to say "I knew her when." I hope I have indeed made you all proud. Thank you to the members of my dissertation writing cohorts, who not only included (at various times) members of my doctoral cohort, but also: Robert LaRue, Rachel Mariboho, and Natalya Cherry. Since graduating and joining the faculty of Texas A&M University—Central Texas, I have had the pleasure of being the accountibili-buddy of Roslyn Schoen. While I try (and happily fail) to stay within the boundaries, traditions, and conventions of my discipline, I am a better thinker because of my extra-disciplinary friendships.

Certain people leave an impression on our lives more strongly than others. To my dearest friend Mimi, you are the bravest of all. I became vulnerable in the act of writing this book because you believed in me. Thank you for reading my book in full, from the first word to the last, and for reading certain chapters *twice*. I am so blessed to call you my best friend. To my dear friend Robert, thank you for always pushing me to think creatively and critically — even, and especially, when I am tired (of life, of academia, of the burden of feeling so much about everyone and everything). Our conversations over nearly a decade of friendship have made me a sharper writer. I am deeply grateful of the careful attention you offered in reading, responding, and conversing with me about Chapter 3 of this book. I must also thank the graduate students of my spring 2020 "Medical Fiction" course who provided lively discussions and thoughtful engagement about the feminist medical fiction I explore in this book: Katahdin Benard, Shelby Claridge, Danea Dameron, Stephanie Muro, Genesis Roblero, Robin Scheafnocker, Jillian Shanks, Sue Sitton, Stacey Torres, and Nelsie Valenzuela. Our weekly class was a (unlikely!) therapeutic refuge in the midst of the chaos of the pandemic. Thank you for showing up in every sense of the phrase.

ACKNOWLEDGMENTS

I would be remiss if I did not thank all of the mentors—past and present—who encouraged me, believed in me, and guided me toward this point in my career. Many thanks to the series editors of this book: Christopher Hanlon, Sarah Ruffing Robbins, and Andrew Taylor. I deeply appreciate the time and attention you freely gave in reading drafts, providing feedback, participating in virtual meetings with me, and offering advice on your own experience as first-time authors. I am also grateful for the faith and encouragement of my senior commissioning editor, Michelle Houston, and her assistant, Susannah Butler, who diligently worked together to put my book into the hands of readers. Profound thanks to my dissertation committee at the University of Texas at Arlington for their dedicated time and attention to my work, as well as for modeling rigorous scholarship and professional practices: Kenneth Roemer, Stacy Alaimo, Desiree Henderson, and Neill Matheson. To my Master's thesis chair at the University of Texas at Dallas, Theresa Towner: Thank you for encouraging me to challenge my own self-limiting beliefs during such a formative time in my life (and for teaching me how to read William Faulkner). You are *magical*. Thank you to Barbara McCaskill, who provided vital encouragement and mentorship while I was on the job market, as well as for making introductions on my behalf among key scholars in my field. Who knew that a pre-conference mentorship breakfast might be life-changing? Last, but never least, I thank my earliest teachers of English, who cultivated my love for learning and my love of literature, especially Rhonda Kaufman Gill, my eleventh-grade English teacher, and Julie Leslie (formerly Martin), my eighth-grade English teacher.

It is a remarkable thing when established scholars extend their valuable time and effort to advise early career scholars, especially when such advising occurs outside of prescribed academic spaces. A warm thank you to those established scholars who have freely given the rare privilege of informal advising at lunches, dinners, and in moments of personal downtime at conferences: Sherryl Vint, Marta Werner, Dana Seitler, and Heather Houser. Small efforts matter because they can have a significant impact, and your small efforts are appreciated. I also extend my deep gratitude to those scholars in nineteenth-century American studies who have maintained correspondence and whose published work has been inspirational throughout my own writing process, namely: Sari Altschuler, Britt Rusert, and Kyla Schuller. Any good scholar knows that opportunities to give an invited talk on your research during its formative stages help sharpen your argument. Thank you to David Arditi and Sonja Stephenson Watson for inviting me to give a talk on the research presented in this book at your respective events, the UTA Center for Theory's Fall 2017 Colloquium and the UTA Women's and Gender Studies Program's 2016 Brown Bag Luncheon.

I have had the singular pleasure of working alongside wonderful colleagues throughout my career. While at the University of Texas at Arlington, I had the privilege of ongoing support from: Estee Beck, Paul Conrad, Sean Farrell,

Jason Hogue, Joanna Johnson, Peggy Kulesz, Jennifer Miller, Erin Murrah-Mandril, Amy Speier, Amy Tigner, Jim Warren, and Kathryn Warren. Special thanks to Tim Morris, who introduced me to Charlotte Perkins Gilman's *The Crux* and encouraged me to pursue research on this understudied subject of women's medical fiction once I had discovered that it was "a thing." I also extend my heartfelt thanks to Penny Ingram, whose guidance during and after my doctoral education and general praise among colleagues on my behalf continues to impact me in wonderful ways. At Texas A&M University—Central Texas, I thank the exceptional members of the College of Arts and Sciences and of the Humanities Department, who have provided stimulating conversations that make me think about my subject differently, including: Bruce Bowles, Amber Dunai, Lynn Greenwood, Tim Hemmis, Christine Jones, Cadra Peterson McDaniel, Mienie Roberts, and Allen Redmon. The joy of doing interdisciplinary work is in the opportunity to work alongside a heterogeneous group of scholars whose own disciplines affect my identity as a scholar and my work in positive ways. Special thanks to Allen for mentoring me as an early career faculty member, and for listening to me as I think through the specifics of my theorizing on this book. I do hope readers find it as "compelling" as you.

I would be remiss if I did not acknowledge the support and advocacy of those university staff members who have made my work possible and my life a little easier. For every travel reimbursement, financial aid disbursement, and faculty load form, among other kinds of paperwork that you have processed on my behalf, I sincerely thank: Margie Jackymack, Yael Sasley, and Rosemarie Torres. Sometimes the perspective of librarians helps us think about the complexities of making our work visible in an increasingly digital world. To Margaret Dawson, our humanities librarian at A&M—Central Texas, thank you for helping me settle on a title for this book because of your expertise on cataloguing. I extend deep thanks to Karen Clos for advocating on behalf of the faculty at A&M—Central Texas in the wider world of media production. You put us on the map. Finally, I must thank my provost Peg Gray-Vickery for her ongoing support of my research and scholarly identity in medical humanities, or "medicine and literature," and for welcoming me as a member of the A&M—Central Texas family. Only at a small, regional university like A&M—Central Texas can faculty like myself build a kind of professional working relationship with the university provost, and what a privilege it has been.

Whether or not they ever read my book from cover to cover (And it's totally okay if you don't. No pressure!), there are family members whose ongoing love and support allowed for the production of this book and for my growth as an individual and a scholar. To my parents, Steve and Christine Peebles, thank you for raising me in a loving home and for always encouraging me to be my best self. A mis suegros, Alicia Morales Meneses y Carlos Tavera Vargas, gracias por su apoyo, ahora y siempre. Primero Dios, y todo lo demás seguirá. Thank you also to Lara Best, our nanny, who made my job of caring for an infant-turned-toddler manageable in the midst of a pandemic and while writing this book.

This book would not have been possible without institutional research and writing support. Profound thanks to the Jacob Rader Marcus Center at the American Jewish Archives in Cincinnati, Ohio for hosting me during Spring Break in March 2015. The intensive research conducted in the AJA archives during that week provided me with material on Annie Nathan Meyer, portions of which have been used for the fourth chapter of this book. Special thanks to archivist Kevin Proffitt, who arranged my visit to the American Jewish Archives, and to Gail Madden, who arranged my stay in the Sisterhood Dormitory at Hebrew Union College. I extend a warm thank you to the Moorland Spingarn Research Center at Howard University for sending me archival materials in the midst of a pandemic when I could not travel to the archives themselves. Special thanks to archivist Sonja Woods who orchestrated this "distance-learning" version of archival research on the Angelina Weld Grimké papers, portions of which appear in the conclusion of this book. I also wish to thank Eric Hayot for his book *The Elements of Academic Style: Writing the Humanities*, which taught me how to find my voice within and beyond the conventions of academic writing.

For financial support in completion of this manuscript, I thank the College of Arts and Sciences at Texas A&M University—Central Texas, which generously awarded me a research grant during the spring 2021 semester. For early financial support of this project, I thank the College of Liberal Arts at the University of Texas at Arlington for multiple awards including a Dissertation Research Travel Award to the American Jewish Archives.

DEDICATION
For my boys

INTRODUCTION

Early in Annie Nathan Meyer's medical novel *Helen Brent, M.D.* (1892), the titular woman physician Dr. Helen Brent examines her future protégé, Lotus Bayley, as a patient when Lotus's mother brings her to the clinic for what she considers the signs and symptoms of "nervous prostration." Mrs. Bayley offers a litany of complaints on behalf of her daughter, all of which underscore Mrs. Bayley's discomfort with her daughter's choice to attend college and study chemistry: "'She is very headstrong,'" Mrs. Bayley reports, "'and she will persist in going on with those ridiculous studies of hers,'" causing her to not eat well and grow "round shouldered and pale" from poring over books.[1] Even in 1892, before an audience of white male physicians, Mrs. Bayley's complaints would be considered legitimate and would be further legitimized by a patriarchal medical authority who considers deviant social behavior a sign or symptom of disorder. Physician and author of medical advice literature Dr. Edward H. Clarke popularized the belief that young women suffer from nervous prostration, or hysteria, when the minimum standards that society requires for academic and professional success are too rigorous, given that the female sexual system demands more energy to perform its expected functions, namely menstruation, ovulation, pregnancy, and lactation. Clarke's treatise *Sex in Education* (1873), which cites case studies of hysteria among Clarke's own female patients as evidence for the need of a "separate spheres" education system, was so popular that it sold out little more than one week after publication and prompted an additional sixteen editions over the course of the next two decades.[2]

Importantly, Clarke does not argue that the sex organs unique to the female body inherently disable her as a mature woman, a characterization that historians Ben Barker-Benfield, John S. Haller and Robin M. Haller, and Mary Spongberg, among others, espouse in their arguments that nineteenth-century medical theory and practice was foremost a social science. Literary historian Kyla Schuller updates this impression in her recent study, *The Biopolitics of Feeling: Race, Sex, and Science in the Nineteenth Century*. Nineteenth-century scientists actually theorize the body as a "biocultural formation" that is molded by both material and cultural processes.[3] Our twenty-first-century scholarly impression of biological determinism as dominating nineteenth-century scientific discourse persists because of a long-standing commitment to social constructionist frameworks rather than a negotiated framework that accounts for theories of social construction, materiality, and affect. Nineteenth-century scientists did not agree with one another on the biological origins of gender, race, or disability, a point I will examine in R_x 1 (Chapter 1) concerning scientific disagreements over the origins of hysteria. Schuller suggests that we characterize the nineteenth century as a period of scientific disorder during which scientists struggled to impose order on a rapidly professionalizing system of healthcare and its subject of study and practice, the human body. Perhaps the term "sociobiological indeterminism," or as I will write it, "(socio)biological (in)determinism," best encapsulates their attempt to rhetorically impose order, draw boundaries, and regulate stasis on the precarious bodies of individuals and of knowledge during the late nineteenth and early twentieth centuries.[4]

Such a re-characterization of nineteenth-century medical theory and practice does not and cannot rescue its proponents from their sexist, racist, and ableist agenda. Clarke, for instance, conflates sex with gender and disability in his popular treatise *Sex in Education* when he defines the female body under the rubric of disability because of its supposed innate vulnerability to illness, a weakness Clarke locates in the "reproductive apparatus," which includes the uterus, ovaries, and hormones. Annie Nathan Meyer had no truck with this brand of sexist, racist, or ableist medicine. She responds to the sexist medicine that Mrs. Bayley recites with a literal prescription—complete with R_x symbol—that underscores the material affect of social conventions upon the bodies of young women like Lotus Bayley:

> R_x Loose, sensible, plain gowns
> Gymnasium at least twice weekly.
> Horseback or bicycle tri-weekly for an hour in morning, after light breakfast.
> Early hours for retiring.
> Liberty to seek the quiet of her room, if desired.
> Liberty to seek the companionship of her classmates.[5]

Dr. Brent's prescription recognizes no less than three factors contributing to Lotus's oppression: corsets, which physically cause organ displacement and limit the flow of oxygen; passivity, caused by lack of exercise; and constant social interaction, which forecloses engagement in higher education or intellectual discourse. Using the act of prescribing a therapeutic regimen, Dr. Brent "r_xe-scripts" or "(p)re-scribes" the role of the female body in society as an active agent for public change. Instead of continuing the cycle of gender oppression through dressing for society events, gossiping at luncheons, or waltzing "half-naked in a ballroom," all in the service of attracting an eligible husband, Dr. Brent's prescription breaks the cycle by medically authorizing a space for Lotus to study chemistry at the Root Memorial Hospital and College for Women.[6]

Through her spokesperson Dr. Helen Brent, Meyer assumes the authority of medical science to engage her (white) male peers in conversation about gender double standards for physicians in the emerging field of gynecology. She further addresses the animacy of diseases such as syphilis at the expense of the de-animacy of the female body, a false and damaging cultural narrative that many nineteenth-century medical writers and practitioners, Clarke included, were responsible for perpetuating. Meyer was not alone in adopting the genre of medical fiction as a space for theorizing the female body and its potential to affect change. She was in good company among literary contemporaries like Louisa May Alcott, Rebecca Harding Davis, Elizabeth Stuart Phelps, Frances Ellen Watkins Harper, and Charlotte Perkins Gilman, all of whom wrote works of medical fiction that challenge patriarchal medico-legal narratives of the female body during a period of censorship in the United States under Comstock law. Medical fiction as a genre of writing was already gaining in popularity before the arrival of feminist writers to the scene. Frederick Wegener speculates that imaginative portrayals of the woman doctor emerge in earnest during the 1850s, after Elizabeth Blackwell famously became the first woman in the United States to obtain a medical degree in 1849.[7] However, Sari Altschuler locates the medical imagination at work in earlier cultural productions of American fiction as a response to crises such as the yellow fever epidemic (Charles Brockden Brown's *Arthur Mervyn*), the cholera epidemic (Edgar Allan Poe's "The Sphinx"), and debates over the use of anesthesia (Oliver Wendell Holmes's *Elsie Venner*).

Yet the specific concerns of women writers remain absent from this conversation. Scholarship on woman-authored medical fiction as a field remains understudied, even as historians and literary scholars account for the long reach of sexist, racist, and ableist medicine that emerges from the long nineteenth century with the professionalization and specialization of science and continues well into the twenty-first century with ongoing debates about the efficacy of masks or the dangers of vaccination during the COVID-19 pandemic. What might the concept of the medical imagination reveal about the specific concerns of women writers for crises that affect the female body? One such crisis demanded response because of its direct, overt attack against women: censorship under Comstock law. On March 3, 1873, Congress passed the "Act for the Suppression of Trade in, and Circulation of, Obscene Literature and Articles of Immoral Use" (Ch. 258, § 2, 17 Stat. 599), a censorship law that began as an attempt to expurgate birth control and abortion from American society. Called the "Comstock Law" for short in honor of its greatest advocate and "special agent" of the United States Post Office Anthony Comstock, who was given charge of search and seizure of obscene materials, the law evolved over the course of its forty-two-year reign of power. Although Margaret Sanger's birth control campaign largely made Comstock law impotent by 1915, little Comstock laws existed at the state level until well into the 1960s.[8] Significantly, as I argue in this book, the greatest effect of federal Comstock law was its success in manufacturing shame, which women writers of medical fiction oppose through the recommendation of various therapeutic regimens: environmental medicine, coalition-building, empathetic nursing, and access to medical knowledge.

(P)rescription Narratives historicizes and theorizes the role of narrative affect in storytelling as an oppositional act of reclamation and reanimation of the female body writ large. In other words, I argue that women writers of medical fiction practice storytelling as a form of proto-narrative medicine à la Rita Charon, for they prescribe various forms of healing as an antidote to the shame manufactured by an American culture of censorship through the act of narrative itself. American women began producing medical fiction at a greater rate during the period 1873–1915 because they were writing to, against, and within the confines of the Comstock Law. Charlotte Perkins Gilman, in particular, emerges as the most prolific writer of medical fiction as she produces no less than eight short stories, two novels, and one play about women's health in the span of twenty-four years.[9] Women writers of medical fiction felt the pressure of censorship personally as writers of a gender and sex who were barred from engaging in professional medical discourse and were robbed of an authoritative voice within the field of professional medicine in its reliance upon clinical language. They were further individuals whose bodies medico-legal discourse adopts as the subject of definition, diagnosis, and treatment within specific categories of sex, gender, and race to accomplish the work of differentiation and to conscript within specific private spheres for socio-biopolitics.

I refer to this counternarrative practice of concurrently critiquing, rewriting, and prescribing through the deployment of the term "R_xe-scription," which I write as "(p)rescription" in subsequent chapters. Indeed, in playing on the concept of each chapter as an examination of the prescriptions—by which I mean ways of healing—that women writers of medical fiction offer through narrative, I refer to my own chapters in this book as "R_x's," e.g. R_x 1, R_x 2, etc. As a theoretical term, "R_xe-scription" describes how narrative works affectively to perform multiple kinds of interventions that cut through the sociobiological indeterminism of nineteenth-century medicine, interrupt the dissemination of false narratives of the female body, and alter the course of cultural development toward greater inclusivity. I further deploy the term "R_xe-scription" in my own act of intervention that concurrently critiques theories of social construction and materiality, rewrites the trajectory of liberal humanism as a process and product of affect, and prescribes affect theory as an antidote to the social/material tension of twenty-first-century identity politics about gender, race, and disability. Because the subscripted "x" of "R_xe-scription" is burdensome to rewrite (both for *this* scholar and future scholars) and impossible to use as a digital tag, we as theorists cannot have the term "R_xe-scription" as a useful theoretical concept for longer than the length of this paragraph. My deepest apologies. Instead, I offer the term "(p)rescription" as an alternative that adapts itself more readily to myriad rhetorical situations, especially within digital and multimedia contexts. Language, narrative, and storytelling are limited by the systems of power within which they are entangled, and so in a sense, I have failed at my project before I have even begun. Yet Jack Halberstam finds possibility, even hope, in moments of failure—as do I—because failure offers an opportunity for considering how we might be otherwise.[10] In an attempt to consider the utopian possibilities of deploying "(p)rescription" instead of "R_xe-scription," I offer this: Perhaps the parenthetical of "(p)rescription" might better serve to highlight what kinds of boundaries nineteenth-century women writers and twenty-first-century theorists must confront, transgress, cut, or reshape for greater inclusivity of marginalized bodies within and beyond the parenthesis itself—and in a way that a subscript "x" cannot.

I derived my original term "R_xe-scription" from the root word "script," which signifies "writing," or a "distinctive writing system," usually given by hand. It is also the root word of "prescription," which allows for a kind of transcription from "R_x" to "(p)" in the adoption of R_xe-scription's theoretical doppelgänger in the title of this book, (p)rescription. Until the dawn of digital prescriptions and the legalization of electronic medical records (at least in the United States) in 2007, the word "prescription" was historically symbolized by the R_x symbol. Once again, the digitization of writing not only thwarts our attempts at representation but also threatens to erase or cause us to forget that the R_x symbol itself links writing and healing as entangled processes. The R_x symbol, which is signified by placing a line across the elongated right foot of the letter "R," derives from the Latin "recipere," meaning "to take," and was eventually specified further as "to take this medicine." I seek to recall each of these meanings in the prefix + root of my theoretical term, for whether we write it as "R_xe-scription" or "(p)rescription," and whether we invoke a visually silent "x" or an orally silent "p," the term should be phonetically pronounced "re-skrip-shun." This phonetic pronunciation should further invoke the term "rescription," an already-existing theoretical and scholarly concept that signifies "rewriting a narrative," especially a cultural narrative that is limiting to a specific population. Since we cannot have "R_xe-scription," I encourage readers to allow the R_x symbol to haunt or shadow the "(p)" of "(p)rescription" each time that they read it in this book so that, taken together, "(p)rescription" crystallizes a complex ongoing process of resignification.

Importantly, (p)rescription enacts multiple interventions that are simultaneously historically contingent and culturally relevant for twenty-first-century scholars, theorists, and public intellectuals. The act of (p)rescription in the field of American women's literature works to excavate a history of women writers who intercede in medical discourse about the female body using the genre of fiction as a medium. As a framework for genre studies, (p)rescription examines narrative affect, and specifically, how the act of storytelling creates a space for empathy as an antidote to that shame that cultural narratives of the female body engineer under censorship. From the vantage point of medical humanities, and as a form of narrative medicine à la Rita Charon, (p)rescription offers a scholarly reconstruction of the history of women's literature and feminist activism concerned with how medico-legal discourses inform the development of the subject "woman." Finally, as a theoretical intervention into the limitations of social construction and material feminisms using affect theory as a point of departure, (p)rescription theorizes narrative as affective, and by extension, considers identity subject formation—specifically, gender, race, and disability—as affective phenomenon. (P)rescription performs a kind of shadow feminism à la Jack Halberstam that not only inherits the oppositional biopolitics of its feminist theoretical ancestors, including, but not limited to, Michel Foucault, Judith Butler, Donna Haraway, Karen Barad, Mel Y. Chen, and Sylvia Wynter. (P)rescription boldly steps out of the shadows of its ancestors in an effort to also move affect theory into public intellectual discourse about the multiplicity of force relations that participate in the ongoing creation of history, politics, and cultural narratives of gender, disability, and race.

Cripping Affect, Biopolitics, and the Liberal Human(ist) Subject

(P)rescription Narratives and its theory of (p)rescription accounts for how narrative works affectively to construct our identities and identity categories under the rubrics of race, gender, and disability in an ongoing process of becoming. Several recent scholarly studies excavate race, gender, and disability as the locus of biopower not only in their co-evolution during the nineteenth century, but also in their deployment by various nineteenth-century systems or institutions—political, economic, medical, legal—to accomplish the work of population differentiation and control. Ellen Samuels excavates the historical and contemporary reliance upon biocertification for the co-making of race, gender, and disability, criteria that ultimately prove unstable for all three mark-

ers of identity. Like Samuels, Bridgitte Fielder relies upon a social constructionist framework for her study of race-making, or rather re-making, in the counternarratives of white women writers whose antiracist potential Fielder locates in the language of kinship. By contrast, Cristin Ellis and Kyla Schuller excavate the language of contemporary theories of posthumanism and affect, respectively, in the liberal politics of nineteenth-century writers who reclaim the language of an oppressive scientific discourse for racial and sexual liberation. Ellis, for instance, traces a tradition of nineteenth-century writers that includes Frederick Douglass, Henry David Thoreau, and Walt Whitman, who adopt the language of materiality from an empirical (racist) scientific tradition and redeploy it for the cause of Black liberation.[11] Schuller similarly describes how nineteenth-century writers such as Frances Ellen Watkins Harper, Dr. Elizabeth Blackwell, and W. E. B. Du Bois, among others, engage in a negotiated biopolitics that adopts the language of impressibility from evolutionary discourse and redeploys it for the cause of liberation from sexual or racial oppression.

What the work of Samuels, Fielder, Ellis, and Schuller highlights is that contemporary theories of social construction, materiality, and affect are not new and were operative during the nineteenth century but under different language. In fact, Schuller jocularly critiques that "new" materialism is not new. The cultural scripts of new materialism, social construction, and even affect—in the form of "impressibility"—not only circulate in nineteenth-century writing, but also create and preserve hierarchies of sexual and racial difference well into the twenty-first century. If, as contemporary scholars and theorists, we seek to avoid making the same mistake as our literary and theoretical ancestors, Schuller insists we must critically engage the language of materiality rather than celebrate it.[12] *(P)rescription Narratives* takes up Schuller's call from a crip affect perspective. One of the primary reasons that any field of liberal philosophy—including social constructionism, posthumanism, and new materialism—fails to accomplish the work of liberation is because liberal philosophy demands that we recognize the sovereignty of all subjects, both human and nonhuman. Karen Weingarten identifies precisely this tension at the center of abortion discourse during the first decades of the twentieth century even prior to the rhetoric of "life" and "choice": "at its core liberalism emphasizes the autonomous, self-reliant, individual citizen whose singular rights must be protected above all."[13] Liberalism's celebration of sovereignty appears to disregard forms of dependency, including cooperative networks, entanglements, and communities, which places posthumanism and new materialism at odds with its roots in liberal humanist ideology.

Can the liberal human subject ever truly be unfaithful to its origins, as Donna Haraway once suggested in her cyborg manifesto? Weingarten seems to respond with a resounding "no" as she highlights how "liberalism as a basis for securing access to abortion (or any other right) ensures the exclusion of some other marginalized group."[14] And she's right. This is why the rhetoric of Anthony Comstock and Margaret Sanger "can be easily co-opted to argue the exact opposite of their intentions," as both writers/speakers rely upon specific components of liberal ideology to animate either the liberal (white) male subject or the liberal (white) female subject at the expense of another subject whose body is rhetorically de-animated based upon the self-same liberal ideology that inherently relies upon hierarchies of difference.[15] Although I adopt a crip affect framework for my analysis of woman-authored medical fiction, I do not seek to rescue the language of affect theory or disability theory from liberal humanism because it simply cannot be done. As the work of Michel Foucault reminds us, there is no outside of power because it is not a thing but a doing. Power continually moves, and is therefore affective. Power is relational, and it works on multiple local, national, and global levels simultaneously through relationality, always leaving open the possibility of resistance.[16] This is why Bridgitte Fielder can theorize race as relational, as a product of kinship; why Cristin Ellis effectively draws upon posthumanist discourse to theorize racial discourse as a form of materialist ontology, even in the wake of a problematic speciological discourse; and why Kyla Schuller convincingly theorizes race as palimpsest from the vantage point of affect theory.

But, while Ellis rightly observes that "Liberation, as we know it, implies disentanglement" and further seeks to accomplish this liberation of the liberal (human) subject via a "decolonized posthumanism," I do not seek to disentangle twenty-first-century poststructuralism from its roots in liberalism at all. I revel in entanglement because, as a disability studies scholar, I am reminded that people with disabilities are fully relational and reliant upon systems of power for their own recognition as liberal subjects. Tobin Seibers's theory of complex embodiment exposes the sovereignty that liberal humanism celebrates as an illusion under the rubric of disability studies: Disabled subjects rely upon the built environment, nonhuman aids or prosthetics, and their own knowledge and experience of disability in a specific social milieu to assert agency alongside other human and nonhuman active subjects in ongoing reciprocal relationships.[17] Liberation is really about inclusion, accountability, and ethics, which we can only truly accomplish by acknowledging that we cannot disentangle the liberal (human) subject from liberal humanism since there is no outside of power, and therefore, no outside of entanglement in systems of power.

Moreover, turning away from humanity à la posthumanism and new materialism risks escaping the imperfectly human world, or at the very least disengaging from a history of scientific sexism, racism, and ableism that we are not yet done examining, as the legacy of the myth of the black beast reveals each time it rears its ugly head in twenty-first-century cases of police brutality. Or, more recently, each time the myth of biological determinism threatens to condemn women to the role of reproducing subjects once again, this time in the form of legalized anti-abortion laws that enforce compliance by turning civilians into bounty hunters. If we think the legacy of the Comstock Law has passed, we must think again. The US Supreme Court recently upheld the state of Texas's passing of SB8, which is just another Comstock law in disguise in so far as the law draws upon a (false) medical rationale of female passivity and a centuries-old cultural narrative of biological determinism to regulate the reproductive functions of the female body and further shame women for any non-normative decisions they make about their own reproduction.[18] This reality—that we cannot escape our past cultural narratives—is depressing. And the recognition that there is no outside of power appears defeatist. But here is where we turn toward affect to negotiate a theoretical framework that accounts for the affective nature of social construction and materiality in an ongoing process of meaning-making.

Throughout my reading of woman-authored American medical fiction at the fin de siècle, contemporary scholarship on nineteenth-century American literature, and contemporary theories of social construction, posthumanism, and new materialism, I have traced a return to the language of affect even when the writer does not purport to engage in affect theory. In her description of the birth of biopolitics à la Foucault, Ellis characterizes the act of differentiation based upon racial criteria "to make live or let die" as an affective process.[19] She further draws upon scholarship by Christopher Castiglia and Peter Coviello that adopts a more direct approach to affect theory in which the act of nation-building requires the formation of "affective attachments" to create a community, whether real or imagined.[20] Ellis shifts the language of affective attachment to material attachments, and then again to "involuntary material intimacies," a move which not only links the work of affect theory to the work of posthumanism but also understands affect as a kind of movement itself. Fielder likewise draws upon the language of affect in her description of the social construction of race as kinship, not least because both "[k]inship and racialization emerge . . . in structures of feeling."[21] Kinship is both a product of and catalyst to affective attachments. Similarly, race, gender, and disability are products of, catalysts to, and apparatuses for affect.

It should not surprise us that projects of social construction, posthumanism, and new materialism engage the language of affect theory, and indeed might be described as affective apparatuses themselves. The subjects that these theories purport to study emerge from a complex series of intra-actions among history, economics, politics, law, and the bodily differences of human and nonhuman subjects that have their own histories that they bring with them into new social and cultural contexts. Using Karen Barad's theory of agential realism as a framework, Michael Hames-Garcia describes race as both a cultural construction that manifests materially and a material subject visible on the body that we read and interpret through specific cultural contexts, which continually works to shape our world and our behaviors.[22] In other words, Hames-Garcia recognizes the intersections of social construction, new materialism, and affect in his theorizing of race as phenomenon. He resides in the space of both/and, not either/or, and in so doing, he recognizes that theories of social construction and materiality are not at odds with one another but are partners in creating the conditions for the possibility of transformation and liberation. Of course, as I have already critiqued and further demonstrate in R_x 1 of this book on the "matter of hysteria" in medico-legal discourse, theories of social construction and materiality have their limits in effectively and affectively liberating the liberal (human) subject from forces of biopower that oppress them. How then do victims of cultural trauma heal? Where do women writers of medical fiction locate hope for women with disabilities and women of color to gain recognition as subjects before the law? Schuller offers the palimpsest as a model for imagining what Barad might call the superposition of waves, for a palimpsestic process recognizes how "impressions," or affective experiences, "layer upon one another over the life span of the individual and the evolutionary race of time."[23] Palimpsest works on the level of the individual and the population, and further emphasizes the role of writing, of narrative, and of storytelling in the formation of a subject.

I find the palimpsest metaphor valuable in accounting for various kinds of affect—emotional affect, material affect, cultural affect, and narrative affect, among others—specifically because it accounts for how various forms of matter leave traces or marks upon us over a long period of time. Yet I offer (p)rescription as a model for theorizing the superposition of race, gender, and disability, as well as for describing the formation of race, of gender, and of disability as phenomenon, because of its relationship to the professional fields of medicine and health and its emphasis on healing. Arguably, (p)rescription is a palimpsestic model, and it definitely negotiates social construction and materiality as forms of affect. As a newer field of study than its poststructuralist sisters, affect theory set its parameters early on with an inquiry into feeling. Sara Ahmed's concept of "affective economies" describes how emotions bind subjects and objects together, while Ann Cvetkovich's early work not only posits texts as repositories of feeling but also how the traces of affect create new subcultures that emerge as a result of trauma.[24] The titles alone of early academic studies in affect theory betray an emphasis on feeling and emotion: *An Archive of Feelings* (Cvetkovich), *Feeling Backward* (Heather Love), and *The Feeling of Kinship* (David Eng). The work of Mel Y. Chen further expands the purview of affect theory as they prioritize the materiality of language and queer affect: "I include the notion that affect is something not necessarily corporeal and that it potentially engages many bodies at once, rather than (only) being contained as an emotion within a single body."[25] Chen accounts for a phenomenon in theorizing affect that emphasizes its subtlety of movement, which resides in its capacity for excess, for potentiality, for its becoming and "yet-ness," and its constantly "shuttling intensities" that signify an "in-between-ness" that never quite settles before moving on.[26]

In an early turn toward what would become the field of crip affect, Robert McRuer bridges the gap between queer theory and crip theory in his explanation of the cultural work of "crip." Crip takes its cue from queer as simultaneously a noun, a verb, and an adjective that critically attempts to destabilize cultural notions of normative bodies, whether under the rubric of compulsory able-bodiedness/able-mindedness or compulsory heterosexuality, or both concurrently.[27] Alison Kafer extends feminist theoretical discourse about (re)production and futurity into McRuer's crip theory, as she explains that her preference for the phrase "crip theory" or "crip studies" over "disability theory" or "disability studies" arises from its contradictory, provocative, and expansive character. Crip theory "mak[es] room for those who do not or cannot recognize themselves in crip,"[28] which I argue includes women writers of medical fiction, even as they strove to distance themselves from the concept of disability for fear that proximity to disability in the form of hysteria, postpartum depression, passivity, contagion, or even Blackness or queerness might threaten to disavow them of subjectivity and their status as rights-bearing citizens. More recently, David T. Mitchell, Susan Antebi, and Sharon L. Snyder bring discourses of feeling and emotion, materiality, and the social construction of disability under an expansive definition of crip affect in their recent collection, *The Matter of Disability: Materiality, Biopolitics, Crip Affect*. In the introduction, the editors of and contributors to the collection define the field of crip affect as alternatively "matter in motion," "disability as a phenomenon" (not unlike Hames-Garcia's concept of "race as phenomenon"), and a "unique mattering" that marks the subject as "embedded in her environment, in a complex corporeal and interdependent sensory relationship."[29] Admittedly, Mitchell, Antebi, and Snyder emphasize the feeling of disability experience such as "the feel of the materiality of the cane," "sensing the weight of the stick," and "the pressing of the plastic arm" of the wheelchair, which once again risks re-emphasizing physical disability to the exclusion of all else.[30] Yet the essays in the collection also account for a broader definition of affect that includes material relationality, even the dependency of human and nonhuman species on one another ("interspecies affect"), the influence of social environments on shaping our behavior ("biopolitics"), and the impact of literature and film on cognition ("literary affect" or "narrative affect").

I take my cue from this expansive definition of crip affect as theorized by McRuer, Kafer, and Mitchell, Antebi, and Snyder. To this definition, I add another form of affective relationality: empathy. Throughout her body of work, public academic Brené Brown repeatedly argues that empathy is an antidote to shame. In her TedTalks, this catchphrase becomes borderline kitschy.

And yet, in *Daring Greatly*, she convincingly makes her argument for empathy by differentiating empathy from feeling or emotion. Empathy is not an emotion, she explains, though we often confuse it as one: "Empathy is connection," but more specifically, "Empathy is connecting with the emotion that someone is experiencing."[31] Empathy is both an act and a state of being as it involves "simply listening, holding space, withholding judgment, emotionally connecting, and communicating that incredibly healing message of 'You're not alone.'"[32] Empathy is foundational to community-building and it lies at the core of the practice of narrative medicine, as well as at the core of the biopolitics of woman-authored medical fiction, specifically because empathy works as an antidote to the shame that selective censorship engineers under Comstock law. In her definition of narrative medicine as a therapeutic practice, Rita Charon explicitly identifies empathy as the catalyst for an effective—and affective—method of treatment. Narrative medicine begins with the act of affective listening, a form of engagement Charon alternatively calls "listening for" and "living through."[33] Importantly, what practitioners of narrative medicine should listen for is not just diagnostic clues such as signs or symptoms of illness that lead to a definitive diagnosis. They must also engage their imagination and try to inhabit the point of view of the speaker/patient so that they can negotiate with her to find an effective way forward that eases her suffering based upon her specific situation.[34] That is empathy by its very definition.

Charon adopts the metaphor of narrative as an ethical practice of medicine not least because the act of clinical diagnosis begins with the patient speaking about their symptoms, or narrating a story of illness. Charon also describes a meaningful doctor-patient relationship as the "shared creation" of knowledge, which can only unfold over time and when we organize our life experiences into narrative structures. Empathy cannot be taught, Charon explains. But it can be nurtured over a long period of time when we equip listeners with the right kind of skills: to identify suffering, interpret pain within specific contexts and through multiple points of view, imagine the implications of that suffering or pain, and finally, "be moved by it to action."[35] Not only do the skills Charon pinpoints as the prerequisites to empathy align with the skills of narrative analysis; the creation of narrative knowledge further takes up affect as its objective given that the act of storytelling seeks response. Narrative knowledge makes use of specific elements of storytelling: a teller, a listener, a frame, a timeline, a plot, and a point. Yet it also expects affect in the speaker's desire to touch, change, influence, move, or elicit a response from the listener that might work toward easing the suffering of the speaker. Narrative medicine, then, is a term Charon uses "to mean medicine practiced with these narrative skills of recognizing, absorbing, interpreting, and being moved by the stories of illness."[36] If empathy is both the objective and the prerequisite for compassionate response, then narrative medicine is the very deployment of affect, as it invites a communal sharing of emotions and communal building of knowledge about the experience of illness or disability. Charon offers an expansive practice of narrative medicine that includes the act of reading a literary text since the goal of communal sharing, community-building, and knowledge production is the same in written narrative as it is in spoken narrative, even if that community is only initially comprised of two people, the author and the reader. "Narrative knowledge provides one person with a rich, resonant grasp of another person's situation as it unfolds in time," Charon explains, "whether in such texts as novels, newspaper stories, movies, and scripture or in such life settings as courtrooms, battlefields, marriages, and illnesses."[37]

What better way of unfolding a narrative over time, thereby cultivating empathy, or at least sympathy, than before a captive audience in the form of an extended piece of prose such as a novel? Communities further expand, disseminate, and contribute to the creation of narrative knowledge as readers recommend medical novels to others. Affective narrative becomes the site of transformative potential not only for subjects within a biopolitical system such as the writer or reader but also for the system itself, which Charon imagines might re-form from the inside out as subjects become better at cultivating empathy through the act of listening affectively to the stories of others. But, of course, contemporary scholars of nineteenth-century American literature have known all along of the power of affective narrative. This is why in *Affecting Fictions*, Jane F. Thrailkill defends the "affective fallacy" that earlier New Critics disavowed as central to the study of literature and culture. Since Jane Tompkins underscored the cultural work of American fiction in *Sensational Designs*, influential scholars in the field of American literature such as Judith Butler, Rosemarie Garland-Thomson, Thomas Lacqueur, Elaine Showalter, and Priscilla Wald have argued for the capacity of fiction to shape or move a culture, not simply express the values of a culture. Thrailkill builds upon their work by explicitly focusing on the role of emotions in the production of American literary realism. Nineteenth-century realist writers were responding to scientific discourses of emotion, Thrailkill argues, and they understood emotions to be located in the body. They not only sought to represent this principle of embodied feeling in their work but also to exemplify it to their readers by eliciting a response.

Helen Brent, M.D., as a work of realist fiction that specifically engages timely medical discourses of the 1890s, participates in this late nineteenth- and early twentieth-century tradition of affective narrative, though Annie Nathan Meyer employs affect to different ends than her peers. She gives her readers a prescription that directly counters one or more of the cultural narratives of gender, race, or disability difference upheld by hegemonic medico-legal discourse. Her prescription further offers a therapeutic regimen for healing from the traumatic aftermath of these oppressive cultural narratives. In the wake of the cultural narrative of female passivity, Meyer recommends physical activity and prescribes various forms of exercise including the gymnasium, riding horseback, and bicycling. In response to the cultural narrative of separate-sex education and female inferiority, Meyer encourages higher education among women and prescribes that she "seek the companionship of her classmates" for intellectual and moral support (36). The prescription itself is framed before by Dr. Brent's speech about the irresponsibility of using clinical diagnosis to uphold gender double standards and after by a critique of American liberalism as crystallized in one of the most binding legal documents of nation-building, the Declaration of Independence. How can the founding fathers preach the sentiment of equality for all, and then, "with the last flourish of [the] pen," "turn up their aristocratic noses at those lesser mortals that had been unequally created without such distinguished forefathers"?[38] The answer is implied in the question: class privilege and a lack of diverse representation among the signers themselves. Like her contemporaries whom I examine in this study, Rebecca Harding Davis, Louisa May Alcott, Charlotte Perkins Gilman, and Frances Ellen Watkins Harper, Meyer makes the conscious decision to take up the flourish of her own pen and (p)rescribe against the minority majority speakers in power, regardless of the threat of censorship.

Affective Fictions in the Age of Comstock

I recognize censorship under Comstock law not as a passive historical backdrop upon which the act of (p)rescription takes place but as itself an affective narrative that produces the necessity of and engages in ongoing superposition with the production of woman-authored medical fiction. If we take Baradian superposition seriously as an apparatus for theorizing the subject formation of gender, race, and disability as phenomenon, then we must also acknowledge that the incidence of women writers producing medical fiction at an urgent rate from 1873 onward was not coincidental with the timing of the Comstock Law. In other words, women writers wrote medical fiction because of the adverse effects of Comstock law on their personal, professional, and social lives. Comstock law upheld the cultural narrative of compulsory able-bodiedness/able-mindedness, compulsory heterosexuality, and even compulsory whiteness because of its dependence upon the scientific work of men who fit the normative body that the law celebrated: Edward H. Clarke, S. Weir Mitchell, Jean-Martin Charcot, Samuel Morton, Samuel Cartwright, Josiah Nott and George Glidden, and Louis Agassiz, to name but a few influential scientists who appear in this study. Following the work of Tompkins and Thrailkill among others, we must also recognize that woman-authored medical fiction is no mere reflection of the cultural milieu within which the writer lives and works. Women writers actively shape the discourse of censorship, as well as the medico-legal discourse authorizing censorship law, through the act of producing medical fiction that self-consciously politicizes gender, race, and disability.[39]

Of course, women writers did not invent the genre of medical fiction, nor were they the only writers who called out Comstock for his hypocrisy. Sari Altschuler locates the medical imagination at work during periods of crisis in American culture such as how Charles Brockden Brown provides a kind of early public service announcement about yellow fever in his novel *Arthur Mervyn* (1799–1800), while Robert Montgomery Bird challenges Samuel Morton's methods of scientific race-making in his novel *Sheppard Lee* (1836) and Oliver Wendell Holmes inquires about the moral value of pain in his novel *Elsie Venner* (1861). Similarly, Cynthia J. Davis finds scientific authority in crisis during the period of 1845 to 1915 because it conveyed a number of contradicting truths about the medicalized body and embodied subjectivity. The instability of professional medicine during this period opened a space for writers of fiction such as Nathaniel Hawthorne, Oliver Wendell Holmes, Louisa May Alcott, Margaret Fuller, Charlotte Perkins Gilman, and Elizabeth Stuart Phelps to imagine ways of returning medical knowledge to a position of equilibrium. Women writers are responding to an extended crisis in the form of Comstockian censorship and they do seek a kind of equilibrium, though one that is very different from their male peers, because selective censorship unevenly affected the American populace. Arguably some male authors of medical fiction, such as Henry James and William Dean Howells, do more to contribute to the culture of shame under selective censorship than they do to lessen that shame. As Cynthia J. Davis highlights, *Doctor Breen's Practice* (1881) may realistically represent the challenges that a woman physician might face during the late nineteenth century, yet the ending of Howells's novel clearly suggests in no uncertain terms that a woman cannot manage both a career and a marriage at once. Howells accepts the false premise of Edward H. Clarke's "arrested development" of the uterus and ovaries under professional duress, whereas Phelps not only rejects Clarke's premise in her medical novel *Doctor Zay* but also rewrites the script of how women engage in the field of professional medicine.[40]

Similarly, Dr. Mary Prance of *The Bostonians* (1886) performs the stereotype of the androgynous woman physician to such a degree that when one has finished reading James's novel, the idea of a woman physician should appear wholly ridiculous rather than commonplace. It is no coincidence that Henry James's Dr. Prance and Sarah Orne Jewett's Dr. Prince differ in name by merely one letter, "a" versus "i," respectively, for the anti-feminism of *The Bostonians* likely works to rewrite Jewett's own asexual female physician. James offers an unflattering portrayal of the woman physician as a "type" of female who is alternatively cold, detached, unfeeling, and devoid of femininity such that readers are led to infer that women physicians like Dr. Prance and Dr. Prince are not only disabled women due to their lack of sentimentality but also unfit for the field of professional medicine.[41] Clearly, women writers of medical fiction are not the only ones engaging in the act of rewriting or reinscribing cultural narratives of the female body, but they are the only ones engaging specifically in acts of (p)rescription, because they offer prescriptions for healing from the after-effects of cultural trauma. And, of course, male writers of medical fiction were no less aware than women writers of the damaging effects of selective censorship under Comstock law. F. Scott Fitzgerald explicitly and unabashedly names his male protagonist Anthony Comstock Patch in *The Beautiful and Damned* (1922) as a way of commenting upon the adverse effects of Comstockian censorship. Unlike Comstock, who not only outlawed abortion but discursively shamed women for abortion in many of his speeches and written tracts, Fitzgerald appears complacent with abortion as an option for women who are not financially prepared to raise a child. Arguably, Fitzgerald's Anthony drops the "Comstock" from his name as a way of distancing himself from his cruel namesake.

And yet, as Karen Weingarten highlights, Fitzgerald does no better than Comstock himself, as his protagonists Gloria and Anthony confirm Comstock's convictions that abortion encourages lustful behavior and the recklessness and decadence of the 1920s, leading to a slip away from morality.[42] *The Beautiful and Damned* exposes Fitzgerald's privilege and his lack of complex embodiment, given that he fails to imagine how legal abortion or access to medically accurate reproductive knowledge might not only cause the lesser physical and psychological pain, but also liberate women from the destructive forces of Western culture. Langston Hughes would not make the same mistake. His short story "Cora Unashamed" (1933) simultaneously represents the dangers of making abortion illegal for Black and white women alike, as well as exposing white America's anxiety with interracial relationships. Many of the fictional texts about abortion and birth control that Karen Weingarten, Layne Parish Craig, and Beth Widmaier Capo examine in their scholarship we might also consider works of medical fiction given that medical discourse about reproductive health and the medical model of disability repeatedly manifests in their carefully chosen archive, which includes Edith Wharton's *Summer* (1917), William Faulkner's *As I Lay Dying* (1930) and *If I Forget Thee, Jerusalem* (1939), and Nella Larson's *Quicksand* (1928). However, what differs for women writers of medical fiction prior to 1915 and the onset of the birth control movement is the direct threat of censorship and shame from Anthony Comstock and his supporters during the time of their literary production. Conversations about the medicalized female body, reproductive rights for women, and access to sex education and informed consent for women did not end with the death of Anthony Comstock. But the tenor of the conversation and the form it adopts does shift, as I argue in the Conclusion of this book, which reads the anti-lynching plays of Angelina Weld Grimké, Mary Powell Burrill, Georgia Douglas Johnson, and Annie Nathan Meyer as a form of early reproductive justice.

Comstock died in September 1915, just days before the court announced its verdict on the case against Margaret Sanger. Poetically perhaps, Comstock's crusade against obscenity is bookended by two court cases against women activists for reproductive rights, Victoria Woodhull and Margaret Sanger.[43] Less poetically, Comstock was marginally successful at suppressing artistic production of sexual culture and medical knowledge about reproductive health, though historians agree that his crusade affected how Americans talk about sex and sexuality and left a legacy of shame in the wake of his death. Writing in 1927, in the aftermath of Comstockian censorship and the birth control campaign that began the decades-long process of bringing down federal Comstock law, biographers Heywood Broun and Margaret Leech reflect on Comstock's legacy of shame in American culture: "It was not the lustful thoughts which mar human personality," Broun and Leech diagnose, "but only the sense of shame. Comstock spread shame about very widely and it was a force much more debilitating than any exotic notions which might have come from the books he seized."[44] If we return to the work of Brené Brown, we find that shame is defined as the embodiment of wrongdoing. It assumes that because one has behaved badly, then one is a bad person. Shame exposes a fear of disconnection: "it's the fear that something we've done or failed to do, an ideal we've not lived up to, or a goal that we've not accomplished makes us unworthy of connection."[45] Comstock may have felt shame himself for any number of reasons related to upbringing, his military service, or his marriage, but he allowed his own shame to circulate in the form of obscenity law, effectively normalizing shame in discourses of American sexual culture, including medically- and education-based discourses about sex and sexuality. He not only created the feeling of disconnection from society among non-normative bodies through the act of engineering shame, but also materially disconnected individuals and communities from society along the lines of gender, race, and disability differentiation.

Comstock law functions as an affective biopolitical practice primarily because it deploys a specific ideology (defined by Anthony Comstock's own experience as a white upper-class heterosexual male) of what constitutes moral behavior, good taste, and decency over a general population that neither fits the demographics of the author of the narrative nor shares in their dominant ideological values. Moreover, the act of selective censorship under Comstock law determined who counts as a liberal subject with full rights and privileges therein before the law of the land based upon Comstock's image of the normative liberal subject. Historians who study the Age of Comstock and the effects of Comstockian censorship, such as George Chauncey, Amanda Frisken, Helen Lefkowitz Horowitz, and Amy Werbel, acknowledge that Anthony Comstock selectively censored artistic productions of obscenity along the lines of gender, race, and queer subjectivity. His public attacks on women activists like Woodhull and Sanger, as well as on the reproductive rights of women for which they stand, lead many historians to declare women as the population most devastatingly affected under Comstockian censorship. Yet enforcement of the law betrays who the hegemonic power believes merits status as a rights-bearing citizen. Legislators, judges, and executors of law insert a body into the cultural narrative via the act of censorship when that body counts as a normative subject worthy of discourse, whereas they expurgate from representation a body that does not count as a subject worthy of discourse and then further strip that body of status as a rights-bearing citizen. For instance, when Comstock began working with editors and publishers to censor "obscene" or sexually suggestive visual or print material, he notably censored the ankles of white women from public view. In contrast, Comstock did not censor images displaying the frontal nudity of Black women, because he did not consider them liberal subjects or rights-bearing citizens worthy of respect.[46]

Amanda Frisken explains that what some historians might consider an omission in censorship bans was actually Comstock's way of actively courting racist and sexist stereotypes such as the myth of the black male predator and the myth of black female hypersexuality. Comstock explicitly censored representations of white male rape in visual and print material but permitted—even highlighted—depictions of black rapists.[47] George Chauncy finds a similar practice in Comstockian censorship of queer culture. While Comstock himself raided clubs that employed gay performers, and searched and seized gay literature from booksellers and publishers, supporters of Comstock and his censorship practices expurgated any mention of the subject of homosexuality in visual and print culture, as in the case of John Sumner, who publicly attacked *The Masses* for running an essay on the question of homosexuality.[48] Homosexual defendants further suffered unusually lengthy sentences for obscenity convictions that Comstock personally prosecuted.[49] Comstock peddled the cultural narrative of compulsory whiteness, compulsory able-bodiedness, and compulsory heterosexuality, with variations on this theme of white supremacy and straight male hegemony. Predictably, any deviation from this dominant perception of normative subjectivity was rhetorically cast as illness or disability, which is one of the reasons I find crip affect a particularly useful framework for extricating how women writers of medical fiction rescript the cultural narratives Comstock circulated. Comstock caused real damage, and he was fully aware of the affect he created even as his crusade failed to suppress the creation and circulation of sexual culture.

And it did fail. Art historian Werbel traces a predictable trend of emboldened resistance throughout Comstock's reign. Focusing on visual culture specifically, Werbel notes that by the first decade of the twentieth century, "the images he managed to remove from the public sphere were more than matched by the outpouring of work featuring fully realized and anatomically complete nudes in following years made by artists who stood in opposition to his efforts."[50]

Werbel even goes as far as arguing that Comstock put Sanger in the history books, given that his public court case made her a famous victim, even martyr, of the culture of "Comstockery": "Without Comstock's prosecutorial intervention, Margaret Sanger might not have made much of a mark."[51] It is thanks to Comstock that aesthetic productions of sexual culture flourished at the fin de siècle, since the harder Comstock pushed censorship, the more emboldened anti-censorship artists, writers, dramatists, and social reformers were to find loopholes in the law or even publicly undermine it or mock it.[52] In fact, the term "Comstockery" became a public joke at the expense of the United States for the public impression of a prudish culture among foreign audiences. One of my personal favorites from the visual culture of Comstockery is a political cartoon by A. B. Walker published in *Life* magazine, titled "Let Anthony Comstock's Punishment Fit the Crime" (1901), which depicts the corpulent, nude Comstock as a model for an art class. Comstock once attempted his own version of (p)rescription in a published report that redefines "Comstockery" as "the noblest principle of law," but his definition did not catch on.[53] Keeping with the tenor of (p)rescription, Comstock considered himself not just a moral crusader but also a diagnostician and healer of the race: Obscenity "poisons the moral atmosphere. Its breath is fetid, and its touch moral prostration and death... When art lends its enchantments to vice the law quarantines it, and justice applies a disinfectant," Comstock wrote in *Morals Versus Art* (1887).[54]

Comstock, however, was responsible for creating the conditions of mental illness by engineering shame, which is why women writers of medical fiction often depict the adverse effects of medico-legal discourse on the psyche: Alcott's Rose is "pale, heavy-eyed, and listless," even sad, as a result of no outdoor exercise, Davis's Dr. Maria Haynes Muller suffers from neuralgia after her sexist lover rejects her for a domesticated woman, and the narrator of Gilman's "The Yellow Wallpaper" suffers from undiagnosed postpartum depression that her physician-husband writes off as only in her imagination. Comstock made people—people he did not even personally know—feel shame for pursuing sexual knowledge or engaging in sexual behavior such as masturbation, viewing erotic stereographs, or purchasing condoms or douches. Some felt shame so deeply that they committed suicide, while others Comstock made to feel shame through arrest or ridicule.[55] How much more might he have made women feel shame for reading about their reproductive health, even in the form of fiction? Censorship trends during this period give us some clues. Anthony Comstock led a war against obscene books even before the passing of the Comstock Law in March 1873. In his paid leadership role on the YMCA Committee for the Suppression of Obscene Literature, Comstock gave speeches and published essays in periodicals to attack publishers and booksellers for the production of erotica such as *Fanny Hill, or the Memoirs of a Woman of Pleasure* (1748). Additionally, he placed large orders of erotic novels in an effort to personally seize and destroy the "obscene" texts, but his attempts to discourage or destroy the production of erotica only led to an underground economy of erotic books.[56]

Comstock's most high-profile cases offer insight as to the kind of literature he suppressed with the authority of federal censorship law backing him: nonfiction medical texts and popular medical advice literature, including Dr. Edward Bliss Foote's *Medical Common Sense* (1858), *Plain Home Talk About the Human System* (1870), *Science Story* (1872), and *A Fable of the Spider and the Bees* (1876), of which the latter two are sex education texts for young audiences that Foote wrote to directly oppose Comstock law; Ezra Heywood's anti-marriage pamphlet *Cupid's Yokes* (1878); and Margaret Sanger's sex education column in *The Call*, "What Every Woman Ought to Know."[57] Mark Twain once published a satirical essay that pokes fun at Comstock's selective censorship practices of literature, citing the attempt to suppress the work of popular poet Walt Whitman as an example of the ridiculousness of Comstockery.[58] Even after his death, Comstock's supporters successfully and infamously deployed the power of prosecution to suppress James Joyce's *Ulysses* (1918–20), as well as a number of other then-modern and classic works of literature, including Theodore Dreiser's *An American Tragedy* (1925), Ernest Hemingway's *A Farewell to Arms* (1929), D. H. Lawrence's *Lady Chatterley's Lover* (1928), Giovanni Boccacio's *Decameron* (1353; in English, 1886), and Geoffrey Chaucer's *The Canterbury Tales* (c. 1400).[59] Worse, the consequence of censorship or suppression was not just the risk of destroyed texts after search and seizure, or fine or incarceration after trial if convicted. The shame of a trial or media exposure could ruin reputations and livelihoods—as in the case of Margaret Anderson, who not only watched as 500 copies of *The Little Review* containing the serialization of James Joyce's *Ulysses* were confiscated and burned, but in the aftermath of the trial also paid a hefty fine of $50.00 and felt pressured to exile herself to Paris to escape persecution.[60]

Women writers of medical fiction witnessed the high-profile convictions of white middle- to upper-class male and female physicians, writers, and social reformers who defended a woman's right to know about her body, and it shook them, especially women writers like Annie Nathan Meyer and Charlotte Perkins Gilman who not only lived in New York City at the time of these convictions but also personally knew one or more of the victims. If such privileged men and women as these were paying fines and serving full prison sentences, what chance did the average woman writer have of successfully challenging medical discourses about the female body without penalty? Alicia Puglionesi argues that the consequences of censorship or suppression led women writers to publish in alternative venues such as popular subscription periodicals like *Search Lights for Health*, which adopted elusive and euphemistic rhetoric to avoid detection.[61] Women writers of medical fiction took a slightly different tactic by presenting didactic arguments for the right to medical knowledge, and (p)rescribing and citing the medical knowledge that they knew, in works of fiction with such unassuming titles as *Kitty's Choice: A Story of Berrytown* (1873), *Eight Cousins, or The Aunt-Hill* (1875), *Iola Leroy, or Shadows Uplifted* (1892), and *The Crux* (1911). Moreover, their works of fiction appear distinct from earlier works of woman-authored medical fiction such as Sarah Harper Monmouth's *Wimbledon* (1854) and Mary Gove Nichols's *Mary Lyndon* (1855) because woman-authored medical fiction post-1873 not only appears self-consciously aware of its authors' political position in advocating for a new narrative about women's bodies and women's health, but also faced specific forms of hegemonic resistance during and after Comstockian censorship.[62]

R_x Summaries

(P)rescription Narratives follows a roughly chronological order from the immediate aftermath of the Comstock Law in 1873 to the beginning of the federal law's demise in 1915 in the wake of the Progressive-era Anti-Venereal Disease Campaign and Margaret Sanger's birth control campaign. Throughout each R_x, I trace how nineteenth-century medico-legal discourse engineers the conditions of shame in American culture, which emphasizes compulsory able-bodiedness/able-mindedness at the expense of the health of women who suffer debilitating conditions such as postpartum psychosis in Gilman's "The Yellow Wallpaper," psychological trauma during and after slavery in Watkins Harper's *Iola Leroy*, and syphilis or gonorrhea in Gilman's *The Crux* and "The Vintage" and Meyer's *Helen Brent, M.D.* In R_x 1, I argue that women writers of medical fiction rescript the concept of disability as a product of both linguistic and material processes, or what affect theorists Mel Y. Chen and Judith Butler refer to as "the materiality of language," which opens up a space to retheorize gender as affect. Louisa May Alcott, Charlotte Perkins Gilman, and Rebecca Harding Davis counter both the social construction and materiality of hysteria in the medico-legal discourse of Edward H. Clarke, S. Weir Mitchell, and Anthony Comstock, exposing hysteria as a fake illness that masks real mental illnesses such as postpartum psychosis, depression caused by grief and loss, and post-traumatic stress. This tension between social construction and materiality in nineteenth-century medico-legal discourses of hysteria parallels twenty-first-century theoretical conversations that negotiate tensions between social constructionist and posthumanist or new materialist theories. Taking a cue from Alcott, Gilman, and Davis, who describe gender as a product of the affective outdoor environment, I posit affect theory as a useful intervention to the limitations of social construction and new materialism. The failure of language to affect personal, social, or political change in Davis's *Kitty's Choice*, as well as Davis's larger skepticism toward feminist utopian politics and environmental health, opens up a space for imagining creative therapies or (p)rescriptions to heal the pain of disability, illness, and even culturally induced trauma.

I explore the (p)rescriptions of women writers of medical fiction further in R_x 2, R_x 3, and R_x 4, each of which posits a different prescription for healing from the shame engineered by selective censorship under federal Comstock law. In R_x 2, I examine Elizabeth Stuart Phelps's *Doctor Zay* (1882) and Charlotte Perkins Gilman's *Mag-Marjorie* (1912) as representative texts that exhibit the affective function of narrative through the figure of the New Man, whom Phelps invents as an ideological counterpoint to the New Woman doctor. Using the framework of narrative medicine and narrative prosthesis, I argue that Phelps, and later Gilman, deploys the New Man ideal as a prosthetic that works to resolve the tension between readerly expectations of a romantic plot and writerly expectations of the sovereign woman physician. Because readers were strongly affected by the presence of a romance narrative, Phelps and Gilman package their oppositional politics in defense of gender equality and the autonomous woman physician in the form of a conversion narrative. They deploy the New Man as a transformative figure who converts readers to the cause of the New Woman doctor, and by extension, the politics of the feminist writer, by teaching us how to "listen for" the experiences of the New Woman doctor from a narrative medicine standpoint. While Phelps and Gilman prescribe affective listening as a method of healing from the gender oppression of medico-legal discourses, Frances Ellen Watkins Harper prescribes empathetic nursing as a path toward healing from the ongoing trauma of slavery. Using, and problematizing, Cary Wolfe's concept of "before the law," I argue that Anthony Comstock does not recognize Black women as subjects before the law and instead deploys selective censorship practices to perpetuate the false narrative of black animality and black bestiality that underpins the law of hypodescent and anti-amalgamation law. In *Iola Leroy*, Watkins Harper not only counters such false cultural narratives that seek to delegitimize women of color as rights-bearing citizens and to legitimize the rape of Black women during and after slavery, but also imagines empathetic nursing among communities of color as a way to heal from the physical and psychological trauma.

R_x 3 and R_x 4 also turn from theorizing the narrative function of affect in medical fiction to theorizing race, gender, and disability as superposition, as a process, product, and apparatus of affect à la Karen Barad's theory of agential realism. Understanding race and gender as superposition reframes our interpretation of the medico-legal discourses at work in Frances Ellen Watkins Harper's *Iola Leroy*, and at work in our own society as we hold onto the cultural narrative of black bestiality and hypersexuality in the twenty-first century. In R_x 4, I bring disability as superposition into the conversation as well, since Charlotte Perkins Gilman and Annie Nathan Meyer rescript the medico-legal discourse of popular Anti-VD Campaign films whose stock seduction narrative and outbreak narrative represents venereal disease as a rationale for implementing public sex education programs. Meyer and Gilman uproot cultural narratives of contagion that figure disease as originating from the female sex, but they also redeploy the rhetoric of fear from Anti-VD Campaign films in their own counter-campaign narratives, a move which has long-standing implications for queer communities and people of color in cultural narratives of contagion. This is particularly salient for crip/queer characters of color Jeanne Jeaune and Theophile, whom Gilman uses in *The Crux* to appeal to the logic of science through the emotional rhetoric of fear, and specifically, the fear of illness and of disability.

In the Conclusion, I explore how the practice of medical theater throughout the long nineteenth century led women writers, and especially Black women writers, to deploy the act of (p)rescription in the genre of anti-lynching drama rather than the genre of prose medical fiction in the wake of Anthony Comstock's death, Margaret Sanger's birth control campaign, and the end of censorship under federal Comstock law. Just because the legalization of selective censorship practices had purportedly ended, at least on a national level, the culture of shame that the Comstock Law engineered toward the female body did not end with the federal law's lack of enforcement and eventual repeal. Sanger picked up where Comstock left off, as the birth control campaign and its alignment with eugenic (bio)politics worked to shame Black women and women with disabilities into using contraception as a way of protecting and promoting "race health." In response, Black women writers like Angelina Weld Grimké expose how shame engineered under eugenic birth control politics—rather than censorship law—continues to create the conditions of mental illness among Black women through the trauma of reproductive loss. Scholars have long identified Grimké as the "mother of African American drama" and founder of the genre of anti-lynching drama who established the generic conventions for other dramatists to follow. They have also long considered how Grimké's play *Rachel* (1916) and short stories "The Closing Door" (1919) and "Goldie" (1920) directly engage in birth control discourse with Sanger and her supporters.

However, I consider how Grimké engages the medical imagination in her anti-lynching dramas *Rachel* and *Mara* (c. 1920) as a way of enacting a narratological shift that expands the concept of the medical theater into the theater of lynching, as well as expanding conversations about Black women's health into the sphere of reproductive justice rather than simply birth control. Just as I argue in R_x 1 that the medical fiction of Rebecca Harding Davis and Louisa May Alcott enacts a narratological shift in the years immediately following the passing of federal Comstock law, I further consider in the Conclusion of this book how the anti-lynching dramas of Angelina Weld Grimké and Annie Nathan Meyer enact yet another narratological shift that imagines dramatic performance as a more effective way of affecting audiences who can produce meaningful social change. This is not to say that the writing of medical fiction—or even partial medical fiction in the form of "textual contraception"—ceases during the Progressive Era. As we see in the scholarship of Karen Weingarten, Beth Widmaier Capo, and Layne Parish Craig, women writers continue to produce prose fiction about reproductive health well into the 1920s, 30s, and 40s, though their work adopts a more ominous tone than their predecessors in the wake of Jim Crow, the Great Depression, the eugenics movement, and anti-abortion legislation. Importantly, the work of women writers of medical fiction during and after the Age of Comstock highlights for twenty-first-century readers and scholars the power of narrative affect to shape cultural narratives of gender, race, and disability, as well as the potential of empathy to operate as an antidote to the shame our culture engineers in health discourse.

NOTES

1. Annie Nathan Meyer, *Helen Brent, M.D.* (Hastings, NE: Hastings College Press, 2020), 33.
2. Sue Zschoche, "Dr. Clarke Revisited: Science, True Womanhood, and Female Collegiate Education," *History of Education Quarterly* 29, no. 4 (1989), 547.
3. Kyla Schuller, *The Biopolitics of Feeling: Race, Sex, and Science in the Nineteenth Century* (Durham, NC and London: Duke University Press, 2018), 41.
4. Ibid. 41, 16.
5. Meyer, *Helen Brent, M.D.*, 36.
6. Ibid. 35.
7. Frederick Wegener, "The Literary Representation of Women Doctors in the United States, 1860–1920," *Literature Compass* 4, no. 3 (2007), 596.
8. John D'Emilio and Estelle B. Freedman, *Intimate Matters: A History of Sexuality in America* (Chicago: The University of Chicago Press, 2012), 284. During the 1950s, obscenity cases began appearing in federal court, most of which overturned Comstockian censorship at the state level. The last obscenity case which I found was the U.S. Supreme Court case *Griswald v. Connecticut* (1968), which struck down prohibited access to contraceptive devices and information in Connecticut and Massachusetts. The federal Comstock Law was officially declared unconstitutional in 1983, by which time it had largely ceased being enforced.
9. In this book, I discuss the following works by Charlotte Perkins Gilman: "The Yellow Wallpaper" (1892), *Mag-Marjorie* (1912), and *The Crux* (1911), though I would include "A Coincidence," "Turned" (1911), "The Widow's Might" (1911), "Mr. Peebles's Heart" (1914), "Dr. Clair's Place" (1915), "Joan's Defender" (1916), and *Something to Vote For* (1911) as works of medical fiction, as does Frederick Wegener, per his essay, "'What a Comfort a Woman Doctor Is!' Medical Women in the Life and Writing of Charlotte Perkins Gilman," in *Charlotte Perkins Gilman: Optimist Reformer*, eds. Jill Rudd and Val Gough (Iowa City: University of Iowa Press, 1999), 45–73.
10. Judith (Jack) Halberstam, *The Queer Art of Failure* (Durham, NC and London: Duke University Press, 2011).

11. Extensive conversation has emerged in academic and public discourse on the politics of capitalizing the "B" in "black." In a public humanities article for *The Atlantic*, Kwame Anthony Appiah argues for the capitalization of the "B" in black when it signals the presence of a community or social identity. Cristin Ellis similarly explains her choice to capitalize the "B" in black throughout her book *Antebellum Posthuman* when "black" signifies a marker of social identity as a choice made "in support of this usage's instinct to combat, even in this small way, the systematic devaluation of black life" emerging from a history of black abjection in the United States that works to threaten the social identity of Blackness in the present (173, n. 2). However small a choice this may seem, the politics of grammar have a significant affect on our perceptions of individuals and communities, as I will argue alongside Mel Y. Chen, Judith Butler, and Kyla Schuller, among others. The capitalization of the "B" in black performs a kind of linguistic act of reclamation that resists white mediocrity and the "know-your-place aggression" of the past and present (see Koritha Mitchell, *From the Slave Cabins to the White House*). Thus, my own decision to capitalize the "B" in black at specific times throughout this book contributes to this ongoing performance of mechanics. Importantly, I do not capitalize "black" when it describes a mythological concept like "the myth of the black beast" or "black hypersexuality," since the uppercase "B" works to call attention to and reinforce the essence of blackness as it relates to racist science. I employ the capitalization of Black not simply as a statement of presence but also as a declaration of the right of the community to belong in this nation with all of the privileges of citizenship that that declaration entails.
12. Schuller, *The Biopolitics of Feeling*, 26.
13. Karen Weingarten, *Abortion in the American Imagination: Before Life and Choice, 1880–1940* (New Brunswick, NJ: Rutgers University Press, 2014), 6.
14. Ibid. 6.
15. Ibid. 42, 38–9.
16. Foucault theorized the concept of biopower extensively over his body of work, perhaps beginning with the "Method" section of *The History of Sexuality, Volume I: An Introduction*, trans. Robert Hurley (New York: Vintage Books, 1990 [1978]), 92–102. Of course, I am also thinking of *Society Must Be Defended: Lectures at the Collège de France 1975–1976*, ed. by Mauro Bertani and Alessandro Fontana, and trans. David Macey (New York: Picador, 2003), as well as Foucault's interviews, especially "Power and Strategies," where he explicitly claims that there is no outside of power (141–2). Foucault's theorizing of biopolitics and biopower influence my thinking throughout this study even when I do not explicitly reference his work. This is not least because Foucault's concept of biopolitics informs many of the scholarly studies that I draw upon in my analysis of woman-authored medical fiction from 1873 to 1915, including the work of Kyla Schuller, Cristin Ellis, Karen Weingarten, and Ellen Samuels, among others.
17. Tobin Seibers, "Returning the Social to the Social Model," in *The Matter of Disability: Materiality, Biopolitics, Crip Affect*, ed. by David T. Mitchell, Susan Antebi, and Sharon L. Snyder (Ann Arbor: University of Michigan Press, 2019), 39–47; see also Tobin Seibers, "Disability and the Theory of Complex Embodiment: For

Identity Politics in a New Register," in *The Disability Studies Reader*, 5th edition, ed. by Lennard J. Davis (New York and London: Routledge, 2017), 313–32.
18. Senate Bill 8, or SB 8, is also known as the "Heartbeat Bill" because it outlaws a pregnant woman's access to abortion after eight weeks of pregnancy based upon a scientific misinterpretation of the beginning of life at eight weeks' gestation. SB 8 passed on May 19, 2021 during the 87th legislature of Texas State Congress, and went into effect in the state of Texas on September 9, 2021. Similar bills have since been proposed in conservative state legislatures such as that of Florida. SB 8 is also comparable to the Comstock Law in that it enforces the law through citizen policing via the Texas Right to Life's ProLifeWhistleblower.com, where citizens can anonymously report on one another for violating state anti-abortion law. Read the bill text of SB 8 on LegiScan: <https://legiscan.com/TX/text/SB8/id/2395961> (accessed December 12, 2021).
19. Cristin Ellis, *Antebellum Posthuman: Race and Materiality in the Mid-Nineteenth Century* (New York: Fordham University Press, 2018), 11.
20. Ibid. 19.
21. Bridgitte Fielder, *Relative Races: Genealogies of Interracial Kinship in Nineteenth-Century America* (Durham, NC and London: Duke University Press, 2020), 12.
22. Michael Hames-Garcia, "How Real Is Race?" in *Material Feminisms*, edited by Stacy Alaimo and Susan Hekman (Bloomington: Indiana University Press, 2008), 308–39.
23. Schuller, *The Biopolitics of Feeling*, 93.
24. Sara Ahmed, "Affective Economies," *Social Text* 22, no. 2 (2004), 117–39; see also Ann Cvetkovich, *An Archive of Feelings: Trauma, Sexuality, and Lesbian Public Cultures* (Durham, NC and London: Duke University Press, 2003).
25. Mel Y. Chen, *Animacies: Biopolitics, Racial Mattering, and Queer Affect* (Durham, NC and London: Duke University Press, 2012), 11.
26. Melissa Gregg and Gregory J. Seigworth, Introduction to *The Affect Theory Reader* (Durham, NC and London: Duke University Press 2010), 2–3. I enjoy Gregg and Seigworth's definition of affect, especially in their emphasis on temporality and slipperiness. Affect is hard to pin down because it is always on the "cusp of emerging futurity," and yet rooted in the past, as I demonstrate throughout this book. I appreciate how Gregg and Seigworth describe affect as "tiny firefly intensities that flicker faintly in the night, registering those resonances that vibrate" like race, gender, and disability, in momentary encounters that range from "subtle to seismic" (4).
27. Robert McRuer, *Crip Theory: Cultural Signs of Queerness and Disability* (New York and London: New York University Press, 2006).
28. Alison Kafer, *Feminist, Queer, Crip* (Bloomington and Indianapolis: Indiana University Press, 2013), 16.
29. David T. Mitchell, Susan Antebi, and Sharon L. Snyder, Introduction to *The Matter of Disability: Materiality, Biopolitics, Crip Affect* (Ann Arbor: University of Michigan Press, 2019), 8, 23, 25.
30. Ibid. Introduction, 11; see also pages 16 and 12 of Kafer's *Feminist, Queer, Crip* for a critique of the field of disability studies, which has a long trend of focusing on

physical disabilities with little work on the subject of cognitive disabilities or mental illness.
31. Brené Brown, *Daring Greatly: How the Courage to Be Vulnerable Transforms the Way We Live, Love, Parent, and Lead* (New York: Avery, 2012), 81.
32. Ibid. 81.
33. Rita Charon, *Narrative Medicine: Honoring the Stories of Illness* (Oxford and New York: Oxford University Press, 2006), 4, 57, 66.
34. Ibid. 5.
35. Ibid. 8.
36. Ibid. 4.
37. Ibid. 9.
38. Meyer, *Helen Brent, M.D.*, 37.
39. Kristin Swenson, *Medical Women and Victorian Fiction* (Columbia, MO: University of Missouri Press, 2005). Although Swenson focuses on British medical fiction, she acknowledges that works of what she calls "New Woman doctor novels" by American women authors such as Annie Nathan Meyer's *Helen Brent, M.D.* adopt a "self-consciously political" tone during the post-Civil War period. She characterizes this "self-consciously political" tone as purposefully presenting an argument for social or political reform apropos to the author's own period. I am arguing that the reason this self-consciously political tone emerges in woman-authored medical fiction produced post-1873 is explicitly in rejection of the Comstock Law and in the act of rewriting the medico-legal discourse that underpins it.
40. Cynthia J. Davis, *Bodily and Narrative Forms: The Influence of Medicine on American Literature, 1845–1915* (Stanford: Stanford University Press, 2000), 115.
41. Frederick Wegener, "'A Line of Her Own': Henry James's 'Sturdy Little Doctress' and the Medical Woman as Literary Type in Gilded-Age America," *Texas Studies in Literature and Language* 39, no. 2 (1997), 147; 156; 172, n. 14.
42. Weingarten, *Abortion in the American Imagination*, 51.
43. Amy Werbel, *Lust on Trial: Censorship and the Rise of American Obscenity in the Age of Anthony Comstock* (New York: Columbia University Press, 2018), 8, 304; see also Helen Lefkowitz Horowitz, *Rereading Sex: Battles over Sexual Knowledge and Suppression in Nineteenth-Century America* (New York: Vintage Books, 2002), 376–9.
44. Heywood Broun and Margaret Leech, *Anthony Comstock: Roundsman of the Lord* (New York: The Literary Guild of America, 1927), 270; see also Werbel, *Lust on Trial*, 40–1, 306–7. Broun and Leech offer an apologetic portrait of Anthony Comstock the man, whom they describe as a self-proclaimed soldier against vice who once served in the Civil War and likely suffered physical and psychological trauma long after his service.
45. Brown, *Daring Greatly*, 68–9.
46. Amanda Frisken, "Obscenity, Free Speech, and 'Sporting News' in 1870s America," *Journal of American Studies* 42, no. 3 (2008), 558–9.
47. Ibid. 562.
48. George Chauncey, *Gay New York: Gender, Urban Culture, and the Making of the Gay Male World, 1890–1940* (New York: Basic Books, 1994), 146, 232.

49. Werbel, *Lust on Trial*, 259.
50. Ibid. 279.
51. Ibid. 297.
52. Ibid. 265.
53. Ibid. 265.
54. Anthony Comstock, *Morals Versus Art* (New York: Ogilvie & Co., 1887), 11–12.
55. Werbel, *Lust on Trial*, 232, 300, 147.
56. Ibid. 57–8, 30–3.
57. Ibid. 128–30, 297; see also Horowitz, *Rereading Sex*, 404–18, 424–33.
58. Werbel, *Lust on Trial*, 131–3.
59. Margaret A. Blanchard, "The American Urge to Censor: Freedom of Expression Versus the Desire to Sanitize Society—From Anthony Comstock to 2 Live Crew," *William and Mary Law Review* 33, no. 3 (1992), 768–82.
60. Elisabeth Ladenson, *Dirt for Art's Sake: Books on Trial from "Madame Bovary" to "Lolita"* (Ithaca and London: Cornell University Press, 2007), 95; see also Kevin Birmingham's *The Most Dangerous Book: The Battle for James Joyce's Ulysses* (New York: Penguin Books, 2015), which offers a detailed account of the publication of *Ulysses*, including the case against Margaret Anderson and her publishing partner Jane Heap.
61. Alicia Puglionesi, "'Your Whole Effort Has Been to Create Desire': Reproducing Knowledge and Evading Censorship in the Nineteenth-Century Subscription Press," *Bulletin of the History of Medicine* 89, no. 3 (2015), 470, 479.
62. Actually, I agree with Colleen Martell, who argues that Mary Gove Nichols's medical novel *Mary Lyndon* presents a self-consciously political narrative that advocates for a new theory of the female body against sexist medical sciences of the nineteenth century. Nichols is likely engaging in a form of (p)rescription, but I do not include it as a subject of study for this book because medical conversations about the female body, as well as the stakes of woman sex educators like Nichols for engaging in those medical conversations, were entirely different prior to 1873. Nichols lived and wrote during a time of relative acceptance for women in specific fields of medicine such as hydropathy, or the water cure. See Colleen Martell, "Speaking Bodies: Listening for Mary Gove Nichols (1810–84)," *Feminist Formations* 27, no. 2 (2015), 146–64.

R_x I

CRIP MEDICINE: ENVIRONMENTAL HEALTH AND THE MATTER OF HYSTERIA

One month after the passing of the Comstock Law, Rebecca Harding Davis began serializing *Berrytown* in *Lippincott's* monthly magazine. Such an urgency of timing may suggest that the subject matter responds directly to suppression of medical knowledge and social hygiene discourse. In the climactic scene, in which Dr. Maria Haynes Muller decides to confess her feelings to Dr. John McCall, the reader finds Dr. Muller "lecturing," "chattering for two hours on cervical, dorsal and lumbar vertebrae, without stopping to take a breath," and "fumbling over [her mankin's] bones" in the process.[1] Dr. Muller is teaching a social hygiene, or sex education, class at the water cure facility, which Davis well knows violates the conditions of Comstock law. Despite this legalized censorship, two years later, Louisa May Alcott's *Eight Cousins, or The Aunt-Hill* emerges in *St. Nicholas: A Monthly Magazine for Boys and Girls* promoting a similar social hygiene education scene. Intent on turning his recently orphaned ward Rose Campbell into a healthy, vibrant teenager, Dr. Alec Campbell teaches Rose anatomy and physiology to the embarrassment of her aunts, Alec's sisters. Like Dr. Muller, readers find Rose playing with her manikin as she "counted vertebrae, and waggled a hip-joint in its socket with an inquiring expression."[2] Her inquiring expression should signal to the reader Rose's curiosity toward reproductive health, for the "hip-joint" is structurally located around a contested female sex organ: the uterus.

Scholars have long characterized nineteenth-century medical theory and practice as driven by what historians call "medical materialism" and contemporary theorists call "biological determinism," defined as the prevailing belief among physicians that one's sex organs determine social and cultural roles.[3] Historians John S. Haller and Robin M. Haller further emphasize the role of materiality in their assessment of the nineteenth century as the "nervous century," in which neurasthenia defined the industrialized man and hysteria defined the industrialized woman.[4] Yet literary theorist Kyla Schuller updates this scholarly impression. The recursive deployment of affect and impressibility resulting from a legacy of Lamarckian evolution suggests that the operative notion of the body in nineteenth-century scientific writing was sociobiological indeterminism rather than biological determinism.[5] Nineteenth-century scientists theorize the body as a "biocultural formation," molded by both material and cultural processes.[6] Such narratives do not simply prefigure contemporary theories of new materialism and social construction. They open up a space for theorists to inquire how fiction theorizes the body and the concept of disability, especially since sociobiological narratives deploy the concept of disability to accomplish the work of sexual and racial differentiation.

In this R_x, I argue that women writers of medical fiction rescript the concept of disability as a product of both linguistic and material processes, or what some scholars, myself included, refer to as "the materiality of language." As a narratological move, (p)rescription enacts an ideological shift that affects the female body in the medical imagination since a lack of awareness of one milieu at the expense of the other risks misdiagnosing illness. This narratological turn begins in earnest with Louisa May Alcott's *Eight Cousins, or The Aunt-Hill* (1875). Alcott's emphasis on young adult social hygiene education was a direct affront to Anthony Comstock. Alcott rescripts the rhetoric of animacy from Dr. Edward H. Clarke's separate-sex education system and closed-body theory to an audience Comstock explicitly censures because he considers them highly impressible. Her approach adopts environmental health as a form of preventative medicine that involves educating young women about their physiology and how to care for their bodies as they enter puberty. Because Alcott rescripts Comstock's and Clarke's understanding of materiality and social construction, I examine this narratological turn extending from Alcott through a crip affect framework that theorizes the materiality of language, which includes the deployment of animacy and impressibility.

In framing this discourse, I explain how Charlotte Perkins Gilman's "The Yellow Wallpaper" (1892) demonstrates the consequences of censorship and suppression—how what women do not know harms their health—after the federal Comstock Law had been in effect for almost twenty years. In *Eight Cousins*, Alcott suggests how we might reform our education system more inclusively with correct medical knowledge about the female body as a means of preventing the suffering that Gilman experiences. However, given that Gilman narrates a loosely autobiographical tale of her lived, embodied experience of hysteria diagnosis, one must question the efficacy of Alcott's (p)rescriptions. Did she fail at her efforts to counter Clarke and Comstock? If Alcott fails, then so does Rebecca Harding Davis's Dr. Maria Haynes Muller, who cannot convince her future sister-in-law Kitty Vodges of the value of female independence, body autonomy, and professional fulfillment. Moreover, Dr. Muller's own hydropathic treatments fail to heal her impairment from neuralgia. I conclude this R_x with a meditation on "the queer art of failure" à la Jack Halberstam, using Rebecca Harding Davis's *Kitty's Choice: A Story of Berrytown* (1873) as my point of departure. Davis's skepticism of environmental health prefigures contemporary crip affect theorist Alison Kafer's own critique of environmental feminisms as both writers ask whether cure is not only possible but desirable since the process of grappling with our own embodied experience of health and illness means reconciling with losses both personal and professional. Their skepticism not only works to critique Alcott's confidence in environmental health as an effective form of healing, but further suggests that it is in moments of failure that we imagine creative therapeutic regimens.

The Age of Clarke and Mitchell

Before examining how Alcott and Davis respond to the (socio)biological (in)determinism of nineteenth-century medicine,[7] I propose that we first assess the rhetorical affect of hysterical ideology, which permeates popular and professional medical research from the 1870s through the 1910s. Amy Koerber suggests that one of the reasons women writers of medical fiction could engage in biopolitical discourses concerning hysteria is because debates surrounding the subject were unsettled. Scholars have long considered the nineteenth century the Age of Hysteria.[8] Schuller's findings about sentimental biopower reaffirm this characterization, as scientists theorize women, children, and people with disabilities as more impressible and therefore vulnerable to hysteria. Although the etiology of hysteria plays a dominant role in medical discourse throughout the century, Koerber characterizes this discourse during the decade of the 1870s in terms of "stasis." Jean-Martin Charcot's *Lectures on the Diseases of the Nervous System* (1877) reflects this rhetorical movement (or lack thereof). Charcot proposed that hysteria and epilepsy were actually different neurological conditions, and further, that hysteria might originate in the ovaries rather than the uterus. Yet the academic response to Charcot's proposals was "very quiet," since "conflict among these different voices and ideas had become so embattled that the argument reached a standstill."[9] Debates raged in the medical community over the origins of hysteria, whether it emerges from the uterus, the ovaries, or even hormones, but no conclusions were drawn during this decade because no one could hear above the din.

The paralysis created by endless discussion of female bodies allowed women writers to slip in their own perspective under the guise of fictional narrative. After all, who would question such unassuming titles as *Kitty's Choice* or *Eight Cousins* from such highly respected women writers as Rebecca Harding Davis or Louisa May Alcott? Indeed, by 1873, Davis and Alcott had gained a reputation in the literary marketplace as serious novelists. They also were actively engaged in social reform work. Davis earned public acclaim for her novella *Life in the Iron Mills* (1861), in which she drew upon the literary conventions of sentimentalism and social realism to critique working-class factory conditions. Jean Pfaelzer claims that Davis's published work in the 1860s established her as a parlor radical who not only wrote against slavery and the conditions of the working poor but also began "splicing the political and sentimental through her understanding of misogyny and female equality" such that by the 1870s, Davis's New Woman protagonists like Dr. Maria Haynes Muller become "serious threats to bourgeois culture."[10] Pfaelzer, in fact, boldly concludes that the trajectory of Davis's political fiction "is always, regardless of her historical topic, about female subjectivity."[11]

One might also consider Alcott a "parlor radical." Alcott grew up among social reformers and was active in "reforms of all kinds," including as a member of the New England Woman's Suffrage Association.[12] Moreover, Alcott's body of fiction lends itself to feminist critique because her work is full of "unruly" women: Jo March, Nan Harding, Christie Devon, and even Tribulation Periwinkle, the loosely autobiographical nurse of *Hospital Sketches* (1863).[13] Marlowe Daly-Galeano claims that, even as a published work of fiction, Alcott could get away with an unruly female—dare I say, feminist—protagonist because *Hospital Sketches* created the genre of nursing narratives and Trib engages in a fairly new professional sphere of women's nursing. There were no rules to follow.[14] Feminist (male) physician Dr. Alec Campbell and his thirteen-year-old niece and feminist-in-training Rose Campbell might have been a harder "sell" for readers, especially under Comstockian censorship. Readers were scarcely familiar with the New Woman ideal, much less the feminist New Man, who advocated for the rights of women in the face of their disenfranchisement.[15] Ruth Dyckfehderau reads *Eight Cousins* as a work of political fiction, not least because of Alcott's gender-bending "male mother," Dr. Alec Campbell, who actively participates in domestic activities such as cleaning, cooking, and raising children. Alcott further places Dr. Alec in the role of social hygiene educator who directly undermines Dr. Edward H. Clarke's thesis of the closed-system theory.[16]

Clarke left an impression on professional medicine because of his cult popularity status. *Sex in Education* was a bestseller.[17] His argument that the female biological system could not function at the same advanced levels as the male biological system hinged on the assumption that bodies function as a closed system. Energy circulates through three main biological systems—the nutritive (or digestive) system, the nervous system, and the reproductive system—and this energy is shared equally among those systems.[18] Illness occurs when one system demands more energy than the others do, causing the remaining two systems to experience a depletion of energy. In the context of education and career, Clarke argues that illness manifests among young women when the minimum standards society requires for scholarly and professional success are too rigorous for the female body, since a woman's sexual system demands more energy to perform its expected functions—namely menstruation, ovulation, pregnancy, and lactation. Importantly, Clarke does not make the argument that the female body is inherently disabled by her reproductive system; rather, the female body is vulnerable to illness because her unique reproductive abilities require more energy than her male counterpart does.[19] He explicitly claims, "[N]o organ or function in plant, animal, or human kind can properly be regarded as a disability or source of weakness," and further that "[t]he female organization is no exception to this law" as long as the organization is being "rightly guided and developed."[20]

Clarke's conditions for proper guidance and development of the female body are reminiscent of social construction, for he claims that social systems like education and fashion create the conditions for disability among women. Hysteria, amenorrhea, dysmenorrhea, and other forms of "female weakness" "may be credited to artificial deformities strapped to the spine," and specifically "corsets and skirts," which cause "grievous maladies, and impose a needless invalidism."[21] His insistence that the education system serves as the primary culprit for reproductive disorder undermines what few valid points Clarke makes about the social construction of disability. As Alison Kafer critiques in *Feminist, Queer, Crip*, the social model of disability and its emphasis on the impairment/disability binary misses the experience of disability itself, especially among people with chronic illness or pain, since "social and structural changes will do little to make one's joints stop aching or to alleviate back pain."[22] It further "casts out cure," ignoring those individuals who are searching for a way to heal through medical intervention. I do not disavow the need for social or structural changes during the nineteenth century or today. On the contrary, I argue alongside Kafer that feminist disability studies requires both an attention to the social construction of disability and a relational model of disability for the politics of disability to change.[23] These are not mutually exclusive positions. Nor are they oppositional, constructing yet another binary. Just as Kafer argues that she wants to "twist 'queer' into encompassing 'crip' (and 'crip,' 'queer')," in a kind of "twisted inclusion" that resembles the Möbius strip,[24] I also seek to twist the social into the material (and the material into the social), beginning with the materiality of language.

This kind of twisted inclusion further provides a model for how women writers of medical fiction respond to patriarchal medicine's closed-system theory with their own feminist theorizing of the body as a subject co-constituted by other nonhuman subjects in social and material environments. One of the reasons women writers of medical fiction vehemently reject Clarke not only concerns his claims and evidence but also the rhetorical form of his argument.[25] Clarke's treatise embodies the scientific world's transition to clinical evidence, which drew upon medical jargon that "rob[s]" women of "a ready vocabulary" to engage in conversations about their bodies.[26] Women writers were left in a "hopeless bind": They could respond with their personal lived experience of the female body, which risked being discredited in the face of clinical knowledge, or they could reply in the language of clinical biology, which conceded power to patriarchal medicine.[27] Davis and Alcott chose a third way that prefigures Kafer's "twisted inclusion." Medical fiction opens a space to reclaim female subjectivity through the narrative practice of (p)rescription. This narrative move simultaneously critiques the rhetoric of (socio)biological (in)determinism and imagines the female body as free from socially constructed gender roles. Women writers of medical fiction found that they could draw upon the language of biology without deploying it in a clinical form, and at the same time narrate their lived experience of the female body through the objective distance of a fictional character. As they initiate this turn, Davis and Alcott embrace the rhetoric of "both/and" against Clarke and S. Weir Mitchell, who commit themselves to the "either/or" rhetoric of binary opposition that pits body against mind, female against male, and nature against culture in a humanistic worldview which material feminists and disability theorists still critique today.

Theorist Mel Y. Chen locates this tension between subjectivity and objectivity in the rhetoric of animacy, which they define as a quality of liveness, sentience, or humanness of a noun or noun phrase in the tradition of linguistics.[28] Yet animacy is so much more than a lexical act: "Words more than signify," Chen emphasizes. "[T]hey affect and effect."[29] Women writers of medical fiction and feminist disability theorists share this common belief: Language has the power to govern our thinking. At their worst, words objectify and dehumanize. At their best, they function in oppositional acts of reclamation and reanimation, as in the case of "queer." Most significantly, women writers of medical fiction and feminist disability theorists agree that animacy is political, just as "grammar is politics by other means."[30] Donna Haraway may have been discussing pronouns, but her point dovetails with Chen's: Subjectivity empowers speakers, whether the speaker is a thirteen-year-old girl, a feminist physician, or a cyborg. My theory of (p)rescription necessarily acknowledges that affective grammar may be used to empower the wrong speakers, leading to objectification and dehumanization through the act of de-animating subjects.

Chen explains in their book *Animacies: Biopolitics, Racial Mattering, and Queer Affect* that one method of de-animating subjects involves structurally placing the subject in the position of direct object in a sentence, while another involves universalizing by placing the subject in a larger, impersonal group, or using metaphor to associate the subject with a nonhuman static entity.[31] Thus, when Edward H. Clarke concludes matter-of-factly in *Sex in Education* that "Girls lose health, strength, and nerve by a regimen that ignores the periodical tides and reproductive apparatus of their organization," his phrasing should give us pause as much as the content of his claim.[32] The sentence may begin with the subject of "girls," but the group or "class"—as Clarke refers to them[33]—does not have agency in this sentence. Quite the opposite: The use of "by" and the prepositional phrase that follows signals to readers that the subject of girls is being acted upon. The girls are de-animated. The "regimen" responsible for de-animating "girls" physically and linguistically is the American system of education, which places too many intellectual demands upon them. Clarke, however, does not seek to re-animate girls; he seeks to re-animate their "periodical tides," or menstrual cycles, and their "reproductive apparatus," or system of uterus and ovaries. Clarke repeatedly diagnoses women who display symptoms of hysteria as suffering "an arrest of the development of the reproductive apparatus."[34] Just like the earlier phrase in which girls are de-animated by the intellectual labor that they contribute to the education system, this phrase indicates that the subject under "arrested development" is the uterus and ovaries. Clarke seeks to re-animate the uterus and ovaries at the expense of female subjectivity.

Clarke not only reduces women to their biologies but compares them with nonhuman subjects such as flowers, furthering their objectification under Chen's principle of animacy. In one particularly telling extended comparison, he describes the physician as a gardener who raises "the lily and the rose" in the same environment as "the oak and the vine," but "trains each of them with a separate art" just as he recommends society educate girls and boys differently. Of course, this rhetorical device is not uncommon for the nineteenth century: There has been a tradition in medical discourse of comparing women and girls to flowers ever since *Aristotle's Compleat Master-piece* (1741).[35] Haraway emphasizes that part of the work of feminist science is engaging in "[t]he process of exposing bad science, showing the fictive character of all science, and then proposing the real facts."[36] One of the reasons science maintains a "fictive character" is because the form of scientific knowledge is narrative: "biology tells tales about origins, about genesis, and about nature."[37] Animacy empowers women writers like Alcott and Davis to tell a different story of the female body through (p)rescription, even if they must contend with an inherited patriarchal voice.[38] Scholars must further pay attention to this patriarchal voice if we hope to recognize what is at stake in women writers' efforts to rescript medical narratives of the female body. Like Chen and Haraway, my theory of (p)rescription is indebted to Judith Butler, who argues in *Bodies That Matter* that "language and materiality are not opposed, for language both is and refers to that which is material, and what is material never fully escapes from the process by which it is signified."[39] Alcott and Davis also recognize the materiality of language, and they use animacy to their advantage as they tell a different story about disability and the female body.

When we attend to the materiality of language, we must account for the theoretical frameworks of both social constructionism and new materialism in our theorizing the concept of disability. Moreover, we must also theorize with a critical awareness of the biopolitical potential underlying each of these theoretical fields. Just as the imprint of social construction appears in Clarke's critique of women's dress, so too the imprint of new materialism appears in nineteenth-century evolutionary science and sentimental fiction as a result of the legacy of Jean-Baptiste Lamarck. Kyla Schuller argues that the legacy of Lamarckian evolution throughout the long nineteenth century supersedes Charles Darwin, who did not gain cultural prominence until the 1920s and 1930s in the wake of the rediscovery of Mendelian genetics.[40] Dynamic matter was a central tenet of the American School of Evolution, which touted the work of Lamarck. They express their understanding of affective matter as the "impression theory of sensation": Impressions, or marks made on a body through contact with another substance, result in changes rendered and retained by both subjects; the degree of affect determines impressibility, which became a taxonomical field used to classify the vulnerability and stability of subjects.[41] Women were, of course, more impressible and therefore more vulnerable to sentimentality and the material affect of feelings, which made them an unstable force susceptible to hysteria.[42] One leading neo-Lamarckian paleontologist argued that because women inherit the "disability" of reproduction, they not only are naturally more impressible, but also responsible for carefully regulating their exposure to subjects that easily impress and adapt since impressions are liable to be transmitted to offspring.[43]

Clarke only uses the language of impressibility twice in *Sex in Education*. Both times he makes the case that the female sex is more impressible "in girlhood," and that neglect of a girl's health during puberty "breeds the germs of diseases that in later life yield torturing or fatal maladies" such as hysteria, amenorrhea, and dysmenorrhea.[44] Clarke theorizes from both a materialist perspective and a social constructionist one, which not only confirms Schuller's claim that "notions of dynamic matter" akin to contemporary new materialisms "were alive and well in the nineteenth century," but also upholds her critique of new materialism in its failure to "account for the coconstitution of material and cultural processes over time," the result of which risks redeploying agential matter as a form of biopower.[45] We would be doing no better than our theoretical ancestors, whether hegemonic or feminist, if we continued to uphold a false dichotomy between materiality and language or new materialism and social construction. Language matters. Clarke's closed-system theory, which he articulates through language, caused real damage. In an effort to validate the theory, which posited that girls and young women must reserve their energy for reproductive functions rather than intellectual endeavors, Clarke cites S. Weir Mitchell's *Wear and Tear* (1871) in subsequent editions of *Sex in Education*.[46] Both physicians, unsurprisingly, use the language of hysteria and define the female body in terms of disability. Clarke considers hysteria one possible diagnosis resulting from woman's intellectual exhaustion, or extended "brain-work."[47] Others include disorders of the menstrual cycle such as amenorrhea or dysmenorrhea. Mitchell agrees, blaming women for their status as "self-made invalids" because they spend as many hours in intellectual pursuits as their male peers.[48]

The crux of this rhetorical danger lies in animacy, for Clarke and Mitchell use language to construct hysteria as a viable diagnosis and then actively promote social barriers in higher education and professional spheres as preventative for this fictive condition. One of their peers even cites hysteria as evidence for disenfranchising women in the wake of suffrage.[49] As treatment, Mitchell prescribes the rest cure in *Fat and Blood* (1884), which supposedly heals hysteria through prolonged periods of rest, "massage, electricity, and over-feeding," as well as seclusion.[50] In extreme cases, "rest" involves confinement from a period of six weeks to two months, which would predictably cause or exacerbate mental illness, as we have learned from quarantine during the recent COVID-19 pandemic. Mitchell insists, "The ennui of rest and seclusion is far better borne by women than by the other sex,"[51] which seems to suggest that he finds the female sex more resilient than the male sex. Yet his advice contradicts this understanding of female "constitution," or physiology, for he not only treats women as the "weaker sex" but also actively weakens them through prolonged rest, seclusion, and the prohibition of creative endeavors.[52]

The Matter of Hysteria

Charlotte Perkins Gilman not only confirms the treatment guidelines from Mitchell's *Fat and Blood* but further mocks them in her short story "The Yellow Wallpaper" (1892) and its follow-up essay "Why I Wrote 'The Yellow Wallpaper'" (1913). As Gilman famously writes of the treatment: "[Dr. Mitchell] sent me home with solemn advice to 'live as domestic a life as far as possible,' to 'have but two hours' intellectual life a day,' and 'never to touch pen, brush or pencil again, as long as I lived.'"[53] His advice nearly drove Gilman to "utter mental ruin."[54] Gilman's own language turns our attention toward what is actually at stake in the rest cure: undiagnosed and untreated mental health conditions. Like Chen, Butler, and Haraway, Gilman recognizes the materiality of language, which hinges on the power of animacy to move the listener toward or away from normalized behavior. However, if we were to follow only the social model of disability, which emphasizes the role of language in social construction, we would risk missing the embodied pain Charlotte Perkins Gilman experiences and records in her short story as postpartum depression and psychosis. Is sexist medicine responsible for relegating women to the domestic sphere? Yes. Are Clarke and Mitchell forcing their medical evidence of hysteria to fit already-existing gendered social roles? Absolutely. We could—and should—blame the patriarchal systems at play, as well as seek to end, replace, or reform those systems, and this includes academic research. Clarke and Mitchell engage in an academic form of research—complete with footnotes and references that build upon their (male) peers—that reduces the female body to a kind of simple machine in an effort to make it knowable and controllable using clinical diagnosis.

Yet this level of social awareness is not enough. Scholars must also pay attention to the physical signs and symptoms of illness, since Gilman deploys her experience of postpartum depression into the narrator whose narratological embodiment actively resists a reductive reading of the female body. In what follows from this section, I examine "The Yellow Wallpaper" as a work of medical fiction that theorizes feminist medicine as beholden to environmental health, which I argue serves as a narratological move that resists clinical diagnosis in favor of a more holistic approach. In other words, Gilman uses her short story to retheorize the human body as a dynamic, porous subject co-constituted by a reciprocal relationship with other nonhuman subjects within and beyond the human body. She makes "strange bedfellows" of chemical hormones and arsenic-laden wallpaper. Gilman rebukes physicians like Mitchell and Clarke who willfully ignore such environmental factors as part of their diagnostic and treatment methods. Their exclusive focus on internal biological factors not only approaches the body as a machine experiencing system breakdown but also objectifies the body in its universalizing process of diagnosis and cure. As we have seen in their popular medical treatises, Mitchell's and Clarke's rhetorical practice of de-animating the female body involves the principle of universalizing subjects by speaking of the subject as part of a group or class. Navigating general versus particular causes of illness is one of the responsibilities of medical practitioners in their good-faith practice of narrative medicine, according to Rita Charon.[55] One-size-fits-all diagnostics miss the unique phenomena of the patient's situation, while considering every patient a special case risks overlooking possible therapies that practitioners have successfully employed for patients with similar cases.

The act of missing, overlooking, and misdiagnosing is an act of failure. Of course, the medical system fails Gilman and her narrator because of its hyperbolic emphasis on gendered diseases and cures. It cannot help but fail her. But the theoretical frameworks animating sexist medical practices, as crystallized in and popularized by the works of Edward H. Clarke and S. Weir Mitchell, fail

Gilman too. Because Clarke and Mitchell interpret the female body through a negotiation of social constructionist and materialist worldviews, even our contemporary oppositional revisions—or (p)rescriptions—of social constructionist theory and new materialist theory must inevitably fail to explain Gilman's experience of postpartum depression. However, as Jack Halberstam reminds us, failure is not always a bad thing: "Under certain circumstances failing, losing, forgetting, unmaking, undoing, unbecoming, not knowing may in fact offer more creative, more cooperative, more surprising ways of being in the world."[56] Like Halberstam, I eschew "thinking on the bright side," as the popular saying goes; rather, I find the failure of women writers of medical fiction offers an opportunity for readers of medical fiction to reimagine the medical system and the larger hegemonic structure in which it exists as being otherwise. "Why not think in terms of a different kind of society than the one that first created and then abolished slavery?" Halberstam asks, echoing the inquiry he perceives across animated "Pixarvolt" films such as *Chicken Run*, *Over the Hedge*, *A Bug's Life*, and *Finding Nemo*.[57] In a way, this eventually becomes Gilman's project, first in *Moving the Mountain* (1911) and then in *Herland* (1915). Gilman's flawed socialist feminist utopia is emphatically not the anarchic feminist utopia of *Chicken Run*. But the utopian impulse underlies much of the work of feminist medical fiction, including the medical novels of Gilman, Alcott, and Davis—and it is driven by failure.

Because Gilman's narrator in "The Yellow Wallpaper" fails to heal, Gilman herself finds her voice as the narrator's spokesperson and as the spokesperson for other women who might be suffering from postpartum depression. This was, in fact, her self-proclaimed reason for writing "The Yellow Wallpaper": "It [the story] was not intended to drive people crazy, but to save people from being driven crazy" by alerting them to a popular yet dangerous method of treatment, "and it worked," she concludes.[58] At the very least, Gilman's short story affected one reader enough to "save [her] from a similar fate" and convinced "the great specialist," S. Weir Mitchell, to "alter[] his treatment of neurasthenia since reading *The Yellow Wallpaper*." Even if these anecdotes of success are mere fables, Gilman's failure to heal herself and others enacts a kind of "shadow feminism" that questions alongside Babs of *Chicken Run* why women suffering from mental illness only have two choices: "freedom in liberal terms or death."[59] Failure—of the system to treat her, of Gilman's ability to heal—provides Gilman with an opportunity to imagine "a sex-neutral medical model" that considers multiple environmental factors including domestic spaces, outdoor spaces, nonhuman actors, and the agents within one's own biological ecosystem as responsible for affecting health.[60] Scholars have written extensively about "The Yellow Wallpaper," often reading the narrative as an early feminist work of social or political fiction that symbolically explores gendered oppression. Yet, as Sari Altschuler highlights, few scholars have read this seminal late nineteenth-century text as a work of medical fiction: "[I]t took until the twenty-first century—an age in which medical and health humanities programs are flourishing—to see the story as a medical text."[61]

We need new theoretical frameworks like (p)rescription, animacy, sentimental biopower, and crip affect to (re)imagine and (re)theorize the oppositional power of nineteenth-century women writers of medical fiction, even if it means failing in our attempts to do so. Jane Thrailkill characterizes this "epistemological reorientation" as "a deceptively simple" move grounded in a narrative medicine practice that shifts "from looking at a patient's body" à la clinical practice "to listening to a patient's story," and she specifically cites "The Yellow Wallpaper" as an early form of theorizing narrative medicine in fiction form.[62] Narrative medicine is "deceptively simple" because it requires the audience to "listen for" the experience of illness, which is an exercise Rita Charon distinguishes from active listening in its engagement of empathy, or the act of sharing the burden of the speaker's experience through imagining oneself in the speaker's position. Empathy is hard and uncomfortable. For instance, the narrator of "The Yellow Wallpaper" feels exhaustion at even the thought of performing small tasks such as writing or getting dressed. She further confesses, "I cry at nothing, and I cry most of the time."[63] She describes her nerves as "dreadfully depressing," which signifies clinical depression (6). When the narrator first encounters the yellow wallpaper, she animates the "sprawling flamboyant patterns" as "pronounced enough to constantly irritate and provoke study, and when you follow the lame uncertain curves for a distance they suddenly commit suicide" (5). This is not just a description of wallpaper. The narrator communicates her embodied experience of mental illness, which she perceives through her interaction with the wallpaper: She is constantly irritated and is contemplating suicide. For a reader with lived experience of postpartum depression—or even a reader with lived experience of clinical depression that is not pregnancy-related—the signs and symptoms trigger memories that place the reader in the text.

Even without this complex embodiment, as disability theorist Toibin Seibers calls it, readers can learn to empathize with the narrator of "The Yellow Wallpaper," and by extension Gilman herself, through the act of occupying her emotional space.[64] Gilman evokes the experience of postpartum depression by situating the events in close succession after the birth of the narrator's baby. And her experience of mental illness aligns with the clinical signs of postpartum depression: depressive mood, excessive crying (often for no reason), overwhelming fatigue or loss of energy, intense irritability, restlessness, thoughts of harming yourself, and recurrent thoughts of death or suicide. The narrator further expresses an aversion to the nursery in their country house retreat and struggles to bond with her newborn, both of which are symptoms of postpartum depression: "I *cannot* be with him, it makes me so nervous," she declares (6, her emphasis). Gilman herself experienced postpartum depression after the birth of her daughter, Katherine.[65] If we take seriously biological criticism in disability scholarship, as do David Mitchell and Sharon Snyder, then this means considering how disabled authorship reorients readers to "yield important insights into the inevitable impact of disability upon the creator's worldview."[66] Moreover, if we as scholars take into account our own positionality, then we must further follow Mitchell and Snyder as "politicized scholars [who] encourage the development of reading practices that embrace, transform, and reckon with our inherited disability storylines."[67] For me, such politicizing means acknowledging that my own experience of postpartum depression after the birth of my oldest son biases my reading of Gilman's "The Yellow Wallpaper" as a work of medical fiction about postpartum depression. It also means acknowledging that Gilman and I seek to raise awareness of the embodied truth of postpartum depression because we desire appropriate medical intervention.

And yet, my experience of postpartum depression is not the same as Gilman's experience of postpartum depression. The onus is still on me as a reader to empathize with her specific experience of loss, grief, and failure, as well as her hope for healing. Like Rebecca Harding Davis before her, Gilman imagines artistic endeavors as one possible means of healing until treatments that are more effective are developed. Many scholars have commented upon Davis's own experience of postpartum depression and rest cure therapy under the care of S. Weir Mitchell. Although there are few references to postpartum depression—and none to the rest cure—in "The Wife's Story" (1864), the despondency Hester (Hetty) Manning feels may be attributed to postpartum depression, given that Davis wrote the short story around the time of her son's birth in April 1864.[68] Hetty explicitly links her sadness to the birth of her daughter, observing, "since my baby was born, my soul as well as my body had been weak and nauseated."[69] However, she dismisses her feelings as the result of sleeplessness from struggling with the fussiness of her baby, who is constantly "crying night and day like any other animal," thereby "wearing out in me the strength needed" just to get by.[70] Although it is helpful to recognize "The Yellow Wallpaper" and "The Wife's Story" as fictionalized accounts of the authors' respective experiences with postpartum depression, our goal should not simply be diagnosis of characters or the author. Scholars must also pay attention to the ideological worldview of the author if we are to reconcile with their proposed methods of healing and prevention.

Jean Pfaelzer describes Davis's experience with Dr. Mitchell as "radically" different from Gilman's, for although he "recommended the same cure of rest and sensory deprivation that he later prescribed to Charlotte Perkins Gilman," Davis does not follow a strict regimen of abstaining from literary endeavors.[71] In fact, Davis confides in a letter to her friend Annie Fields that "the doctor forbids the least reading or writing for fear of bringing back the trouble in my head," yet she clearly disregards this advice in the very act of writing a letter to Annie and in drafting "The Wife's Story" at the exact same time.[72] In a move that echoes her own experience of art as a source of healing, Hetty fervently pursues music and operatic singing in "The Wife's Story." Gilman alternatively warns that a lack of artistic endeavors opens up a space for psychosis as her narrator does not just obsess over the yellow wallpaper but further hallucinates a woman trapped in the wallpaper. Both authors ultimately agree that art serves as a source of healing in direct opposition to the advice of their physician, Dr. Mitchell. Yet, even if Davis and Gilman had experienced similar effects of the rest cure, they might still experience postpartum depression differently and thereby produce divergent narratives of their experience. Clinical signs and symptoms guide practitioners toward a diagnosis so that they can appropriately intervene, but no two individuals experience the same signs and symptoms in exactly the same way. Moreover, many of the symptoms apply to other mental health conditions among both men and women, including bipolar disorder, dissociative disorder, and psychosis.

Gilman's experience figures postpartum depression as a complex phenomenon in "The Yellow Wallpaper" in direct opposition to Mitchell and Clarke, whose theories and treatments strove to reduce the supposedly mystical female body to discrete, knowable parts. One cannot reduce diagnosis of postpartum depression to a single knowable cause or biological organ, Gilman suggests. Our volatile environments play as much of a role as our biological systems, creating the conditions for ever-evolving collisions and reactions. Gilman animates both the wallpaper and the narrator's body in a reciprocal push-pull kind of relationship that recognizes how nonhuman subjects co-constitute human identities. The wallpaper "stares" at the narrator with "two bulbous eyes," evoking an emotional reaction from the narrator, who becomes "positively angry with the impertinence of it" (7). This is no "static entity," nor is the wallpaper a "blank slate, surface, or site passively awaiting signification," as Karen Barad might say.[73] It is agential, both in its material affect upon the narrator and in her linguistic reconstruction of its movement. It crawls, and she crawls with it. They crawl together as a kind of companion species, co-evolving toward psychosis.[74] Although the narrator expresses surprise at "so much expression in an inanimate thing," Gilman intentionally describes the wallpaper as an affective agent. It evokes a range of emotional responses from "infuriating" to "torturing" (12), as well as acting upon the narrator's body, leaving sensory marks such as "yellow smooches on all [her] clothes" and a "foul," "awful" odor that "creeps all over the house" and "gets into [her] hair" (14–15).

Historian Lucinda Hawksley further nuances our reading of Gilman's "The Yellow Wallpaper" when she remarks in her study of Victorian wallpaper that the smell to which the narrator refers is arsenic. Hawksley correctly summarizes the impression among contemporary scholars that nineteenth-century readers consider "The Yellow Wallpaper" a tale of insanity, while "modern readers interpret it as a portrait of a woman stifled by her era."[75] Like Hawksley, I find both readings too simplistic. Hawksley explains that, by midcentury, arsenic had become a popular binding agent for adhering wallpaper. It retained its common usage even after the owner of Morris & Co. famously dismissed its fatal effects to an anxious consumer public.[76] Since the narrator's experience of hallucination and smell "corresponds to toxicology reports of wallpaper containing arsenical pigments emitting a distinctive smelling gas," we might do well to consider this detail in our reading of Gilman's short story.[77] Several disability scholars have adopted a new materialist approach (and vice versa) in their critical examinations of toxicity and environmental health, among them Mel Y. Chen, Stacy Alaimo, and Alison Kafer.[78] They remind readers that invisible substances do not exist "out there," somewhere distinct from us, but are always already within and around our bodies, threatening our health on a daily basis.[79] Much like the narrator of "The Yellow Wallpaper," many unsuspecting middle-to upper-class women were vulnerable to arsenic poisoning because of prolonged exposure as they performed daily domestic tasks in their living spaces, especially if they were confined to home for rest cure therapy. As citizens of a risk society, women writers of medical fiction became acutely aware of the nature of their vulnerability, which emerged from a complex network of systems including sexist medicine, legal censorship, and gendered private and public spaces. Gilman theorizes a feminist practice of diagnostics that accounts for the role of affect, both the material subjects enmeshed with the body and the social circumstances placing that sexed body at risk.

Comstockian Impressions

At the same time that Clarke and Mitchell pathologized hysteria in their professional medical treatises, Anthony Comstock set limits upon what may (and may not) be publicly said about the female body, and by extension, hysteria, through the act of passing a federal censorship law. Congress passed the "Act for the Suppression of Trade in, and Circulation of, Obscene Literature and Articles of Immoral Use" (Ch. 258, § 2, 17 Stat. 599) on March 3, 1873, and appointed Comstock as a "special agent" of the United States Post Office.[80] Called the "Comstock Law" for short, this piece of legislation began as a direct act against Victoria Woodhull and her free lovers.[81] However, the law adopted a life all its own, since it gave the US Postal Service—and Comstock himself as "special agent"—"broad and vague powers" to "search, seize, and arrest" potential violators. The Comstock Law was comprehensive. It not only outlawed the publication or distribution of "any obscene book, pamphlet, paper, writing, advertisement, circular, print, picture, drawing or other representation, figure, or image on or of paper or other material"; it also prohibited "any drug or medicine, or any article whatever, for the prevention of conception, or for causing unlawful abortion" and the "advertisement" of any drug, medicine, or abortifacients, whether via print or word of mouth. Instead of rhetorically de-animating the female body like his contemporaries Clarke and Mitchell, Comstock and his federal law attempted to omit the female body from medical discourse through the act of censorship.

Of course, it did not work. Comstock strove for "suppression," but he utterly failed, as his indictments and prosecutions led to media attention, which in turn led bold artists, writers, and dramatists to create more risqué content. Amy Werbel claims that by the 1880s, "Comstock was well aware of the boost in sales his censure could provoke,"[82] forcing him to adjust his censorship approach from overt measures of legal proceedings to more subtle measures of search and seizure, intimidation, and media shaming. But in the immediate aftermath of the passing of the Comstock Law, writers were not sure how seriously to take legal censorship. Werbel documents multiple covert yet creative methods of erotic cultural production, from transparent playing cards to trick cigar cases with racy images to penis-shaped liquor bottles. She even briefly discusses a satirical essay by Mark Twain and sexually explicit poetry by Walt Whitman, both of which were meant to mock and resist Comstock.[83] Women writers had it harder. As Alicia Puglionesi explains, women writers and readers of sexual hygiene—much less erotic content—were forced to adopt creative methods of evading censorship, such as publishing and purchasing subscription presses like *Search Lights for Health*. Comstock may have appeared to win the war on obscenity, at least for a period of forty-two years, but he failed to stop the production of obscenities, which ultimately led to the creation of new subcultures.[84] His failure may be our gain, at least in the sense of gaining fictional texts that creatively resist Comstockian censorship, rewrite the medical narratives animating female subjectivity, and reimagine the medico-legal system with greater inclusivity for non-normative bodies.

Comstock recognized the (bio)power of animacy just as much as Clarke and Mitchell, which is why he prohibited the publication of obscene texts: "He was defending the youth of the country against forces of evil that worked in secret to carry into homes obscene books and pictures inciting lust and leading to masturbation and prostitution," Horowitz explains of Comstock's motivations.[85] Comstock himself says as much in his treatise *Traps for the Young* (1883), a defense of his methods of censorship and suppression which he wrote approximately one decade after the passing of federal Comstock law, when he realized that his methods were neither working nor being taken seriously by the public. "This is a plea for the moral purity of children," Comstock proclaims on the opening page of the treatise.[86] He warns his audience of parents against the dangers of "evil reading," charging them to watch and censor what their children read, including "half-dime novels and story papers," which receive an entire chapter unto themselves. Much like the patient case studies of Clarke's *Sex in Education*, Comstock offers a series of anecdotes that demonstrate the effect of evil reading upon the behavior of children and young adults. This is peppered with commentary that imagines how Satan uses evil reading to trap children and young adults into sinful behavior in a move that is oddly reminiscent of C. S. Lewis's *The Screwtape Letters* (1942), though it might be worth pointing out that *The Screwtape Letters* is a novel, whereas Comstock is wholly sincere when he asserts in his nonfiction treatise that "[Satan] resolved to make another trap for boys and girls especially," which Comstock identifies as the novel.[87]

What Comstock describes throughout *Traps for the Young* is the power of narrative affect. Comstock recognizes the materiality of language when he repeatedly asserts that novels not only breed impure thoughts, but also present young audiences with radical ideas and dangerous scenarios that they cannot help but act out in the real world. In other words, Comstock assumes that young audiences are incapable of discerning for themselves between fiction and reality. "The boy cheats himself by imagining he is doing a manly thing when he naturally follows a base example" from a novel, Comstock warns his own audience of parents.[88] Young women and girls similarly debase themselves through "evil reading" as they act out romantic scenarios that cheapen their virtue, causing them to lose their virginity and marry to hide their shame, or alternatively, become runaways and criminals. Instead of animating the body at the expense of the female subject, as does Clarke, Comstock animates the novel at the expense of the minds of "youth who [are] unaccustomed to analysis" and mere "creature[s] of impulse."[89] Comstock imagines the minds of children and young adults as passive recipients of relata, which is an ideological holdover of Lockian tabula rasa from the Enlightenment period that Paolo Freire would critique eighty-two years later in *Pedagogy of the Oppressed* (1968; in English, 1970). How the court system would interpret and enforce this ideology further links the impressionability of the minds of children and young adults with the impressionability of women, and specifically, the supposedly feeble minds of women. For further evidence of Comstock and his contemporaries' faith in animacy, we must consider *United States v. Bennett* (1879), a federal court case that not only upheld Comstock law but also established the Hicklin test as an appropriate means of censoring literature.

In *United States v. Bennett*, free love reformer D. M. Bennett was tried and convicted for marketing and selling obscenity in the form of *Cupid's Yokes* (1876), a free love pamphlet written by Ezra Heywood that argued against government regulation of sexual relations via the legal institution of marriage. Heywood had already been tried and convicted for the writing of *Cupid's Yokes* by the time Bennett's case arrived in the United States Circuit Court in New York. Although Heywood's case was significant for enforcing Comstock law, as well as discouraging writers and publishers from violating obscenity regulations, Judge Samuel Blatchford wrote a landmark decision in *United States v. Bennett* that had far-reaching power for over fifty years, and he specifically adopted the Hicklin test as the appropriate rubric for defining and censoring obscenity.[90] First adopted by British law after *Regina v. Hicklin* (1868), the Hicklin test defined obscenity based upon impressibility, or the capacity of an individual to receive a mark from external objects created by pressure from the giver and resulting in changes rendered to the receiver.[91] In American law, the Hicklin test incorporated a secondary feature beyond general impressibility; it further demarcated a specific audience of "the young and the inexperienced" as most vulnerable.[92] In a nearly word-for-word parroting of his British counterpart Chief Justice Alexander Cockburn, Blatchford states in his decision:

> It is not a question of whether it would corrupt morals, tend to deprave your minds, or the minds of every person; it is a question whether it tends to deprave the minds *of those open to such influences* and into whose hands a publication of this character might come. It is within the law [to convict] if it would suggest impure and libidinous thoughts in *the young and the inexperienced.*[93]

Blatchford defines the vulnerable, or impressible, as young adults and unmarried women of all ages, as denoted by his rhetorical act of linking "those open to such influences" with "the young and the inexperienced." The Supreme Court of the United States would later bolster Blatchford's ruling by adopting the Hicklin test to convict Lew Rosen for distributing an obscene newspaper titled *Tenderloin, Number, Broadway* in the case of *Rosen v. United States* (1896).

Although Blatchford's ruling concerned a nonfiction pamphlet that was explicit in its argument against the institution of marriage and in favor of casual intercourse, the Hicklin test would eventually apply to convictions against works of fiction like James Joyce's *Ulysses*. In 1918, *The Little Review*, an American literary magazine published by feminist anarchist Margaret Anderson, began serializing episodes of *Ulysses*. The magazine came under attack during the 1921 trial of *United States v. One Book Called "Ulysses,"* in which the US District Court in southern New York ruled *Ulysses* obscene based on the Hicklin test for the novel's explicit depiction of masturbation. This effectively banned *Ulysses* in the United States for over a decade until the Second Circuit Court of Appeals overturned its ruling in 1933, after which Joyce's novel returned to the American literary market and the US courts abandoned use of the Hicklin test.[94] But not before US courts ruled several classic works of fiction as obscene, including Theodore Dreiser's *An American Tragedy*, Ernest Hemingway's *A Farewell to Arms*, D. H. Lawrence's *Lady Chatterley's Lover*, and even Geoffrey Chaucer's *The Canterbury Tales*.[95] Although the majority of these convictions occurred during the decade of the 1920s, women writers of medical fiction took precautions in the immediate aftermath of the passing of the federal Comstock Law, since they knew that they were challenging the sensibilities of male lawmakers, physicians, and writers who wielded power over them with the potential threat of reporting.

Censorship does not stop animacy, and yet Comstock's fear of this acknowledged link between animacy and impressibility drove him to censor reproductive health discourses, whether medical or literary, in his effort to sanitize a potential audience of young adults and unmarried women. Nineteenth-century physicians and politicians share an anxiety of imagination with twenty-first-century conservatives who defend literary censorship to protect children and young adults. They fear that imaginative exploration of the body in fiction will incite—even excite—youth to engage in risky behavior in the real world, and if they further adhered to the principles of Lamarckian evolution as Schuller suggests, then they might also believe that risky behavior could permanently affect race health through hereditary transmission.[96] Louisa May Alcott did not agree with this hegemonic notion of impressibility as a function of gender and sex differentiation. For her, as for other women writers of medical fiction, so-called "illicit" knowledge does not negatively impress the body; rather, danger to the impressible body lies in medical ignorance. Alcott rescripts threads from Clarkian animacy, Mitchellian etiology, and Comstockian notions of impressibility into her medical novel *Eight Cousins*, even when she agrees with Clarke, Mitchell, and Comstock that young women are impressible. Yet, from Alcott's perspective, the fact of their impressibility is not something to fear, because it opens up a space for properly educating young adults in how to care for their bodies. Stephanie Browner observes that, in an ironic turn of events that directly satirizes Clarke's treatise and Mitchell's rest cure, Mac in *Eight Cousins* suffers anxiety and eyestrain from too much study and "is confined like a female neurasthenic to rest in a dark room for several months."[97] For Alcott, "[i]llness is gender-blind,"[98] but I would also add that Alcott recognizes illness as a product of co-mingling social and material forces. Mac gains "very little comfort" from a consultation with his doctor concerning the efficacy of solitary rest, so Rose takes it upon herself to be "head-nurse and chief-reader," helping Mac successfully heal from eyestrain (132). In yet another jab at Clarke's treatise, Alcott mocks the disbelief of the other six male cousins and the aunts at the efficacy of Rose's care. "'Odd, isn't it, what a knack women have for taking care of sick folks?'" (135–6), Charlie rhetorically questions. Nope, not odd at all, Alcott discerns. Women can be nurses and physicians, just like men. Any suggestion otherwise is a social construction meant to privilege one gender at the expense of another.

In writing a young adult novel that presents the medical knowledge a young woman ought to have, Alcott flagrantly challenges Comstockian censorship and the Clarkian education system. "'I intend to know what kills me if I can,'" Rose declares in her justification for studying physiology (224). Alcott desires the same for her readers. She chooses one of the most impressible figures according to Comstockian ideology, a thirteen-year-old female orphan, and gives her access to medical knowledge about the body. If the premise alone did not incite the ire of Clarke and Comstock, then the form and content of the narrative would have done, since Alcott contradicts the closed-system theory before an audience of impressible young (mostly female) readers. One substance that threatens to "kill" Rose is the corset, a diagnosis with which Clarke concurs. However, Alcott's scientific rationale diverges from Clarke in her ungendered approach, which animates the respiratory rather than reproductive system. "'[T]here are 600,000,000 air cells in one pair of lungs,'" Rose reports to Aunt Myra after her first physiology lesson, "'so you see what quantities of air we *must* have'" for proper functioning of the human body (223, her emphasis). Alcott animates the alveoli in an effort to reveal the actual dangers of the corset, which prohibits the flow of oxygen into the alveoli that "open and shut" like "little doors" (223). This function has nothing to do with uterine displacement or the menstrual cycle, as Clarke suggests. Her rescripting of the Clarkian education system should impress young readers with a counternarrative of how bodies perform the same respiratory function regardless of gender or sex.

No Sex in Outdoor Education

New materialists and disability theorists often focus on the dangers of our environs in theorizing environmental health such that we cannot help but refrain alongside Stacy Alaimo, "No place is safe."[99] Heavy metals lace the building materials of our homes. Allergens in our gardens cause swelling or difficulty breathing. Even our own minds become cavernous places of obsessive thought. Nevertheless, we cannot deny the therapeutic experience of encountering life outdoors. Even Kafer concedes, "I cannot deny that I feel different 'outside,' away from traffic and exhaust pipes and crowds of people. That I have been conditioned to feel this way does not change the fact that I feel more peace in my body when perched on the side of a cliff, or gazing over a meadow, or surrounded by sequoias."[100] Charlotte Perkins Gilman, Louisa May Alcott, and Rebecca Harding Davis agree with Kafer in their shared attempt to imagine nature as a space for healing and of the healthy (female) body as co-constituted by its nonhuman environs, though Davis is perhaps more skeptical of the efficacy of outdoor therapy than her peers. In this section, I examine how Alcott and Davis theorize the environment as an affective form of preventative medicine or therapy that heals the body of the mal-effects of medico-legal discourse. Neither Alcott nor Davis uses the term "hysteria" in their medical novels, yet the etiology of hysteria informs their theorizing given that Rose Campbell and Dr. Maria Haynes Muller perform variations of disability depending upon their intra-actions with their environs. Ultimately, I argue that Alcott and Davis "crip" medicine, since their representations of disability force nineteenth-century and contemporary readers to self-reflexively question what constitutes disability and how we cleave embodied experience from/to socially constructed contexts in our readings of disability both written on the body and in fiction. As Kafer emphasizes, "crip" destabilizes identity formation in its function as noun, verb, and adjective.[101]

In the nineteenth century, "woman" was already an unstable gender identity given its conflation with the female body, which physicians and lawmakers could not seem to regulate in the body's failure to conform to cultural notions of restraint. The female body exceeds boundaries. It literally overflows with all manner of secretions, from blood to vaginal discharge to breastmilk. Alcott and Davis recognize the failure of hegemonic professional medicine to regulate female embodiment. They further turn to nonhuman material bodies to destabilize our notions of the medicalized human body. Following crip theory, I find Alcott's and Davis's narratological practice oppositional in their resistance to normative cultural ideologies of the body as established by Clarke, Mitchell, and Comstock, as we have already seen of Alcott, who shifts the conversation around the corset from the reproductive system to the respiratory system. Alcott seems to indicate that if women suffer hysteria, then they do so as a product of cultural practices—such as fashion—and cultural readings of those practices, as in the case of Clarke's etiology that draws upon the "arrested development" of the uterus under duress from the corset. Alcott pushes back, but "does not completely reject medical authority" or medicine as an organized institution.[102] She expressly favors "reforms of all kinds," including the reform of institutional healthcare,[103] and she grounds her alternative vision of medicine in environmental health. Davis may be skeptical of the efficacy of outdoor therapy, yet she shares with Alcott a vision to "collectively transform" the system of medicine itself and "imagin[e] bodies and desires otherwise."[104]

In contemporary material feminisms, and especially new materialist approaches to disability studies, environmental health refers to a branch of public health that accounts for the role of physical, material, chemical, and biological factors on an individual's well-being. The United States' Centers for Disease Control and Prevention focus on protecting people from environmental hazards. In contrast, the American Public Health Association adopts a broader definition that "focuses on the relationships between people and their environment," whether natural or built.[105] They cite the Zika virus outbreak, Hurricane Katrina, and the drinking water crisis in Flint, Michigan as failures of environmental health policy and practice, drawing our attention once again to the invisible dangers threatening our well-being, much like the arsenic-laced wallpaper of Gilman's short story. Importantly, APHA emphasizes relationships in the more-than-human-world, which perhaps evolves from and echoes nineteenth-century notions of what Linda Nash calls the "ecological body" and Schuller traces from the legacy of Lamarckian evolution.[106] Meanwhile, the growing popularity of "environmental medicine" or "ecological medicine" emphasizes the complexity of environmental factors in diagnosing and treating illness. The American Academy of Environmental Health not only pays attention to the potential for adverse relationships among human and nonhuman subjects but also acknowledges that milieu as a complex network. "Rarely is there only one offending agent responsible for causing a diseased condition," the AAEH explains of the "total load" concept, which further accounts for physical and emotional stress, genetic predisposition, environmental toxins, and nutritional practices as part of the diagnosis and treatment process.[107] Still much of the theoretical, professional, and activist discourse of environmental health concerns adverse effects of the environment, toxicity in our ecological systems, and a fear of exposure that creates the conditions for disease and disability.

Can our environments heal us? Alcott says yes, for the longer Rose Campbell spends outdoors in nature, the stronger and healthier she becomes. Readers meet Rose on the first page of the novel, awaiting her Uncle Alec Campbell's arrival from Calcutta. We learn she is recently orphaned. Her father died one year prior, while her mother passed away in childbirth. Alcott admits that Rose's grief may owe much to her poor constitution. Nevertheless, Uncle Alec diagnoses the "pale, heavy-eyed, and listless" Rose, who complains of headaches and fatigue, as suffering from lack of sleep and exercise, poor diet and dress, and too much rich food, coffee, and medicine (3, 26, 32). In other words, Rose is sick and weak from "the effects of too much culture," Browner explains, which includes "sentimental novels" like those of Sir Walter Scott "and modern habits" for women such as "tonics, pills, frequent naps, limited activity, and corsets."[108] Uncle Alec outlines the cure, which consists of "three great remedies": "Plenty of sun, fresh air, and cold water" (73). He later amends, adding manual labor such as milking cows, sweeping floors, and baking bread. Importantly, Alcott does not gender domestic activities. Uncle Alec performs these so-called "feminine" skills alongside Rose, a move which leads Ruth Dyckfehderau to consider Uncle Alec as a "Marmee" figure whom Alcott adapts in *Eight Cousins* from a model that worked for her successfully in *Little Women*. Uncle Alec attracts Alcott's existing readership, yet softens her moralizing approach that draws upon the medical authority of Uncle Alec in his subversive role as an anti-Clarke figure.[109]

Education outdoors appears a cornerstone of Alcott's rescription of 1870s medico-legal discourse. Drawing upon two of his remedies, plenty of sunshine and fresh air, Uncle Alec prescribes running laps around the garden to "get up a glow" in Rose's skin (51). As Rose gains strength and endurance, Uncle Alec prescribes additional forms of physical education alongside her seven male cousins, including rowing, swimming, horseback riding, and even football. Alcott repeatedly describes the reformed Rose as a "little Amazon" (155), which not only recalls but further rejects Clarke's belief that the "appearance of Amazonian coarseness" among girls with "more muscular tissue," "coarser skin," and "generally a tougher and more angular makeup" is responsible for reproductive dysfunction. Clarke further describes female masculinity as akin to "a third class" of species "who have no reproductive apparatus."[110] In this ultimate dehumanizing rhetorical move, Clarke concludes that, "Such persons are analogous to a sexless class of termites."[111] Alcott desires precisely this "Amazonian coarseness" for American young women, as Rose represents a model for her readers to emulate. Like Dr. Alec, Alcott considers a "stout," "muscular" physique among young women as a sign of good health, since one can only achieve such a physique through good exercise, diet, and exposure to sunshine and fresh air. As a former nurse, Alcott well knows the benefits of sunshine and physical exercise, which includes reduced stress and anxiety, alleviated depression, elevated mood, and improved memory, even if neither Alcott nor her representative Uncle Alec could yet articulate it as "vitamin D" and "endorphins." Readers witness all of the benefits of Rose's "runner's high" during the narrative. At the end of the novel, and the conclusion of his yearlong experiment, Uncle Alec offers a visual comparison for the aunts (his sisters) of Rose's physical changes in the form of two photographs, one "before" and one "after" the experiment. His approach rings of infomercials for Jenny Craig or the season finale of a weight-loss-centered reality television show like *The Biggest Loser*. Predictably, readers witness a "striking contrast" between the "weak," "melancholy" waif of the before photo and the "blooming smiling face, full of girlish spirit and health" of the after photo (292–3).

Cathlin M. Davis compares Alcott's outdoor education method in *Eight Cousins* with the pedagogy of John Dewey, since both Alcott and Dewey emphasize active, hands-on learning that occurs beyond the traditional classroom. For instance, Mac and Rose vacation in the mountains, teaching each other botany and geology (151), which embodies Alcott's belief in "learning and teaching as a natural outgrowth of exploration of their environment."[112] Although Rose's anatomy and physiology lessons occur in Uncle Alec's office, where he practices medicine, substances derived from outdoor environments play an important role in treatment when environmental conditions threaten her health. Alcott does not disavow the potential for our environments to make us ill. Rose catches pneumonia from extended exposure to winter weather. It is not, however, the chilling wind alone that makes Rose ill; rather, her static position leaves her vulnerable to cold as she waits for Mac to arrive. After Rose finishes her "grand skating bout," she tries her best to "get up a glow again," or generate body heat, "by trotting up and down the road" (251). Eventually, she succumbs to exhaustion and "cuddled disconsolately under a pine-tree to wait and watch" for Mac instead of returning home (251). Her inanimate state causes her to catch pneumonia. As any good homeopathic practitioner would do, Dr. Alec turns to natural remedies for the cure, including a cup of sage tea and cordial (252), the latter of which is a herbal medicine made from the clary sage plant (salvia sclarea), rosa solis (also known as sundew or drosera), cardamom, apple, cinnamon, and either lemon or orange peel. Alcott had a personal history with homeopathy as her own uncle, William Alcott, belonged to "a vibrant network of health reformers who included Thomsonians, eclectics, homeopaths, and those opposed to drug and allopathic doctors."[113] Louisa May Alcott not only appears to sympathize with her uncle; the fictional Dr. Alec Campbell may be a homage to Alcott's real-life Uncle William, who wrote several single-authored social hygiene books including *The Young Woman's Book of Health* (1855), which defended women's education in the wake of sexist medicine.[114] One can only imagine Uncle William Alcott would have loathed Dr. Edward H. Clarke as much as his niece did.

Homeopathy not only advocated for women's rights, but also supported women physicians as practitioners.[115] Feminist medical fiction mirrors this cultural development since characters are often homeopathic practitioners who defend women's rights, including Dr. Zay in Elizabeth Stuart Phelps's *Doctor Zay* (1882), Dr. Nan Prince in Sarah Orne Jewett's *A Country Doctor* (1884), Dr. Alec Campbell in Alcott's *Eight Cousins*, and Dr. Maria Haynes Muller in Rebecca Harding Davis's *Kitty's Choice*. Homeopathy was popular in America during the first half of the nineteenth century, reaching its peak during the 1840s and 1850s, before allopathic physicians worked to discredit it in the aftermath of the Civil War and with the professionalization of allopathic medicine. Although historians once believed that homeopathy met its demise during the 1870s after the American Medical Association barred homeopaths from membership,[116] Susan Cayleff suggests that it may have evolved throughout the long twentieth century into present-day naturopathic medicine. Nineteenth-century homeopathic physicians encourage the body's natural response to heal itself, using treatments made from organic matter. They eschew the popular practices of cupping, bleeding, or leeching, which allopathic physicians deploy to release toxins from the body and alleviate the symptoms of disease.[117] Twenty-first-century naturopaths likewise promote equilibrium among the interconnections of body, mind, and soul, which they achieve through non-toxic natural therapies, preventative techniques, and an attention to environmental factors. Alcott similarly advocates "the healing properties of the sun and clean, fresh air," as well as supporting alternative medicine treatments such as Chinese herbals and acupuncture just like homeopaths before her and naturopaths after her.[118] Dr. Alec, in fact, gifts Rose a herb pillow from India, which is "filled with saffron, poppies, and other soothing plants" to ward off insomnia and promote better sleep (47). Alcott ultimately expresses her understanding of environmental health in terms of animacy and impressibility, for Uncle Alec insists, "Nature knows how to mould a woman better than any corset-maker" (214), as subjects in nature co-constitute one another for better or worse. "Nature," or rather various relata, molds Rose into an able-bodied individual who is distant from and resistant to the signs and symptoms of hysteria.

Cripping Medicine

In her emphasis on able-bodiedness as the product of nature's molding and evidence of good environmental health, Alcott characterizes the outdoors as a space for performing adventures such that the outdoors risks excluding physically disabled bodies. I say "physically disabled bodies" because Alcott encourages the outdoors and outdoor activity as a preventative therapy for mental illness. Similarly, Gilman suggests that the narrator of "The Yellow Wallpaper" suffers a worsening case of psychosis the longer she is cut off from the outdoors and kept inside with the wallpaper. Sarah Jaquette Ray locates the origins of adventure culture in the tradition of American natural history, ecology, and the wilderness movement of the long nineteenth century. Unsurprisingly, white heterosexual men develop this cultural trend in literature: Ralph Waldo Emerson, Henry David Thoreau, John Muir, and Teddy Roosevelt, among others. Adventure culture defines the physically fit adventuring body against the category of disability, since the threat of disability itself—the act of successfully overcoming the risk of harm while performing a physical feat—makes the adventure meaningful.[119] Alcott is complicit in advancing this culture among young women. Rose risks her health while ice-skating not only because she exposes herself to cold and catches pneumonia, but also because of the potential for falling through thin ice as did Amy March in *Little Women*. The fact that Rose overcomes pneumonia and returns to a state of vitality by the end of the novel suggests Alcott believes young women to be resilient against animate nonhuman subjects that might otherwise threaten to disable them.

In *Kitty's Choice*, Rebecca Harding Davis adopts a more ambivalent position toward the efficacy of environmental medicine than Alcott does. Yet, like Alcott, Davis draws upon the feminist potential of hydropathy and homeopathy given that her protagonist Dr. Maria Haynes Muller manages a water cure facility, which promotes one of our most valuable resources—water—as a source of healing. However, hydrotherapy cannot cure the pain of Dr. Muller's physical and emotional losses. After being twice spurned by her erstwhile lover Dr. John McCall, once at the water cure and again at a Woman's Club meeting, Dr. Muller suffers neuralgia, "an attack of syncope," or what we might simply call a nervous breakdown (41). Whereas Alcott might turn to organic resources for healing, Davis questions the efficacy of naturopathic medicine, for "no pack or sitz proved a remedy" for Dr. Muller's neuralgia (41). Considering that Dr. Muller is a homeopathic physician who specializes in water cure, the inefficacy of hydrotherapy might not only prove disheartening but also cause self-doubt, especially given that Dr. McCall had previously denounced hydropathy as mere "flummery" (33). Even though the episode of neuralgia "almost destroyed her usefulness as a surgeon" (41), Sharon Harris emphasizes Davis's use of "almost," since the conditional phrase opens up a space for possible recovery.[120] Davis finds hope in the disabled woman physician because she masculinizes the female body in a way that challenges medical narratives of the hysterical woman. Dr. Muller emphatically does not suffer from hysteria. Davis chose the diagnosis of "neuralgia" because of its masculine connotations. As the disabled male body became increasingly commonplace in the aftermath of the Civil War, Harris explains, "that made the able-bodied, domestic image of the female even more important as a site of purity and return to 'normalcy.'"[121] Dr. Muller upsets this cultural paradigm in her role as a woman physician, which physicians like Clarke and Mitchell and politicians like Comstock would deem oxymoronic.

Although Davis gives readers hope for a better future for progressive women, her hope appears tempered by the conservative characters Hugh Guinness and Kitty Vodges, who learn nothing from their schemes and manipulations. Berrytown may be a so-called utopia, "the capital of Progress, where social systems and raspberries grew miraculously together" (4), yet Davis suggests that as long as conservative families like the Guinnesses and Vodges reside in Berrytown, progressivism will not spread within or beyond the community. Both Hugh Guinness and Kitty Vodges are selfish, manipulative individuals who do horrible things to people with disabilities. Guinness, formerly Dr. McCall, commits his wife to a sanatorium because she is an opium-eater. Kitty discovers the truth of Guinness and his wife Louise when Kitty comes into possession of a note from Louise Guinness, who has called for her husband in the wake of her impending death. Although Kitty could help Maria by disclosing what she knows, she selfishly chooses not to, even though she is aware of Maria's feelings for Dr. McCall and that Maria's neuralgia likely emerged from Dr. McCall's absence. Kitty instead follows Guinness to the sanatorium in Philadelphia, where Hugh and Kitty visit Louise Guinness just before her death. They spend one week with Louise, tending to her pains and chills and nausea before she "died at last, alone with Kitty," and Kitty, for her part, takes little pity on this woman "of a low type at birth [who] had grown more brutal with every year of drunkenness and vice" (47). In a move reminiscent of Mr. Rochester and Jane Eyre, Hugh Guinness expresses relief at being free from his wife, who is an addict and therefore a madwoman.[122] He immediately marries Kitty Vodges once he gains his freedom, while Kitty, in choosing to marry Guinness, chooses against Maria, against women's rights, against progressivism.

For Davis, the issue is not simply male medical professionals like Dr. John McCall (or Dr. Edward H. Clarke or Dr. S. Weir Mitchell) who reinforce cultural narratives of disability upon the female body—rather, women are just as responsible for maintaining the status quo, even when they do not derive their authority from the power of sexist medicine. Kitty choses to marry Hugh Guinness because it gives her power within the domestic sphere and authority within Berrytown society. Unlike Maria, Kitty cannot imagine the possibility of power beyond her own home and her own husband, perhaps because she lacks creativity. Creativity is precisely what we gain from failure, queer theorist Jack Halberstam argues. Failure opens up "a grammar of possibility" with which we can describe a new, alternative political vision.[123] Small-minded Kitty has neither the grammar nor the political vision, and she rejects Dr. Muller's attempt to give her one. Kitty chooses to remain trapped in Berrytown, while Maria leaves the increasingly toxic small-town environment that fails to support her professional contribution and her feminist politics. Because of and through her multiple experiences of failure, Dr. Muller creatively reimagines her life after social hygiene lecturer Mary Gove Nichols. Perhaps Davis concedes that environments do heal us, or at least she acknowledges that a change in environment offers us distance from which we might glean new perspective on life.

Halberstam traces a queer utopian vision through his theorizing the art of failure. He not only reads *Chicken Run* as a feminist anarchist utopia that serves to critique consumer capitalism, but rhetorically constructs a utopian vision for us through the act of "tak[ing] failure apart" and reassembling it as an alternative political vision of meaning-making through struggle.[124] Utopia, by definition, is both a "good place" and "no place." Thomas More coined the term in the act of titling his 1516 work of fiction *Utopia*, which is a pun on the Greek prefixes *eu*, meaning good, and *ou*, meaning no, alongside *topos* or place.[125] Lyman Tower Sargent deftly summarizes the definition of "utopia" as "a non-existent society described in considerable detail and normally located in time and space that the author intended readers to view as considerably better than the society in which the reader lived."[126] Utopian studies scholars generally agree with Sargent that the goal of utopian literature like More's *Utopia* is to construct a better world—not a perfect world—and it accomplishes this by performing two primary functions: (1) critique of the writer's contemporary sociopolitical conditions and (2) suggestions for a better way of being. The Aunt-Hill has the markings of a domestic utopia and Alcott draws upon the conventions of the utopian novel in *Eight Cousins*. Alcott critiques nineteenth-century sexist medico-legal discourse through her utopian guide Dr. Alec Campbell, who further offers a better way of defining female subjectivity and caring for the female body. By this definition, Berrytown is no utopia, even though Davis describes Berrytown as "the Utopia in actual laths, orchards, and bushel-measures of the advance guard of the reform party in the United States. It was the capital of Progress, where social systems and raspberries grew together miraculously" (4). By the end of the novella, Davis's description of Berrytown as a utopia sounds tongue-in-cheek.

In fact, Jean Pfaelzer argues that *Kitty's Choice* is a critique of utopian feminism as a form of politics. Davis witnessed the founding of multiple "utopian" intentional communities, all of which failed due to their patriarchal structures that disregarded the physical and emotional labor of women. Pfaelzer claims that Davis specifically satirizes Bronson Alcott's Fruitlands (founded by none other than Louisa May Alcott's father), but she likely had in mind any number of failed intentional communities that were in vast majority founded by men: George Ripley (Brook Farm), Robert Owen (New Harmony), and John H. Noyes (Oneida). Maria Haynes Muller might be a physician, but she must still fight for authority in the wake of community skepticism. "'I earned my right to the title of physician too hardly to give it up for that which belongs to every simpering schoolgirl,'" Dr. Muller chastises one of her patients who calls her "Miss Muller" instead of "Dr. Muller" (34). Even in utopia, conservative women marry and become homemakers while progressive women become professionals who retain their status as spinsters. Consequently, Davis must masculinize her protagonist, since she recognizes that even her readers might not accept the idea of a woman physician, whether or not they are self-professed "progressives," reformers, or feminists. If, as Pfaelzer argues, Davis's work as a parlor radical "is always, regardless of her historical topic, about female subjectivity," then how do we read this critique of utopian feminism within the context of her medical fiction? Might Davis be questioning whether a utopian health system is possible, and if so what such a utopian health practice might look like?

Davis does not give readers any clear answers as to how to pursue a utopian health program. The fight between Dr. Muller and Dr. McCall, which typifies the broader societal tensions between homeopathic and allopathic medicine during the nineteenth century, ends in a draw, though the patients surmise "[h]omeopathy ... had the worst of it, for the lady was visibly agitated and McCall apparently unmoved" by the intense and "earnest converse" (34). Although Davis suggests that homeopathy and the woman physician will prevail, even if it must go on the road, she ultimately leaves readers guessing as to whether American society and professional medicine as a microcosm of American society will heal from sexism. In other words, Davis does not leave us much hope. In spite of Halberstam's claim that his book is not about hope but what comes "after hope,"[127] the concept of utopia is about hope. Even dystopias must have a scrap of hope. Reading Alcott after Comstock law does not give us much hope either, since Gilman continues to grapple with the effects of Clarkian animacy, Mitchellian etiology, and Comstockian censorship some twenty years later. But perhaps failure is the point of crip medicine, since, as Kafer suggests, "a feminist/queer/crip ecology might mean approaching nature" and medicine "through the lenses of loss and ambivalence" and failure.[128] After all, Dr. Muller loses her (sexist) would-be lover as well as her ability to perform surgeries. The narrator of "The Yellow Wallpaper" loses her mental health as long as she remains indoors, undiagnosed and untreated.

Even Rose will eventually lose her innocence and the protection of her feminist physician uncle as she ages into womanhood and puts her medical knowledge to work against a sexist society that does not acknowledge her autonomy. Crip medicine is about ambivalence and loss, but also about the capacity for healing that loss and the grief that inevitably follows as women writers work to shift ideologies of disability and the female body for future generations.

Notes

1. Rebecca Harding Davis, *Kitty's Choice: A Story of Berrytown* (Philadephia: J. B. Lippincott and Company, 1874), 33, 32. Hereafter cited in the body of the text. The novella was first serialized in *Lippincott's* magazine from April to July 1873 as *Berrytown*. It was then republished as a stand-alone novella one year later as *Kitty's Choice: A Story of Berrytown*. I cite the full-text version from 1874 from this point forward, but the original serialized version is available on *HathiTrust* here: <https://babel.hathitrust.org/cgi/pt?id=chi.74725787&view=1up&seq=404&q1=davis> and <https://babel.hathitrust.org/cgi/pt?id=chi.74725845&view=1up&seq=37&q1=davis> (accessed December 12, 2021).
2. Louisa May Alcott, *Eight Cousins* (New York: Puffin Books, 1995), 223. Hereafter cited in the body of the text. The young adult novel was first serialized in *St. Nicholas: A Monthly Magazine for Boys and Girls* from January to October 1875. It was then published as a stand-alone novel later that same year. I cite the bound book version, but the original serialized version is available on *HathiTrust* here: <https://babel.hathitrust.org/cgi/pt?id=mdp.39015068521981&view=1up&seq=150&q1=Alcott>, <https://babel.hathitrust.org/cgi/pt?id=mdp.39015068522146&view=1up&seq=361&q1=Alcott> (accessed December 12, 2021).
3. Ben Barker-Benfield, "Sexual Surgery in Late Nineteenth-Century America," *International Journal of Health Services* 5, no. 2 (1975), 279; see also Thomas Laqueur, *Making Sex: Body and Gender from the Greeks to Freud* (Cambridge, MA: Harvard University Press, 1990). Ben Barker-Benfield specifically refers to this phenomenon as "gynecologic materialism," since the uterus and ovaries defined the degree to which women as a class may participate in the public sphere. Prior to the nineteenth century, medical practitioners adhered to the belief that men and women were not biologically different; rather, women were "lesser" versions of men, a model Laqueur refers to as "the one-sex system." Scientific discoveries challenged such an approach to sex, resulting in the emergence of a "two-sex system," which defined women as different from men because of their sexual organs. Twenty-first-century American culture still follows the two-sex system today.
4. John S. Haller and Robin M. Haller, *The Physician and Sexuality in Victorian America* (New York: W. W. Norton and Company, Inc., 1974), 4, 6, 15.
5. Schuller, *The Biopolitics of Feeling*, 41.
6. Ibid. 41.
7. As I point out in the Introduction, Schuller suggests that we characterize the nineteenth century as a period of scientific disorder during which scientists struggled to impose order on a rapidly professionalizing system of healthcare and its subject of study, the human body. She suggests that we characterize nineteenth-century science as driven by

sociobiological indeterminism rather than biological determinism, which makes sense given that Amy Koerber points to how there was no consensus as to the biological origins of hysteria other than its location in the female body. However, in an effort to preserve the slippage between biological rationales for gendered behavior, I use the term "(socio)biological (in)determinism" throughout this R_x.

8. Amy Koerber, *From Hysteria to Hormones: A Rhetorical History* (University Park: Pennsylvania State University Press, 2018), 46; see also Andrew Schull, *Hysteria: The Disturbing History* (New York: Oxford University Press, 2009) and Carroll Smith-Rosenberg, *Disorderly Conduct: Visions of Gender in Victorian America* (New York and Oxford: Oxford University Press, 1985). Andrew Schull traces the history of hysteria from the seventeenth through twentieth centuries, finding that it evolved as a diagnosis from a disease called "the suffocation to the Mother," in which the female body appears tortured by evil spirits, to its nationalization as an "English malady" defined by nervous disorder, to its American transference post-Civil War as evidence of sexual differentiation and a condition of female biology. Schull ends with a consideration of how hysteria led to the development of Freudian psychology and recognition of wartime post-traumatic stress disorder (PTSD). For Schull, the Age of Hysteria seems to be late nineteenth-century America when S. Weir Mitchell gains prominence—and wealth—for developing a popular etiology and treatment method for hysteria. Carroll Smith-Rosenberg opens her chapter on "The Hysterical Woman" by pronouncing hysteria as "one of the classical diseases of the nineteenth century," which was defined as a "peculiarly female" entity that characterizes the Victorian bourgeois family in America (197). Smith-Rosenberg likewise notes the prominent role of Dr. S. Weir Mitchell in defining hysteria as a uniquely American and female malady during the late nineteenth century, yet I also want to emphasize the role of Dr. Edward H. Clarke because of his popularity, his rhetorical influence on Mitchell, and his impetus for Louisa May Alcott's writing *Eight Cousins*.

9. Koerber, *From Hysteria to Hormones*, 73. Significantly, decades prior to Koerber's study, Michel Foucault identified Charcot as "a central figure" complicit in the production and deployment of sexuality as a method of biopower. For Foucault, the objective of Charcot's therapeutic interventions in the diagnosis and treatment of hysteria was to preserve the role of the nuclear family unit as a regulatory or disciplinary power (*The History of Sexuality*, 111–12).

10. Jean Pfaelzer, *Parlor Radical: Rebecca Harding Davis and the Origins of American Social Realism* (Pittsburgh: University of Pittsburgh Press, 1996), 10, 12.

11. Ibid. 4.

12. Sarah Elbert, *A Hunger for Home: Louisa May Alcott and Little Women* (Philadelphia: Temple University Press, 1984), 149, 150. Elbert claims that, during her writing of *Eight Cousins*, "Alcott travelled the full range of this reformers' network" from women's rights to temperance (208). Activism played a significant role in her paternal grandparents' and her parents' lives. Her paternal grandparents were actively involved in reform circles for a broad range of social institutions and issues including abolition, education reform, and prison reform (12). This heavily influenced Bronson Alcott, Louisa's father, who was also involved in social reform

circles such as abolition, temperance, and even women's rights (36–49, 75). Louisa May Alcott also had an uncle, William Alcott, who was a conservative health reformer and wrote many advice manuals such as *The Young Wife* (1838) (Elbert 5), which may have led to Louisa's own interest in social hygiene reform. For more on William Alcott's role in reform physiology, see James C. Whorton, *Crusaders for Fitness: The History of American Health Reformers* (Princeton, NJ: Princeton University Press, 1982).

13. Marlowe Daly-Galeano derives the term "unruly women" from Anne Helen Petersen's *Too Fat, Too Slutty, Too Loud: The Rise and Reign of the Unruly Woman* (2017) and from Roxanne Gay's anthology *Unruly Bodies* (2018). Both texts discuss the "unruly woman" as synonymous with the "too much woman": As an archetype, the unruly woman is either "too strong, too fat, too shrill, [or] too pregnant," or all of the above at once, because she exceeds the boundaries of culturally defined "good womanhood" (61). Katherine Adams warns against the presentism of reading Alcott as feminist since the term "feminism" did not even exist until 1882, and yet Adams acknowledges that scholars frequently frame Alcott's work within the context of feminism whether in terms of anthology or critical study (55). I, personally, have no qualms with presentist readings if the purpose for employing such a methodology is, as Adams concludes in her article, "to investigate our own feminisms and the ways they can and cannot set us free" (64), which is one of my objectives in this book. Adams identifies the same "unruly" women from Alcott's fiction as potential "feminist icons," or at the very least "strong heroines": Jo March, Tribulation Periwinkle, and Christie Devon (53). In this R_x, I suggest that Dr. Alec Campbell performs the role of feminist physician who is raising his niece Rose Campbell as a feminist in his image. See Marlowe Daly-Galeano, "Louisa May Alcott's Unruly Medical Women," *Arizona Quarterly* 74, no. 4 (2018), 61–86; see also Katherine Adams, "Feminist Alcott?," in *Critical Insights: Louisa May Alcott* (New York: Grey House Publishing, Inc., 2016), 52–65.
14. Daly-Galeano, "Louisa May Alcott's Unruly Medical Women," 72.
15. I address the definition and function of the New Man in R_x 2 of this book. Although it is not the focus of either this R_x or R_x 2 to read Dr. Alec Campbell as a New Man, one could certainly analyze his character within such a framework, since he educates Rose to be a New Woman.
16. Ruth Dyckfehderau, "Moral Pap and Male Mothers: The Political Subtexts of Louisa May Alcott's *Eight Cousins or, The Aunt Hill*," *Legacy* 16, no. 2 (1999), 163.
17. Zschoche, "Dr. Clarke Revisited," 547. As Zschoche highlights, the first edition of Clarke's *Sex in Education* sold out in little more than one week and its popularity prompted an additional sixteen editions over nearly two decades.
18. Edward H. Clarke, *Sex in Education, or a Fair Chance for Girls* (Boston: J. R. Osgood and Company, 1875), 32.
19. Ibid. 33. This is an important differentiation. Nineteenth-century scientific discoveries such as French physician Achille Chereau's 1844 discovery of ovaries challenged any belief that the female body was an "inverted" version of the male body, since the female ovaries did not have a male counterpart. Consequently, nineteenth-century society could no longer accept the possibility of similarities between men and women, biological or otherwise, for fear that women would seek

social equality in the public sphere. Sexual difference allowed scientists to define woman as "unique" or "special" because of her reproductive abilities. She may not be less than man, biologically speaking, yet her sexual difference made her an object requiring social protection. For more on how science was used to support social behavior, see Thomas Laqueur's *Making Sex*.
20. Clarke, *Sex in Education*, 25.
21. Ibid. 23, 25.
22. Alison Kafer, *Feminist, Queer, Crip* (Bloomington and Indianapolis: Indiana University Press, 2013), 7.
23. Ibid. 8–9.
24. Ibid. 16. Anne Fausto-Sterling adopts the Möbius strip apparatus as a model for articulating her developmental systems theory, in which biological and social processes are always already intertwined. She describes the Möbius strip as "a topological puzzle, a flat ribbon twisted once and then attached end to end to form a circular twisted surface" (*Sexing the Body* 24). Should one trace or walk across such a surface, they would find that the outside surface moves one to the inside surface and out again, without ever leaving the plane. Each side becomes the other, fluidly moving back and forth, and at one point when traversing the bend, one can inhabit both spaces at the same time. Fausto-Sterling derives the Möbius strip from Elizabeth Grosz, who, in *Volatile Bodies: Toward a Corporeal Feminism* (Bloomington: Indiana University Press, 1994), proposes that we think of the body as co-constituted by this inside-outside relationality. I find the Möbius strip a useful apparatus for imagining the materiality of language because it helps visualize how words fluidly transition into affect, and how we make sense of material actions through language.
25. Although, from Koerber's perspective, the kind of evidence employed among male medical professionals and researchers is telling of their ethical standards and ways of establishing standards for credibility. The debate over how to pathologize hysteria rhetorically centers on what counts as reliable evidence. For Charcot, visual evidence was key to establishing hysteria as a diagnosable condition. This is why he conducted public hypnosis demonstrations and photographed female patients in various stages of hysteria (Koerber 59). In contrast, Clarke drew upon case studies of his own patients as physical evidence as well as citing his peers parenthetically and bibliographically via endnotes. Neither method is ethical, since both medical theater and anecdotal evidence exploit the female body under the medical gaze. Yet Clarke's practice of case study and citational practice would eventually become the modern standard for peer-reviewed research.
26. Zschoche, "Dr. Clarke Revisited," 550. Clarke left a legacy in cultural narratives of the female body, which is evidenced by the nonfiction texts written immediately—and urgently—in response to Clarke's treatise, among them: Julia Ward Howe's collection of essays *Sex and Education: A Response to Edward H. Clarke's "Sex in Education"* (1874), Eliza Bisbee Duffey's *No Sex in Education* (1874), Anna C. Brackett's *The Education of American Girls*, and George F. Comfort and Anna Manning Comfort's *Woman's Education and Woman's Health, Chiefly in Reply to "Sex in Education"* (1874).
27. Zschoche, "Dr. Clarke Revisited," 560.

28. Chen, *Animacies*, 24.
29. Ibid. 54.
30. Ibid. 30; Donna Haraway, *Simians, Cyborgs, and Women: The Reinvention of Nature* (New York: Routledge, 1991), 3.
31. Chen, *Animacies*, 53.
32. Clarke, *Sex in Education*, 127.
33. Ibid. 107.
34. Ibid. 82; also 44, 78, 79, 84n., 87, 92, 93, 94, 97, 107, 113, 115.
35. Horowitz, *Rereading Sex*, 21; see also Londa Schiebinger, *Nature's Body: Gender in the Making of Modern Science* (New Brunswick, NJ: Rutgers University Press, 2010), 4. Horowitz includes an image of one of the earliest drawings depicting an anatomical female body with a fetus in utero, which is clearly floral. There are four points that serve as petals, an umbilical cord that serves as a stem, and the head of the fetus that serves as stamen. Schiebinger similarly finds that flowers played a significant role in early gynecological study. Even before gynecology was established as a professional field of medicine, scientists such as Carl Linnaeus compared female anatomy with flower biology as a means of explaining human sexuality, albeit from a decidedly heterosexual position (4). This may account for why young women characters in medical fiction are often named after flowers such as "Rose" in Alcott's *Eight Cousins* (1875) and sisters "Rose" and "Lotus" in Annie Nathan Meyer's *Helen Brent, M.D.* (1892). Women writers of medical fiction may be using flower names subversively to resist biological determinism in medical discourse.
36. Haraway, *Simians*, 78.
37. Ibid. 72.
38. Ibid. 72.
39. Judith Butler, *Bodies That Matter: On the Discursive Limits of "Sex"* (London and New York: Routledge, 1993), 38.
40. Schuller, *The Biopolitics of Feeling*, 24, 31, 63.
41. Ibid. 47, 35–41, 7.
42. Ibid. 59, 37.
43. Ibid. 60.
44. Clarke, *Sex in Education*, 25–6.
45. Ibid. 26, 27.
46. Ibid. 111–12.
47. Ibid. 40–41.
48. S. Weir Mitchell, *Wear and Tear, or Hints for the Overworked* (Philadelphia: J. B. Lippincott Company, 1887), 32, 36. Clarke and Mitchell were not the only (male) physicians who linked hysteria and other reproductive disorders with intellectual exhaustion and overuse of the brain among women. Andrew Schull explains that although Mitchell might seem misogynistic to contemporary readers, his pronouncements "were typical of 'informed' medical opinion on both sides of the Atlantic" (99). Schull cites Dr. Henry Maudsley as an exemplar British physician from the late nineteenth century who "was equally outspoken about the dangers of higher education for women" alongside Mitchell and Clarke. Maudsley likewise held to the closed-system theory (Schull 100).

49. Hysteria was further used to disenfranchise women, as we see in Sir Almroth Wright's *The Unexpurgated Case Against Woman Suffrage* (1913). Here, British immunologist Wright (mis)applies his expertise, arguing in the same vein as Clarke that "the larger question as to the proper sphere of woman," whether public or private, professional or domestic, "finally turns upon the question as to what imprint woman's sexual system leaves upon her physical frame, character, and intellect" (see Preface). The question is rhetorical. Its answer literally appears in the title of Wright's preface, "Letter on Militant Hysteria": The "militant" suffragists suffer from hysteria. Wright further invokes Clarke in his argument that the education system produces the conditions of disability among women. See Sir Almroth Wright, *The Unexpurgated Case Against Woman Suffrage* (New York: Paul B. Hoeber, 1913).
50. S. Weir Mitchell, *Fat and Blood* (Philadelphia: J. B. Lippincott Company, 1891), 52.
51. Ibid. 58, 48.
52. Ibid. 60, 123, 152.
53. Charlotte Perkins Gilman, "Why I Wrote The Yellow Wallpaper," in *The Yellow Wallpaper and Other Stories*, edited by Robert Schulman (Oxford: Oxford University Press, 2009), 331.
54. Ibid. 331.
55. Charon, *Narrative Medicine*, 28. From a narrative medicine standpoint, it is our responsibility as good faith listeners of a person's experience with illness to contextualize the narrative.
56. Halberstam, *The Queer Art of Failure*, 2–3.
57. Ibid. 8.
58. Gilman, "Why I Wrote The Yellow Wallpaper," 332.
59. Halberstam, *The Queer Art of Failure*, 129. Instead of refusing to speak, in the way that Halberstam characterizes "shadow feminism," Gilman does speak through written form whether fictional or nonfiction. In this book, I use "(p)rescription" to advocate for speaking, for telling one's story, for talking as therapy, and, yes, for talk therapy itself.
60. Ibid. 129; Jane Thrailkill, "Doctoring 'The Yellow Wallpaper,'" *English Literary History (ELH)* 69, no. 2 (2002), 529.
61. Sari Altschuler, *The Medical Imagination: Literature and Health in the Early United States* (Philadelphia: University of Pennsylvania Press, 2018), 196.
62. Thrailkill, "Doctoring 'The Yellow Wallpaper,'" 529.
63. Charlotte Perkins Gilman, "The Yellow Wallpaper," in *The Yellow Wallpaper and Other Stories*, edited by Robert Schulman (Oxford: Oxford University Press, 2009), 9. Hereafter referred to in the body of the text.
64. Siebers, "Returning the Social to the Social Model," 42. Siebers defines complex embodiment as an epistemological method of disability formation characterized by mutual transformation between the individual and her environment. In theorizing complex embodiment, Siebers weds the social model of disability with new materialisms, and while he acknowledges that "disability is both affected by environments and changed by the diversity of bodies" (44), he does not quite theorize disability as affect even though the potential is there.
65. Horowitz claims that Gilman experienced depression prior to Katherine's birth (2, 114, 118–19). That does not disavow the possibility of postpartum depression, as

one can experience depression or anxiety-induced depression at any age or stage of life. I struggled with anxiety since the age of eighteen, long before the birth of my first son. Left untreated, anxiety can lead to depression. Horowitz explores whether we can rightly consider Gilman as experiencing postpartum depression from the vantage point of contemporary medical knowledge (205–6). I align myself with disability studies scholars who argue for using present-day terminology to study historical texts that document illness; the illness existed in the past even if the diagnosis was not fully understood or discussed in the same terms. For further information on the medical context of "The Yellow Wallpaper," see Helen Lefkowitz Horowitz's *Wild Unrest: The Making of "The Yellow Wallpaper"* (Oxford: Oxford University Press, 2010).

66. David Mitchell and Sharon Snyder, *Narrative Prosthesis: Disability and the Dependencies of Discourse* (Ann Arbor: The University of Michigan Press, 2000), 30.
67. Ibid. 163.
68. Pfaelzer, *Parlor Radical*, 121–2, 124.
69. Rebecca Harding Davis, "The Wife's Story," *The Atlantic Monthly* 14 (1864), 7, <https://babel.hathitrust.org/cgi/pt?id=mdp.39015030142148&view=1up&seq=19&q1=the%20wife%27s%20story> (accessed December 12, 2021).
70. Ibid. 7.
71. Pfaelzer, *Parlor Radical*, 121.
72. Ibid. 121–2.
73. Karen Barad, "Posthumanist Performativity," *Material Feminisms*, edited by Stacy Alaimo and Susan Hekman (Bloomington and Indianapolis: Indiana University Press, 2008), 139.
74. Donna Haraway updates her cyborg metaphor with the companion species, of which cyborgs are a member (*Companion Species Manifesto* 21). Companion species denotes a kinship among human and nonhuman organisms in which each member participates in a reciprocal process of co-evolution alongside one another. Companion species shape each other's subjectivity over a long period of time. In nineteenth-century terms of affective kinship, companion species impress upon and are impressed by one another. Haraway first introduces her theory of companion species in *The Companion Species Manifesto: Dogs, People, and Significant Otherness* (Chicago: Prickly Paradigm Press, 2003), but updates it further in her study of and meditation on dogs in *When Species Meet* (Minneapolis: University of Minnesota Press, 2007). Haraway explicitly links her theory of companion species (and by extension, the cyborg) to material feminisms when she cites Karen Barad's theory of agential realism and intra-action (*When Species Meet* 220).
75. Lucinda Hawksley, *Bitten by Witch Fever: Wallpaper and Arsenic in the Victorian Home* (New York: Thames and Hudson Ltd./The National Archives, 2016), 38.
76. Ibid. 225–6.
77. Ibid. 39.
78. Both Stacy Alaimo and Alison Kafer discuss environmental health in relation to toxicity and multiple chemical sensitivities (MCS), which both theorists read as a hidden disability that places vulnerable bodies at risk in otherwise benign environments. Because of its invisibility, some medical practitioners are skeptical of patient claims to MCS. Kafer extends this discussion further, asking how we might challenge the

rhetoric of toxicity and environmental injustice. In other words, how do we talk about diseases like MCS without replicating ableist language and attaching stigmas of disease/disability as tragedy? Alcott and Davis seem to circle around the same question, though they draw different conclusions. Alcott reconfigures the outdoors as a space for healing, while Davis wonders if we must move ourselves—as in, physically change our environments—to restore health. Like Mel Y. Chen, I find that Alaimo, Kafer, Alcott, and Davis pay close attention to how we construct narratives about disability, eschewing negative representations that recast disability as toxic because of its proximity to sex, class, nationality, or even, and especially, race.

79. Stacy Alaimo, *Bodily Natures: Science, Environment, and the Material Self* (Bloomington and Indianapolis: Indiana University Press, 2010), 148.
80. Horowitz, *Rereading Sex*, 358, 376–9, 385.
81. Ibid. 382.
82. Werbel, *Lust on Trial*, 205.
83. Ibid. 131–3.
84. It's important to remember that this was not an era of sexual repression. Michel Foucault disproved this now-outdated scholarly consensus of the "repressive hypothesis," arguing in *The History of Sexuality, Vol. 1* that people discussed sex and sexuality *ad infinitum*. This ongoing conversation about sexuality, including sexual health, appears in discursive form, especially written, and was exploited as a secret that must be confessed. Both Kyla Schuller and Helen Lefkowitz Horowitz confirm Foucault's rejection of the repressive hypothesis. Horowitz acknowledges the existence of legal suppression during the late nineteenth century because of Comstock law (as do I), yet finds a vibrant and complex American vernacular sexual culture, which she categorizes into four primary voices: humoral theory, evangelical Christianity, scientific discourse, and moral physiology. At times, these frameworks overlap, but arguably medical fiction falls within scientific discourse while legal censorship emerges from moral physiology. Similarly, Schuller draws upon Foucault in her theorizing of sentimental biopower, ultimately finding that animacy—and, I will add, censorship—acts as a form of biopower that governs by unevenly enforcing laws among a population based on a hierarchy of values such as degree of impressibility, which in turn determines who experiences the effects of biopower to a greater or lesser degree based on gender, race, or disability.
85. Horowitz, *Rereading Sex*, 387.
86. Anthony Comstock, Preface to *Traps for the Young* (New York: Funk & Wagnalls Co. 1883), ix, <https://babel.hathitrust.org/cgi/pt?id=uva.x000491476&view=1up&seq=1> (accessed December 12, 2021).
87. Ibid. 20.
88. Ibid. 25.
89. J. M. Buckley, Introduction to *Traps for the Young* by Anthony Comstock (New York: Funk & Wagnalls Co. 1883), v. Buckley summarizes Comstock's main arguments in the Introduction. The fact that Buckley comments upon the impressibility of young adults indicates that Comstock not only recognizes the power of narrative affect, but also that Comstock views it as a danger. Neither Buckley nor I miss Comstock's argument, even if we are using different language to describe its affect.
90. Horowitz, *Rereading Sex*, 433–5, 410–18.

91. For a comprehensive definition of "impressibility" and "impression," as it is used during the nineteenth century, see Schuller, *The Biopolitics of Feeling*, 6–10. Horowitz briefly summarizes *Regina* v. *Hicklin* (1868) in n. 31 on page 491 of the endnotes. In the chapter "Constitutionality and Resistance: Bennett, Benedict, and Blatchford," Horowitz does not reference the trial by name, but discusses its influence on Judge Blatchford's ruling (*Rereading Sex*, 433).
92. Horowitz, *Rereading Sex*, 433.
93. United States v. Bennett 24 Fed. Cas. 1093, No. 14,571 (S.D.N.Y. 1879), <https://law.resource.org/pub/us/case/reporter/F.Cas/0024.f.cas/0024.f.cas.1093.pdf> (accessed December 12, 2021). Emphasis mine.
94. Elisabeth Ladenson offers a useful analysis of the censorship trial on James Joyce's *Ulysses*, both the trial against *The Little Review* for publishing "obscene" excerpts and the appeal made by Random House. However, John E. Semonche places the *Ulysses* trial within a broader context of censorship efforts under Comstock law. In fact, Semonche discusses two censorship cases that prosecute a work of fiction in which Anthony Comstock was personally involved: One case prosecuted a bookseller for selling copies of Gabriele d'Annunzio's *The Triumph of Death* (1894) and the second case prosecuted a clerk for sending Daniel Carson Goodman's *Hagar Revelly* (1913). Eventually, Comstock went directly to the source: publishers.
95. Blanchard, "The American Urge to Censor," 768–82. For the full court ruling, see United States v. One Book Entitled "Ulysses" 72 F.2d 705 (2d Cir. 1934), <https://law.justia.com/cases/federal/appellate-courts/F2/72/705/1549734/> (accessed December 12, 2021).
96. Schuller, *The Biopolitics of Feeling*, 47–8.
97. Stephanie Browner, *Profound Science and Elegant Literature: Imagining Doctors in Nineteenth-Century America* (Philadelphia: University of Pennsylvania Press, 2005), 153.
98. Ibid. 153.
99. Alaimo, *Bodily Natures*, 125.
100. Kafer, *Feminist, Queer, Crip*, 140.
101. Ibid. 17.
102. Browner, *Profound Science and Elegant Literature*, 150.
103. Alcott once signed a letter to the editors of the *Woman's Journal*, "Yours for reforms of all kinds." The letter is dated 11 October 1879, and was published in volume 10 of the *Woman's Journal*. The letter primarily addresses property rights and suffrage. Several scholars have written on Alcott's reform work and feminist writing, including Sarah Elbert, Elizabeth Lennox Keyser, Madeleine Stern, Birgit Spengler, Elizabeth Young, Cathlin M. Davis, Claudia Mills, and Ruth Dyckfehderau. All of them read Alcott as a feminist who was indeed for "reforms of all kinds," including abolition, temperance, dress reform, education reform, social hygiene reform, and women's rights. This particular letter to the editors of the *Woman's Journal* appears in full and is discussed in Madeleine B. Stern's "Louisa Alcott's Feminist Letters," *Studies in the American Renaissance* (1978), 429–52.
104. McRuer, *Crip Theory*, 32; see also Kafer, *Feminist, Queer, Crip*, 16–17. As I explain in the Introduction to this book, McRuer first established the parameters for crip

theory as a subfield of disability studies, which critically resists the demands of compulsory able-bodiedness in the same vein as queer theory's resistance of compulsory heterosexuality. He explicitly links "crip" to "queer" as functions of oppositional and relational being. Kafer participates in the subfield of crip theory, extending it into feminist theoretical discourses about (re)production and futurity. Like McRuer, Kafer reads "crip" as simultaneously a noun, verb, and adjective. It is a disabled identity, an act of critique, and a description of an oppositional subject.

105. "Environmental Health," American Public Health Association: <https://www.apha.org/topics-and-issues/environmental-health#:~:text=Environmental%20health%20is%20the%20branch,any%20comprehensive%20public%20health%20system> (accessed December 12, 2021).
106. Linda Nash, *Inescapable Ecologies: A History of Environment, Disease, and Knowledge* (Berkeley and Los Angeles: University of California Press, 2006), 80–1.
107. "The Voice of Environmental Medicine," American Academy of Environmental Health, <https://www.aaemonline.org/> (accessed December 12, 2021).
108. Browner, *Profound Science and Elegant Literature*, 152.
109. Dyckfehderau, "Moral Pap and Male Mothers," 154.
110. Clarke, *Sex in Education*, 92–3.
111. Ibid. 93.
112. Cathlin M. Davis, "An Easy and Well-Ordered Way to Learn: Schooling at Home in Louisa May Alcott's *Eight Cousins* and *Jack and Jill*," *Children's Literature in Education* 42 (2011), 349.
113. Susan E. Cayleff, *Nature's Path: A History of Naturopathic Healing in America* (Baltimore: John Hopkins University Press, 2016), 29.
114. Ibid. 30; see also Whorton, *Crusaders for Fitness*.
115. Cayleff, *Nature's Path*, 26, 33. Susan Cayleff also finds hydropathy, or the water-cure movement, inherently feminist, a point she discusses at greater length in *Wash and Be Healed: The Water-Cure Movement and Women's Health* (Philadelphia: Temple University Press, 1985). Hydropathy may have become popular among women physicians not because they were excluded from allopathic practice (which they were), but because they found the field more effective for social reform activism.
116. For evidence of this older position in the history of homeopathy, see William G. Rothstein, *American Physicians in the Nineteenth Century: From Sects to Science* (Baltimore: The Johns Hopkins University Press, 1972).
117. Cayleff, *Nature's Path*, 17.
118. Ibid. 6.
119. Sarah Jaquette Ray, *The Ecological Other: Environmental Exclusion in American Culture* (Tucson: The University of Arizona Press, 2013), 44.
120. Sharon Harris, "Rebecca Harding Davis' *Kitty's Choice* and the Disabled Woman Physician," *American Literary Realism* 44, no. 1 (2011), 41.
121. Ibid. 44.
122. I am purposefully invoking Sandra Gilbert and Susan Gubar's *The Madwoman in the Attic: The Woman Writer and the Nineteenth-Century Literary Imagination* (1979) in my reference to Charlotte Brontë's *Jane Eyre* because there are obvious parallels between the circumstances of Bertha Mason and Louise Guinness.

123. Halberstam, *The Queer Art of Failure*, 2, 19.
124. Ibid. 174.
125. Lyman Tower Sargent, "The Three Faces of Utopianism Revisited," *Utopian Studies* 5, no. 1 (1994), 5.
126. Ibid. 9.
127. Halberstam, *The Queer Art of Failure*, 1.
128. Kafer, *Feminist, Queer, Crip*, 142.

R_x 2

LISTEN FOR THE NEW MAN: FROM NARRATIVE PROSTHESIS TO NARRATIVE MEDICINE

Godey's Lady's Book and Magazine offers a singular criticism of Rebecca Harding Davis's medical novel *Kitty's Choice: A Story of Berrytown*: Although "Mrs. Davis's style is brilliant," as characteristic of her many stories, *Kitty's Choice* "is somewhat marred by extravagance and burlesque in depicting certain classes of people," namely physicians.[1] Reviews are storied texts themselves. This particular 1874 review frames its narrative in terms of health and medicine as it appears nestled alongside the Health Department's column offering treatments for gout. The column concludes just a half-inch above the column "Literary Notices," which not only includes a review of *Kitty's Choice* but also Dr. Justus Liebig's *The Complete Works of Chemistry* and Dr. D. Lambden Fleming's *The Art of Preserving Health*. Such a context suggests we are to read *Kitty's Choice* as a work of medical fiction, and yet the reviewer considers the novella "marred" by the so-called comedic presence of a female physician. *Godey's* is not the only periodical to publish a book review that mischaracterizes the genre of medical fiction. Annie Nathan Meyer was so horrified that book reviewer Edna Kenton missed the gender satire of *Helen Brent, M.D.* she wrote a scathing letter of critique to the editor of *The Bookman*, which they published: "[I]t is a little trying to have such palpable satire as this entirely overlooked," Meyer rebukes Kenton.[2] Meyer cites a passage from her own novel that speaks to one such "palpable" instance of satire, a scene early in the novel in which newspaper reporters scrutinize Dr. Helen Brent's dress at a public address. The point of the passage is precisely as Meyer states in her novel and again in her letter to the editor: No one would dare comment upon "a costume worn by Grover Cleveland when he delivers an address," but everyone scrutinizes "the details of a woman's dress" if she appears in a position of public authority "whether at a suffrage caucus or a prayer meeting."[3] Society holds different standards for men and women. Satire allows writers like Meyer a means of exposing the hypocrisy in such gendered social behaviors.

The affective nature of narrative might fail for any number of reasons, resulting in reviewers like Edna Kenton missing the very purpose of these "stories with a purpose."[4] Something happens during the experience of reading that causes a narrative to either work upon us or leave us unmoved. The degree to which the narrative affects us depends on our position as readers: Are we the intended audience? In fact, the book reviewer may not be the intended audience for the encoded message. When readers miss contextual clues because they are not the intended audience, the message itself is—unsurprisingly—lost in translation. That may be the case with Kenton's review of *Helen Brent, M.D.* Edna Kenton is not the ideal reader, or at least not the kind of reader Meyer had in mind when she published her medical novel in 1892. But if we make the mistake of presupposing that the social issues—plural—of 1892 are no longer relevant at the time of Kenton's review in 1917, then we commit the same egregious error as Kenton. In fact, the reviewers of 1892 were quite often none the wiser about Meyer's political message. Several book reviews published within the first six months following *Helen Brent, M.D.*'s release identify the "social problem" of the novel as alternatively a "defence of the higher education of women," commentary "on the subject of professional careers for women," and "a protest against the demands of society that woman shall subordinate her individuality" in favor of domesticity.[5]

This R_x considers woman-authored medical fiction within the context of two specific narrative theories—narrative medicine and narrative prosthesis—as a means of examining both the affective nature of narrative itself and the efficacy of narrative affect in producing the expected readerly response of the writer. What happens when narrative seems to fail in the culture in which it was created? How might it still leave an impression on subjects in a culture and on the ongoing process of cultural development itself long after its heydey? Feminist medical fiction is political, for in its attempt to retheorize the female body as the product of sociobiological indeterminacy—that is, an agential subject that co-constitutes and is co-constituted by social and material forces—women writers of medical fiction perform political discourse. And, as Judith Butler reminds us, any "theory of the performative is already a work in the exercise of political discourse" as theory works "in implicit and fugitive ways" to challenge existing power structures.[6] In R_x 1, we witnessed this very affect as women writers subversively repurposed the power of animacy to distance the female body from the concept of disability generally, and from one specific illness that confined their sex to domesticity: hysteria.

In this R_x, I not only defend the affective function of narrative but also redefine affect as an ongoing process of signification that produces subjects but cannot be successfully measured, captured, or observed. Any attempt to do so fails. Yet, as we saw in R_x 1, failure creates opportunities to creatively resist the hegemonic cultural narratives that we have inherited. Comstock law failed to curb the production of risqué cultural texts. It also failed to curb the production of feminist medical fiction, as women writers like Charlotte Perkins Gilman increasingly published medical fiction—and with greater frankness—over the course of the next three decades. In my defense of narrative affect, I examine Elizabeth Stuart Phelps's *Doctor Zay* (1882) and Charlotte Perkins Gilman's *Mag-Marjorie* (1912) as representative texts that exhibit the affective function through the figure of the New Man, which Phelps invents as an ideological counterpoint to the New Woman doctor. Phelps, and later Gilman, deploys the New Man ideal as a prosthetic who works to resolve the tension in the cultural narrative between readerly expectations and writerly revisions or (p)rescriptions. Nineteenth-century readers were strongly affected by the presence of a romance narrative, so Phelps and Gilman package their oppositional politics in defense of gender equality in the form of a conversion narrative. Women writers of medical fiction deploy the New Man as a transformative figure who converts readers to the cause of the New Woman doctor—and by extension, the feminist writer—by teaching us how to "listen for" the experiences of the New Woman doctor from a narrative medicine standpoint.

Book reviews from the period capture the possibility of readerly resistance among a late nineteenth- and early twentieth-century audience. This snapshot in time offers contemporary scholars a point of reference for how readers may have responded more broadly to a cultural text produced within a specific cultural milieu. As such, book reviews function as an instrument for measurement or observation of the cultural milieu, which interrupts the ongoing process of material-discursive becoming, producing a false impression of the material-discursive subject. The documented failure to convert nineteenth-century book reviewers to the cause of the feminist writer further exposes the limits of theory, for in the moment we deploy an apparatus to interpret a cultural text and its material-discursive subject, we try to pin it down, to observe it, and to make meaning of it in stasis. Butler has long theorized performativity as a function of gender construction (*Gender Trouble*), of the material body (*Bodies That Matter*), and of language itself as a material subject (*Excitable Speech*). Karen Barad builds upon the work of Butlerian performativity in her theory of agential realism, which extends the performative to nonhuman matter on a quantum level. Because narrative itself is a material subject that acts upon the reader and elicits a response, meaning is co-created during intra-action of the two material subjects, the reader and the text. Moreover, the ideologies operative in the text that act upon the reader engage in an ongoing process of superposition or entanglement, and they do this on a quantum level as ideologies circulate invisibly, neurologically, and somatically. "When we observe a system" such as American patriarchal medicine through the lens of a cultural text such as medical fiction, the material-discursive subjects acting in that system "cease[] to be in a superposition."[7]

In other words, what we observe as race, disability, or gender is actually affect, or the after-effects of the superposition or entanglement, and not the material-discursive subject itself. Recognizing the affective nature of narrative places significant responsibility on readers, a point of emphasis that women writers of medical fiction fully recognize in their deployment of the New Man ideal as a method of conversion. So much was at stake in the act of storytelling. Indeed, theorists past and present agree upon one main truth: Narrative matters. Anthony Comstock believed narrative mattered so deeply that he broadly criminalized "any obscene book" as a catchall phrase for nonfiction and fiction about reproductive health. The women writers of medical fiction studied in this book were willing to risk fine, incarceration, or public shame for their belief that oppositional narrative matters. They share with theorists Judith Butler, Karen Barad, Rita Charon, and David Mitchell and Sharon Snyder a belief in the power of narrative to (re)shape our sense of reality. While this places a significant onus on the reader/listener to respond to the writer's message, the responsibility of listening affectively is a space of hope. The cultural narrative is never complete. It is an ongoing process. The affective nature of narrative and of language becomes foundational for theorizing race, disability, and gender, since the performativity of each of these material-discursive subjects becomes readable in our cultural milieu when we attempt to capture their ongoing movement through cultural artifacts like fiction. And yet those cultural artifacts can never fully represent the raw authenticity of material-discursive subjects in their specific cultural milieu. This slippage might seem like a failure—and it is—yet I revel in that failure because the act of failure offers a space for imagining the cultural narratives of race, gender, and disability as otherwise.

Affective Narrative, Narrating Affect

In *Affecting Fictions: Mind, Body, and Emotion in American Literary Realism*, Jane F. Thrailkill responds to perhaps the earliest theoretical text initiating an "affective turn": "The Affective Fallacy" by W. K. Wimsatt and Monroe Beardsley. Of course, Thrailkill rejects Wimsatt and Beardsley's contention that affect threatens the organizing principles of a literary work. These New Critics predictably eschew any kind of cultural context for literary texts, and affect is certainly cultural. Ironically, Wimsatt and Beardsley demonstrate the cultural nature of affect when they make an impassioned argument against affect: "why, in an essay urging the irrelevance of feeling to literary studies, is the rhetorical register of such emotional intensity?"[8] Thrailkill asks. Why, indeed? Perhaps because the specific flight from affect belies a broader cultural flight from feeling. As a culture, Americans are afraid to get in touch with their feelings, as though displays of emotion—especially among the male sex—might weaken one's credibility, making them "soft," and therefore vulnerable to shame or ridicule. Nineteenth-century writers were just as committed as contemporary writers to the regulation and banning of certain emotions based upon culturally constructed valuations of those emotions. Self-pity is one particular emotion that frequently falls under the censor. As Laura Otis points out in *Banned Emotions: How Metaphors Can Shape What People Feel*, expressions of self-pity are often accompanied by expressions of emotional pain, of loss, and of grief, which American culture censors through the pervasive dissemination of cultural texts that associate self-pity with being a "loser." They further aphorize individuals to self-regulate expressions of emotional pain with pithy statements meant to shame and censor, like "buck up," "let it go," or "move on."[9]

Otis finds that this control of emotional expression is not just a marketing ploy of twenty-first-century self-help books such as *Who Moved My Cheese?*, *The Power of Positive Thinking*, and *The Four Agreements*, many of which do eschew "negative" emotions that the writers perceive as threatening to mental health and emotional stability. Popular cultural texts such as the films *G. I. Jane* (1997) and *Bridesmaids* (2011) promote self-censor and the self-regulation of emotions by associating negative emotions like self-pity with metaphors of dirt and filth, a move that works to shame people against public displays of negative emotions. This has deep roots in the nineteenth century as writers Henry James and Virginia Woolf represent expressions of suffering and pain in a negative light to promote a culture of emotional self-control. But, even before James and Woolf, Anthony Comstock manufactured shame through legal censorship of sexuality and the female body, a move which women writers of medical fiction strove to counter by encouraging expressions of sympathy and empathy even among men, as in the case of New Man Mr. Waldo Yorke in Phelps's *Doctor Zay*. Many of the women Comstock prosecuted in court of law chose to commit suicide rather than endure the public shame of a trial, including women's rights activist Ida Craddock and abortionist Madame Restell.[10] Amy Werbel similarly documents the suicides of several young women with whom Comstock had no direct relationship, yet who were adversely affected by his culture of shame.[11] Clearly, affect matters, as cultural narratives of shame have a more corrosive long-term impact than so-called unregulated emotional expression.

Nineteenth-century lawmakers like Anthony Comstock feared the affective nature of narrative, not least because fiction disseminates "dangerous" ideas that might inspire readers to act out the imaginative scenarios of reproductive health, and thereby engage in behavior Comstock deemed risky to the reader, his/her partner, and society at large. Comstock also feared the affective nature of narrative because it engenders an emotional response. As we might recall from R_x 1 of this book, one of the earliest court cases that established Comstock law as precedent for censoring literature explicitly ruled on the grounds of the potential for literature to cause psychological or emotional damage to impressionable minds.[12] In his ruling, Judge Samuel Blatchford declares, "[I]t is not a question of whether it would corrupt morals, tend to deprave your minds, or the minds *of every person*; it is a question whether it tends to deprave the minds *of those open to such influences* and into whose hands a publication of this character might come."[13] The phrase "of those open to such influences" betrays a fear of affective cultural texts whether artistic, literary, or dramatic. He further identifies the impress(ion)able audience as persons with pre-existing mental illness or those vulnerable to mental illnesses such as white women (hysteria) and Black men and women (panmixia and drapetomania, among others). Comstock and his cronies were not concerned about the everyman reader, by which they imagine a white middle- to upper-class male readership. They were concerned about readers whom medical science designated "open," or vulnerable, because their biological condition predisposed them to emotional influences: Women are vulnerable because of their uterus; young adults and children are vulnerable because of their lack of mature development; and people of color are vulnerable because their melanin predisposes them to being ruled by emotion rather than reason (and in the case of women of color, this manifests in the form of hypersexuality).

How then does language make us vulnerable? Vulnerable to what? And why are we so afraid of vulnerability? In *Excitable Speech: A Politics of the Performative*, Judith Butler specifically examines injurious speech acts such as hate speech and insults, finding that language makes us most vulnerable when we suffer a loss of context because the words themselves wrest control from the addressee. Dr. Armstrong performs just this kind of injurious speech when he declares Dr. Margaret Yale, or the titular "Mag-Marjorie" of Gilman's novel, "ridiculous" because she is a woman physician: "'She'll outgrow it,'" he declares. "'A woman is a woman, and that's enough. Anything beyond that is ridiculous'" (*MM* 109). Dr. Armstrong infantilizes Dr. Yale, who is a full-grown woman with a degree in medicine, by dismissing her professional interests as a fanciful yet unrealistic childhood dream that she will "outgrow," just as a young child outgrows their dreams of being a firefighter, a ballerina, or an astronaut. This, of course, suggests yet another cultural narrative operating beneath the surface of Dr. Armstrong's injurious speech: not only that children fail to follow through on their dreams, but also that children's dreams are silly because they originate from the impressionable minds of a population who have yet to experience the harsh realities of the world.[14]

Just as Butler observes, injurious speech enacts a loss of context. In this case, the speech act metaphorically transfers Dr. Yale out of the sphere of professional medicine and into the kindergarten classroom. Such a rhetorical loss "put[s] its addressee out of control."[15] Since Dr. Armstrong talks about Dr. Yale behind her back, the direct addressee, Dr. Newcome, must determine whether to defend Dr. Yale, and if so, what to say to recover her reputation and authority. Dr. Yale herself may eventually catch word of Dr. Armstrong's injurious speech, which he deploys to sow seeds of doubt in the community about her commitment to the profession. Dr. Yale becomes vulnerable when the speech act threatens to leave her "open to an unknown future,"[16] as she cannot predict how her patients might respond to the public perception inculcated by the speech act—slander—itself. It's no wonder Phelps portrays her woman physician, Dr. Zay, as "cold, unnatural," "hard-hearted," and "cruel" (131, 141, 119), as Phelps feels her protagonist must overcompensate for a cultural narrative of gender that forecloses her ability to perform the masculine art of medicine. Because Dr. Armstrong expresses dismissiveness toward woman physicians generally, and Dr. Yale as a representative, he not only articulates the woman physician as an unworthy subject of conversation but is also unwilling to discuss the political subject further because the subject and the person are unworthy of attention. Dr. Armstrong, in other words, censors Dr. Newcome, and by extension, Dr. Yale, however benign and ineffective his censure might be.

Yet the act of censorship is itself an injurious speech act. Censorship determines what is and is not speakable. Importantly, Butler differentiates between individual acts of censorship such as the one Dr. Armstrong imposes upon Dr. Yale (and her advocates like Dr. Newcome) and state-level censorship that seeks to establish a "constituting norm by which the speakable is differentiated from the unspeakable" as crystallized in Comstock law.[17] This differentiation is important for understanding what or whom is left vulnerable by the invocation of the unspeakable. Comstock identifies sexuality and the female body as unspeakable in his enforcement of obscenity law. It was white women's bodies that were completely covered down to the ankle in aesthetic production, while Black women appeared scantily clad due to a cultural perception of the always-available Black female body. Meanwhile, references to amalgamation were censored to discourage conversations about repealing anti-amalgamation law. What was censored and what was not creates a differentiation between subjects that are so awful as to require protection from disgust or horror, and subjects not worthy of the attention of the censor. In sum, white female bodies required protection; Black female bodies did not. And if we think that this cultural narrative of the unspeakable white female body is past, consider how infrequently we publicly discuss menstruation or miscarriage even now, two decades into the twenty-first century.

In *Against the Unspeakable: Complicity, the Holocaust, and Slavery in America*, Naomi Mandel examines what the rhetorical practice of invoking the unspeakable produces for speakers. She finds that invoking the unspeakable masquerades as an ethical injunction that supposedly protects trauma survivors: "don't speak the unspeakable," she summarizes of this injunction, "for to do so is to violate the integrity of the historical truth, to desecrate the memory of the victims, and to perpetuate the survivor's pain."[18] But what this act of censorship actually invokes is our discomfort with the emotional expression of trauma, for the act of empathy threatens to highlight our complicity in the violence of the narrative. In R_x 3, I discuss how complicity functions as a component of narrative affect in Frances Ellen Watkins Harper's *Iola Leroy* (1892), which threatens to make the reader complicit in American slavery, broadly, and the medico-legal discourse of black sexuality during and after slavery, specifically. For the sake of this R_x, I simply wish to draw out our cultural discomfort with feeling, since like injurious speech, the experience of emotion—even vicariously—through the act of engaged, affective reading threatens the reader with a loss of context; it puts the reader out of control, opening her up to an unknown future in which she must respond, and hopefully, respond ethically.

And yet, much like complicity, this is not something to fear. Complicity helps us to engage ethically with difference, for only when we recognize acts of exclusion, discrimination, and oppression can we respond with compassion for future change. Similarly, only when we recognize our personal and cultural discomforts with a subject do we self-reflexively investigate the source of that discomfort and respond with compassion. If, as Butler and Mandel independently claim, the act of censorship and invoking the unspeakable produce speech, then not only does affective narrative produce emotion, it also plays a role in the formation of identities as gendered, racialized, and disabled. But if we are to stir up emotions among our readers, we best have a therapeutic method of grappling with our newfound emotions. Rita Charon prescribes narrative medicine as a therapeutic practice for both patient/speaker and practitioner/listener that draws upon narrative skills to identify and interpret the stories of illness. Charon invokes narrative medicine as a new framework for a broken healthcare system that emphasizes practitioner productivity over patient well-being. Narrative medicine teaches how to listen affectively, or what Charon calls alternatively "listening for" and "living through." These should not be separate functions. Empathy, by definition, requires that we inhabit the same emotional space as another person; in this case, the speaker or writer. It's not just "trying to inhabit her point of view," although that is part of it, but also "*join[ing]* with the one who suffers" so that both speaker and listener can work toward healing.[19] Narrative medicine is "genuine intersubjectivity" that promotes "authentic relation" among people, for "suffering does not separate" the speaker and the listener.[20] It is shared through the act of narrative, and "[o]nce shared, the suffering is lessened."[21] Suffering is also part of their shared humanity. But we do not like to discuss the things that make us suffer: sexist medicine, racist medicine, American slavery, Comstockian censorship, banned books. Narrative medicine may be the only way forward, for only when we share our experiences of suffering—and listen affectively to the suffering of others—will we finally lessen the burden of cultural trauma.

The Birth of the New Man

Scholars have previously determined that women of all populations were adversely affected by Comstockian censorship.[22] Yet this historical narrative fails to account fully for the role of disability in legal and medical suppression of sexual knowledge. This is particularly significant because, historically, disability, race, and gender co-emerge and co-evolve, so the one vector always already affects the others. Moreover, almost no scholarly studies account for Anthony Comstock's relationship to race or the effect of Comstockian censorship on communities of color, an omission I seek to rectify in R_x 3 of this book. Perhaps this omission occurs because our narratives—historical, cultural, medical—are themselves defined by disability rupture. In *Narrative Prosthesis: Disability and the Dependencies of Discourse*, David Mitchell and Sharon Snyder theorize that the trajectory of narrative itself depends upon the concept of disability. Both the function of plot in narrative acts and the development of literary narratives throughout history rely upon a "textual obstacle," or conflict, in need of resolution. Often that obstacle draws upon disability rhetoric for definition, even when the experience of disability or impairment is not central to the events of the narrative.[23] In pursuing a resolution that masks or eliminates disability, the writer creates a prosthetic through language that resolves the tension in the script in a way that is socially and culturally acceptable to the contemporary reader. Tiny Tim gains the resources necessary to cure his limp from Ebenezer Scrooge. Ahab dies pursuing revenge upon Moby Dick because the pain from his whalebone prosthetic causes madness. Benjy is castrated and institutionalized and Quentin commits suicide, for there is no space in genteel Southern society for deviants.[24] All of these fictional forms of narrative prosthesis expose patriarchal society as responsible for any number of social ills, from class-based allocation of resources (or lack thereof), to the redeployment of racial and ethnic oppression (and genocide) aboard ship, to the erasure of sexually deviant women.

Yet, at the same time, each of these narratives relies upon one or more persons with disability and the language of prosthesis for social critique—and they are all written by (white) men. At least, this normative authorship of disability characterizes the nineteenth-century literary examples that Mitchell and Snyder cite as evidence of narrative prosthesis. What happens when the writer is a woman whose body is medically and socially defined by disability? Or who is herself disabled? Will her experience of disability culturally shape her perspective of disability, and therefore her representation of disability in narrative? Mitchell and Snyder respond with a resounding yes. Disability logic dictates that a writer's experience of disability will inevitably affect her worldview.[25] Yet the same is also true of nineteenth-century critics and twenty-first-century scholars: "What we 'see' in these texts is often dependent on our own orientation or demeanor toward disability."[26] As a woman scholar with a history of physical disability and mental illness, I find myself in a unique position to respond to Mitchell and Snyder's call for scholars to apply "reading practices that embrace, transform, and reckon with our inherited disability storylines" developed from specific embodied experience and academic training.[27] Because the bodies and minds of women writers of medical fiction are defined by disability rhetoric, they expect a different kind of reader for their narratives, just as Mitchell and Snyder expect a different kind of scholar for the future of disability studies.

For women writers of medical fiction, this reader manifests in the narrative through the figure of the New Man. He appears in the person of Waldo Yorke in Elizabeth Stuart Phelps's *Doctor Zay* (1882), Dr. Henry Newcome in Charlotte Perkins Gilman's *Mag-Marjorie* (1912), and Uncle/Dr. Alec in Louisa May Alcott's *Eight Cousins* (1875). He wholly fails to manifest in Davis's *Kitty's Choice* (1874), resulting in Dr. Maria Haynes Muller's neuralgic episode and subsequent impairment, which forces her to adapt her role from surgeon to medical lecturer. Sometimes the narrative remains open-ended to the possibility of transformation beyond the boundaries of the narrative itself, as in the case of Harold Skidmore in Meyer's *Helen Brent, M.D.* (1892). Ultimately, by inscribing the New Man as a prosthetic in the narrative itself, readers are meant to "listen for" him as one prescription regimen in the larger treatment plan for healing the discrimination that ails American society post-Comstockian censorship. Moreover, the practice of narrative medicine complements the theory of narrative prosthesis specifically because the act of imagining the sociocultural context of the speaker's medical condition produces "profound dividends" for negotiating therapeutic regimens.[28] "The hypothesis act[s] like a prosthetic device or tool with which to get to the truth," Charon explains of her own experience practicing narrative medicine.[29] Narrative medicine, and its corollary apparatus of narrative prosthesis, helps bring the listener closer to the experience of the speaker, as the listener seeks to understand and empathize with the speaker's behavior.

The New Man was a creature of imagination in transatlantic fin de siècle narrative. Like his female counterpart the New Woman, he was an archetype readers should aspire to achieve. Margaret D. Stetz refers to him as "The Man Who Never Was," for she finds him an anachronism who emerges in neo-Victorian novels and films from the 2010s as a so-called rediscovered figure. For Stetz, the New Man is revisionist history, not once-lost recovered history. He reveals more about present-day cultural anxieties in the wake of the #MeToo backlash, Trumpist misogyny, and calls for "men's rights" than a utopian figure from the past who might reshape our present. Although Stetz acknowledges that there may have been early calls for the New Man in feminist essays of the 1890s, she finds that he does not appear to have arrived.[30] At least, not in Victorian England. Stetz may be correct about the New Man arriving late to the party: He does not emerge in England even as an imaginative ideal until the First World War, and specifically, 1913. In *The New Man: A Portrait of the Latest Type* (1913), British reporter Sir Phillip Gibbs defines the New Man as a character type "created, largely, by the New Woman" for the promotion of a new worldview.[31] "He is a feminist by conviction," and not just a suffragist for the cause of women, Gibbs explains: "For the New Man has accepted the equality of women without mental reservations," acknowledging their departure from the private, domestic sphere and their emergence as equals in public and professional spheres.[32] The New Man may have been late(r) to emerge in England. Nevertheless, he does exist as a literary paradigm if not a lived embodiment. Gibbs seems to think he manifested in both forms.

Gibbs reminds readers that his book *The New Man* is a product of sociological study, and as such he sketches the natural habitat of the New Man whom Gibbs "has met" drinking in beer taverns, picketing at strikes, working in the industrial center of the city, and at home listening to his gramophone. The New Man is just as real as Gibbs, though Gibbs would not define himself as a New Man.[33] Gibbs further acknowledges the presence of the New Man in the United States, where he appears more effeminate, domestic, and even "emasculated" than his British counterpart. Scholars similarly describe the New Man of Elizabeth Stuart Phelps's *Doctor Zay* (1882) as "emasculated," which suggests rhetorical crossover. Anticipating Gibbs's proclamation of a "new type of man," Phelps directly refers to the New Man as a product of and partner to the New Woman during Waldo Yorke's proclamation of love for Dr. Zay. She initially rejects his proposal, which opens up a space for Phelps to call for the New Man through the regret of her female physician protagonist: "'You see, Mr. Yorke, you have been so unfortunate as to become interested in a new kind of woman. The trouble is that a happy marriage with such a woman demands a new type of man.'"[34] Dr. Zay does not believe this New Man exists at all, much less in the person of Waldo Yorke. It takes several chapters for Dr. Zay to accept Mr. Yorke's conversion, fearing that he would feel "neglected" over time, and therefore, become resentful of her for pursuing professional ambition (164). Dr. Zay makes it clear that she will not give up her profession in favor of marriage. Waldo Yorke points out that he never asked Dr. Zay to give up her profession. On the contrary, he insists that he "'never thought of asking'" because "[i]t would make another woman of [her],'" and he loves her just as she is (165). Perhaps the New Man appears just as mythological to Dr. Zay as he does to Margaret Stetz because he did not exist prior to the publication of Phelps's medical novel, even as a figment of the cultural imagination.

Upon first glance, the New Man seems to function as a counterpoint to the New Woman. Like her male counterpart, the New Woman appears to have first emerged rhetorically when British novelist Sarah Grand wrote her into existence in her essay "The New Aspects of the Woman Question" (1894), declaring that "the new woman . . . has been sitting apart in silent contemplation all of these years, thinking and thinking, until at last she solved the problem and proclaimed for herself what was wrong with Home-in-the-Woman's-Sphere, and prescribed the remedy."[35] I say "appears" because American writer Elizabeth Stuart Phelps references both the New Woman and the New Man in her medical novel *Doctor Zay* twelve years prior to Grand's essay. Nevertheless, Grand's oft-quoted passage in scholarly studies of the New Woman is useful because it properly contextualizes the first usage of the phrase "New Woman."[36] Moreover, the rhetoric Grand employs is significant because she defines the New Woman as a "remedy," medical treatment, or "(p)rescription," for a "problem" or social illness. Grand further articulates education as central to her remedy for woman's oppression:

> Man, having no conception of himself as imperfect from the woman's point of view, will find this difficult to understand, but we know his weakness, and will be patient with him, and help him with his lesson . . . He must be taught consistency. There are ideals for him, which it is presumed that he tacitly agrees to accept when he keeps an expensive establishment to teach them: let him live up to them.[37]

Grand places the role of re-educating man squarely on the shoulders of the New Woman. Her expectation that he "live up to" her lessons suggests the expectation that a New Man will emerge who meets the needs of the New Woman. Indeed, Grand draws upon the rhetoric of futurity that Alison Kafer claims is central to disability discourse when she concludes that the result of re-education is that "[t]he man of the future will be better, while the woman will be stronger and wiser."[38] The New Woman may serve as a remedy for the disabling conditions of gender oppression, but the New Man functions as a prosthetic who works to suture our cultural narrative together while social institutions work toward reform, and eventually, generational healing.

Grand is not alone in her act of cultural narrative prosthesis. In *Doctor Zay*, Phelps prescribes the New Man in partnership with the New Woman as a remedy for the exact same illness. Scholars frequently eschew the New Man in favor of the New Woman in both Phelps's novel and Grand's essay because medical debates evolved in response to the New Woman writer and figure. Edward H. Clarke's thesis struck a nerve with women writers on both sides of the Atlantic, and Phelps was one of many writers who used fiction and nonfiction platforms to disprove his thesis and convert readers to her perspective.[39]

Cynthia J. Davis acknowledges the presence of this conversion plot in *Doctor Zay*: "His total conversion, then, could be seen as a model for skeptical readers," Davis concedes.[40] Because Mr. Yorke's conversion to New Woman thinking occurs during the first half of the narrative and Dr. Zay's conversion to marriage occurs during the second half of the narrative, Davis seeks to find balance in narrative form just as Phelps sought to balance her response between Edward H. Clarke and William Dean Howells. And yet (!) Mr. Yorke's conversion is central to Phelps's narrative. It occurs by the middle of *Doctor Zay* so that Phelps can open up a space for Mr. Yorke to follow through upon his newfound knowledge. Readers are further meant to listen for the experience of the New Woman alongside Mr. Yorke in the first half of the narrative since, upon conversion, they might learn how to enact change as a New Man. It is no coincidence that Phelps tells Dr. Zay's story from Waldo Yorke's perspective.[41] Phelps expects readers to empathize with Mr. Yorke and experience his conversion alongside him.

If this all sounds too utopian—well, it is. The traditional narrative structure of utopian fiction employs a journey motif in which a visitor travels to utopia and embarks upon a guided tour of utopian society. This narrative model, which likely originated with Thomas More's *Utopia* (1516), has witnessed various adaptations in the form of the dystopia and the critical utopia. Regardless of whether utopian fiction appears in the traditional form of dialogic, dystopian narrative, or self-conscious critique of utopianism, scholars agree that what defines utopian fiction is the dual function of social critique of the present and alternative suggestions for constructing a better future.[42] Davis finds just this narrative structure at work in *Doctor Zay*, for aside from Mr. Yorke's "total conversion"—and ours alongside him—Phelps situates the novel "as both a reply to its predecessor and a call to arms, a revision of the past and a vision for the future."[43] Chris Ferns claims that this traditional model shadows adaptations of utopian narrative form, creating a tense paradigm for contemporary utopian fiction since the possibility of radical reform is restrained by this traditional (read: patriarchal) narrative structure.[44] Readers should vicariously experience an ideological shift emerging from the unfolding narrative and respond with enthusiasm as co-converts alongside the protagonist visitor. Yet how enthusiastic could readers possibly be if they are not liberated from patriarchal influence?[45] Enter the New Man, who does not simply replace the visitor of utopian fiction in narrative structure. His function is decidedly feminist. The result is not just conversion, but reformation. Indeed, the writer re-forms her readers in the image of the New Man.

The work of Charlotte Perkins Gilman merges utopian narrative structure with the New Man motif in such a way as to offer a more concrete image of how readers become the New Man through the transformative, affective act of reading. Ferns finds the traditional paradigm of utopian fiction inverted in Gilman's *Herland* (1915) specifically because Herland is a matriarchal society, and sympathetic men like Van or Jeff function as both the fictional visitors and the intended readers guided toward conversion.[46] Because Gilman employs gender satire, readers must actively participate as critics of Herland and Ourland, and they should ultimately draw the conclusion that society will continue to reinscribe oppressive patriarchal values unless and until both genders are social equals.[47] In other words, both matriarchal societies and patriarchal societies hold the potential to oppress because one gender is dominant over another. Gilman suggests that parity and partnership among the genders may begin to resolve this potential for gendered oppression. Yet it will only fully resolve when society has a new man—literally. The birth of Van and Ellador's baby boy in *With Her in Ourland* (1916) is heralded as the solution to ending gender stereotypes and as the beginning of a non-gendered utopia, or at least a society in which gender roles are not determined by biological sex, for only the product of an enlightened Ourlander man and a feminist Herlander woman can produce "a new kind of men," or the New Man himself.[48] In a strange reversal of the creation story from Genesis, (New) Man is created from (New) Woman. She must exist in order to give birth to him.

Gilman's use of satire in both *Herland* and *With Her in Ourland* ridicules the concept of reproduction, since feminist writers often turned toward education rather than gestation to (re)produce the New Man. Like utopian fiction, social critique emerges as a defining feature of feminist medical fiction, or what Kristin Swenson calls the New Woman doctor novel.[49] Given that medical fiction prior to 1873 was largely written by white middle- to upper-class men such as William Dean Howells, Oliver Wendell Holmes, and Henry James, this shift in narrative function speaks volumes about the purpose women writers deploy in assuming the mantle of medical fiction. Phelps seems to take this gender critique one step further than her male contemporaries, namely Howells. She not only critiques patriarchal society for denying women freedom of choice in professional or marital contexts, but also imagines a future in which professional medicine and marriage are no longer patriarchal, because the New Man has opened up a space for women to enter professional medicine and marriage as equal partners with men. Dr. Zay literally occupies that space at the end of the novel, "glid[ing] across the little distance that lay between" herself and Mr. Yorke, standing in for the New Woman and the New Man respectively (Phelps 173). She occupies this space not for herself, but "for the sex, for a cause, for a future," because "a woman in my position . . . ceases to be an individual" as a female physician (Phelps 79). It is not enough to speak up for her own sex. She must also educate sympathetic men who might be willing to collaborate on her project of reforming society.

The New Man in Medical Fiction

What defines this New Man? Does his character align with Philip Gibbs's sociological assessment, or did American women writers envision an altogether different kind of New Man? As an archetype, the New Woman is more recognizable even if hard to define because she appears more frequently in late nineteenth-century fiction. Charlotte Rich locates the New Woman in several works of American fiction from the 1870s and 1880s, including works of medical fiction by Charlotte Perkins Gilman, Elizabeth Stuart Phelps, Sarah Orne Jewett, and even William Dean Howells. Their early work "placed at the forefront of their fiction the New Woman's objectives," especially higher education, a professional career, and ultimately, the goal of economic independence.[50] Scholars agree that as an archetype the New Woman functions as a self-consciously political figure who rejects social convention and critiques any patriarchal practice that seeks to relegate her sex to conventional gender roles. If, as the saying goes, contemporary feminism is the radical notion that women are people, then as a self-consciously political figure bent on gender equality, the New Woman is a feminist. Sarah Grand might herald her arrival in 1894 just as Philip Gibbs heralds the arrival of the New Man in 1913, yet both feminist ideals of New Woman and New Man appear as early as 1882 in American fiction, and specifically, the medical fiction of Elizabeth Stuart Phelps.

In most works of feminist medical fiction, the New Woman always already appears politically active. She guides others through the journey of conversion toward awareness, enlightenment, or what we in the twenty-first century might call "woke"-ness. The New Man is often the subject of conversion, but he need not manifest for the narrative to be rhetorically effective, since the reader de facto takes the position of the New Man as the writer's message affectively works upon the reader. The New Man performs different functions depending on his degree of conviction, but ultimately his material-discursive presence opens up a space for readers to listen to the New Woman's message. In *Doctor Zay*, for instance, we learn about her politics through the narrator Waldo Yorke, who in turn learns from Mrs. Isaiah Butterwell. Mr. Yorke's initial interest in Dr. Zay is superficial. He comments upon her physical beauty, repeatedly describing her as a "blue caryatid" (12, 15, 16, 33). The epithet portrays Dr. Zay on multiple accounts. She may have a classical kind of beauty reminiscent of a Greek sculpture from Mr. Yorke's perspective. Yet Dr. Zay also serves as a pillar, literally and metaphorically, supporting Mr. Yorke through his physical injury and his ideological conversion. During Mr. Yorke's third profession of love to Dr. Zay, she rejects his advances, exclaiming "'I have been nothing but a crutch to you, Mr. Yorke!'" and refuses to entertain any further "expressions of [his] supposed feeling for [her]self" (142). (Spoiler alert: He professes again, she entertains, and they become engaged.)

Dr. Zay likely feels the emotional burden of re-educating a resistant audience, an experience white women and women of color have expressed in the aftermath of #MeToo and Black Lives Matter, respectively. Like a caryatid, Dr. Zay often appears stone-cold, unemotional, and burdened by Mr. Yorke's emotional displacement upon her. She dismisses his emotions—including his professions of love—as mere "symptoms" (88, 128, 132, 141). Her masculine air at the expense of her patient's emasculation is the only way she feels she can effectively assert authority within a professional sphere that is hostile to women. Xtine Yao characterizes Dr. Zay's unfeeling nature as "queer frigidity" or "professionally frigid," both of which function as a kind of controlled disaffection akin to anesthesia. The performance of queer frigidity allows professional women physicians like Dr. Zay and her real-life counterparts such as Dr. Elizabeth Blackwell to rescript the pathologization of the New Woman doctor apart from hysteria and the demands of heteronormative hegemony, while the act of professional frigidity grants the woman physician a necessary clinical distance to treat patients and engage colleagues without emotional investment.[51] Disaffection is an act of preservation. Readers might expect such callous behavior to be off-putting rather than endearing. Nevertheless, Mr. Yorke persists. Curious, he asks his hostess Mrs. Butterwell about the good doctress, and after "entertain[ing] the young man with a graphic account of his accident and its consequences," Mrs. Butterwell reveals a few basic facts such as the origin of her nickname and where she resides (36–7). Later, Mr. Yorke asks Dr. Zay directly about her education and she reveals a little of herself to him. She confesses that she became a doctor in honor of her mother, who died after a long, painful illness: "'I took care of her through it all,'" she reminisces. "'My mother was greatly comforted, during a part of her illness, by the services of a woman doctor in Boston. There was one when we were in Paris, too, who helped her. I said, When she is gone, I will do as much for some one else's mother'" (49). Such vulnerable episodes from Dr. Zay are rare. Because Dr. Zay is guarded, Mr. Yorke learns more from Mrs. Butterwell about the goodness of Dr. Zay than from Dr. Zay herself: that she treats patients of all classes, sometimes without payment; that her father, who was also a doctor, died when she was fifteen; that she is independently wealthy, but also industrious and generous. Mrs. Butterwell concludes, admiringly, "'Seems to me as if there was love enough invested in her for half the world to live on the interest, and never know they hadn't touched the principal'" (56). That's a lot of love, which readers might not have known if Mr. Yorke had not pursued his curiosity.

I rehearse these episodes to emphasize how Mr. Yorke becomes enamored with Dr. Zay, leading to his and the reader's conversion to a New Man ideology. Only when the New Woman appears human can readers empathize with her and be receptive to her message. In fact, empathy is the goal: Dr. Zay asks Mr. Yorke to "'Put yourself in my place for a moment. Reverse our positions'" (134). On the surface, Dr. Zay may be asking Mr. Yorke to consider her position as a professional woman facing a marriage proposal. She fears losing some degree of independence should she change her status. Yet the entire narrative plays on this theme of healing through empathy, for only when we recognize the specific challenges women encounter socially can we register the challenges female physicians face in the wake of sexist medicine. Scholarship on *Doctor Zay* often attends to the suffering of Mr. Waldo Yorke, whose injury from a carriage accident initiates the conflict of the narrative.[52] Thus, from a narrative prosthesis standpoint, the goal appears to be Mr. Yorke's physical recovery from his injuries: a dislocated ankle, a severed artery in the arm, and a concussion (34). However, Mr. Yorke's growing relationship with his physician Dr. Zay uncovers another form of suffering, one that remains largely invisible until Mr. Yorke shadows Dr. Zay on her day-to-day activities: systemic sexism. Cultural trauma such as the gender oppression wrought by systemic sexism (or racism, or ableism) is borne on the body but does not necessarily leave a visible mark, because it foremost affects our psychological state. Subsequently, we best bear witness to the experience of suffering under cultural trauma when we "listen for" and "live through" the suffering alongside the victim. Dr. Zay asks a lot of Mr. Yorke, just as Phelps asks a lot of her reader. They are asking us to sit in the same emotional space as the speaker, sharing in their pain.

Mr. Yorke practices affective listening over the course of several conversations with Dr. Zay, beginning with their first date, which creates a safe space for Dr. Zay to share her challenges as a woman physician. Dr. Zay admits surprise at Mr. Yorke's careful attention, admiring "'I've never heard a man talk like that before . . . It is something even to say it'" (161). The "something" she admires in this specific conversation is Mr. Yorke's acceptance of her core identity, which is not reducible to her gender or profession.[53] Yet the admission applies to Mr. Yorke's recursive practice of "listening for," as Charon reminds readers that affective listening is not honed during a single exercise of narrative medicine but "over time."[54] Mr. Yorke does make mistakes, calling Dr. Zay alternatively "cold, unnatural," "hard-hearted," and "cruel," and privately questioning her professional abilities because of her gender (131, 141, 119). His eventual conversion as a New Man earns the trust of Dr. Zay such that at the end of the novel, Dr. Zay anticipates Charon's patients who express relief at being heard: "No one ever let me do this before," they chorus.[55] Dr. Zay shares the same sentiment of relief at being heard by Mr. Yorke directly and the fictional audience indirectly. Such an expression testifies to the value of affective listening specifically because narrative medicine is a vulnerable act, one both Rita Charon and Dr. Zay liken to religious confession.[56]

At first, what Mr. Yorke hears is Dr. Zay's ethics of care toward her patients, just as Mrs. Butterwell witnesses, but ultimately what both Mr. Yorke and readers should hear is Dr. Zay's experience of gendered oppression as a woman physician. Phelps offers readers multiple opportunities to watch Dr. Zay at work, not only in her care of Mr. Yorke's wounds, but also when Mr. Yorke accompanies her on house calls for patients including Molly, Jim Paisley, and Mr. Beckwith. As a converted New Man, Mr. Yorke expresses pride in Dr. Zay and her ethics of care. Phelps expects this admiration to translate into political action in partnership with the New Woman doctor. Mr. Yorke attempts to flatter Dr. Zay during their first date when he compliments her exceptional skills and ethics of care. She does not accept his compliment, but instead uses the emotional space as an opportunity for sermonizing about gender equality in professional medicine:

> Until recently [the profession] needed force rather than finesse to bring the woman to the surface of a great progressive movement. We are coming to a point where both are to be absolutely necessary to success in the art of healing. A union of these qualities will be demanded of women, because they are women, such as has never been expected of men, or been possible to them. We have a complex task before us. (109)

Contemporary readers might understand this passage in gendered terms, especially since the context for this sermon emerges from Dr. Zay and Mr. Yorke's discussion of the proportion of men to women in professional medicine. As such, we might read "force" as masculine and "finesse" as feminine, echoing Regina Morantz-Sanchez's claim that nineteenth-century women physicians felt a union between masculine science and feminine sympathy was necessary for their success as credible practitioners.[57]

Phelps may also be commenting upon the trajectory of the women's rights movement in which a "union" between the New Man and New Woman may be "absolutely necessary" to heal gender divisions in the profession and society. From a narrative medicine perspective, Phelps shares an expectation with Charon that affective listening will help the listener "translate the news of the body" from these pathographies back to the speaker so that they might work together to create a remedy for healing.[58] Phelps does not offer a vision for this remedy beyond partnership between the New Man and the New Woman. However, Gilman's New Man in *Mag-Marjorie* does offer readers some indication of what kinds of political action might help the medical profession reform. Like Phelps's Dr. Zay, Gilman's medical novel ends with the marriage of her New Woman doctor to a New Man, the latter of whom Gilman overtly names for his role in the narrative, "Dr. Newcome." Gilman's Dr. Margaret Yale—Mag, for short—struggles more overtly than Dr. Zay to gain respect as a female physician among male physicians and male patients when she returns from her education abroad and tries to establish a practice in New England. Yet it is not Mag who laments the struggles of female physicians; rather it is Dr. Newcome, the New Man, who acknowledges the unique challenges Mag must face as a result of patriarchal medicine's conflation of gender with disability. In a direct reversal of S. Weir Mitchell's pathologizing of the female body as diseased, Dr. Newcome asserts, "'Men do have hysteria, you know, in spite of the name's derivation,'" to which Dr. Yale responds that she does, in fact, know the origins of the sexist diagnosis.[59]

Nineteenth-century readers should recognize the term "hysteria" as a catch-all diagnosis for female illnesses ranging from menstrual cramps to postpartum depression. Gilman lampooned the diagnosis—and Dr. S. Weir Mitchell's Rest Cure—in her now (in)famous short story "The Yellow Wallpaper" (1892), which I examine through the lens of crip affect in R_x 1 of this book. What remains unspoken but hinted at here in Dr. Newcome and Dr. Yale's conversation is the Greek origin of "hysteria," which means "suffering in the uterus." Although cis-men do not have a uterus, Dr. Newcome acknowledges that mental illness may affect anyone regardless of gender. Conversely, even though cis-women do have a uterus, Dr. Newcome knows that this one sex organ is not responsible for any illness that might befall a woman, whether her symptoms are mental or physical. Thus, one of the defining characteristics of a New Man figure in fictional narratives is an awareness of the social construction of gender. In the case of medical fiction, specifically, the New Man figure is defined not only by an awareness of gender construction but also sexist practices in medicine. Gilman prefigures Judith Butler's theory of gender performativity in many of her novels, medical or otherwise, even to the degree that Gilman's Herlanders dress androgynously with short hair and pants. Dr. Newcome furthers this critique on Gilman's behalf when he chastises Dr. Armstrong for praising Dr. Yale's appearance before her professional accomplishments: "'Such hair—such color—such shape!'" Dr. Armstrong admires, to which Dr. Newcome revises, "Such brains! Such courage! Such achievements!" (*MM* 109).

However, what truly defines Dr. Newcome as a New Man is his acceptance of Dr. Yale as a professional equal and his willingness to collaborate with her in a future business enterprise. Indeed, as part of his marriage proposal, Dr. Newcome invites Dr. Yale into a professional partnership: "'*Newcome and Yale. Yale and Newcome, M.D.'s*, looks rather well, I think. You see, as you say, our work touches and overlaps. You have the women and I'll take the children, and between us we can undertake any man that comes along, too—" (*MM* 144). Mag is taken aback at first, wary of mixing business and pleasure, but Gilman comments upon the intersections of Dr. Newcome's work as a pediatrician and Dr. Yale's work as a gynecologist throughout the narrative. The reader knows precisely where this is going long before she arrives at the marriage proposal in the final chapter. They are made for each other. Dr. Armstrong, on the other hand, is ill-suited for Dr. Yale for many reasons, not least because he devalues her contribution to professional medicine. He makes no secret of his disdain for female physicians, declaring "[p]rofessional titles do not belong to a woman" and insisting that Dr. Yale only practices medicine because she is bored (*MM* 135). "'She'll outgrow it,'" he declares, and for the traditional, patriarchal Dr. Armstrong, it is better that way, for "[a] woman is a woman, and that's enough.

Anything beyond that is ridiculous'" (*MM* 109). In referencing the ridiculousness of a female physician, generally, and Dr. Yale as a gynecologist, specifically, Dr. Armstrong cites the myth of hysteria, for he implies that the very notion of a female physician appears "laughable," "absurd," or "nonsensical." To take her seriously might border on mental illness.

Gilman also self-consciously anticipates that readers may not be willing to take her seriously as a woman writer who does not have a medical education or degree. Consequently, she attempts to strengthen her credibility by citing—literally, name-dropping—the scientists and theorists most influential to her worldview. In *Mag-Marjorie*, Gilman directly cites feminist activist Ellen Key. Similarly, in *The Crux* (1911), she directly cites venereologist Dr. Prince Morrow and nurse and social activist Lavinia Dock, as well as indirectly citing sociologist Dr. Lester Ward. Gilman is in good company in her deferential appeals to credibility. Rebecca Harding Davis fashions her protagonist Dr. Maria Haynes Muller after hydrotherapist Mary Gove Nichols. Elizabeth Stuart Phelps twice references *Materia Medica*.[60] However, Gilman further appeals to the New Man for political support. In fact, unlike Phelps, who leaves the sermonizing to her New Woman Dr. Zay, Gilman has Dr. Newcome perform the role of sermonizing in *Mag-Marjorie*. During his open office hours, readers bear witness to Dr. Newcome's ethics of care as a physician as he diagnoses and remedies at least two social conditions, lack of sex education and oppressive gender roles. On the one hand, Dr. Newcome meets with Jim Battlesmith upon the counsel of Mrs. Murray and Gerald Battlesmith, who are concerned that young Jim may become sexually active with Mrs. Murray's ward, Elma. Dr. Newcome provides his patient Jim Battlesmith with a complete sex education that includes "facts and figures" and "plates, diagrams, and statistics" of individuals who contracted venereal diseases. He does this not to "preach morality," but to emphasize the consequences of not knowing preventative medicine, and especially of leaving "those helpless, unwilling girl victims" ignorant of the choices they have to protect themselves (*MM* 64–5).

Gilman was certainly an advocate of sex education, though admittedly one of her reasons for promoting both sex education and birth control was eugenics.[61] Even Dr. Newcome's conversation with Jim Battlesmith preaches on the consequences of a lack of sex education for women, children, and "the health of the whole population," consequences which include crippled children as well as future generations of people with "locomotor ataxia, with paresis, idiots, lunatics" (*MM* 65). Yet, in *The Crux*, Gilman most passionately bewails how society disables women via censorship of medical knowledge: "'[W]e bring up girls to think it is not proper to know anything about the worst danger before them. Proper!—Why my dear child, the young girls are precisely the ones *to* know! It's no use telling a woman who has buried all her children—or wishes she had!—that it was all owing to her ignorance, or her husband's. You have to know beforehand if it's to do you any good."[62] No less than one paragraph before this speech, Gilman cites Dr. Prince Morrow as an expert on syphilis of the innocent. Gilman's warning against ignorance speaks to the experiences of women under Comstockian censorship: Readers need to "know beforehand" about venereal disease prevention, but they also need to know about anatomy and physiology, menstruation, and methods of birth control. Since *The Crux* and *Mag-Marjorie* were serialized in *The Forerunner* one year apart, we might consider them companion works of medical fiction in which Gilman diagnoses the condition based on the symptoms women experience, and then offers a remedy in the form of clinical sex education.

Gilman further emphasizes the dangers of sexist medicine in *Mag-Marjorie* during Dr. Newcome's second appointment of the day in which he meets with Miss Daisy Briggs, who complains of depression. Although she has been socially conditioned to minimize her complaints, dismissing them with a flippant, "'I don't suppose there's anything the matter,'" she confesses "'there are times when I can't sleep, and I don't eat, and nothing interests me. I get so depressed! I feel sometimes as if there was nothing to live for—as though I'd better be dead'" (*MM* 67). Dr. Newcome listens. Indeed, we are told he listens, as "He nodded, understandingly" and asks follow-up questions. In direct opposition to his real-life contemporary Dr. S. Weir Mitchell, Dr. Newcome prescribes activity: "'I would most earnestly advise you to take up some kind of work and stick to it. A full-grown woman with fifteen waking hours to fill has to do something to earn her sleep'" (*MM* 67). This is emphatically not the Rest Cure. Dr. Newcome recognizes that gender roles and the boredom of domestic life are precisely what causes Miss Daisy's depression, for as they engage in narrative medicine, Miss Daisy cites as oppressive her parents' ideology of "a girl's place is at home" and their expectations that she study art at Radcliffe. Of course, this scene is potentially problematic for two reasons. First, it reinforces white middle- to upper-class men as the gatekeepers of medical knowledge. Granted, this scene occurs prior to Dr. Yale's return to New Hampshire; Miss Daisy does not yet have the option of a woman physician. Second, the scene reinforces heterosexual marriage as a key factor in the New Woman's success. One of the questions Dr. Newcome asks of Miss Daisy concerns her marital status. Although Miss Daisy is not opposed to marriage, she claims the ratio of girls to boys in her town was too high. Her options are limited. Gilman suggests in her exposition that Dr. Newcome schemes to introduce Miss Daisy and Gerald Battlesmith in the hope they will begin courting. Indeed, Dr. Newcome himself marries Dr. Yale at the end of *Mag-Marjorie*, resulting in the merger of their medical practices.

Because readers make meaning of a narrative reflectively based on its conclusion,[63] the fact that Gilman and Phelps conclude their works of medical fiction with marriage of the New Woman doctor to a New Man suggests their feminist politics rely upon a legal union rather than a "union of qualities" embodied in the New Man and New Woman ideal. Davis agrees, offering two possible readings of Phelps's *Doctor Zay* based on its ambiguous ending: one that suggests Dr. Zay gave up her practice upon marrying Mr. Yorke, and another that suggests she did not. From Davis's perspective, the former interpretation would reinforce Clarke's and Howells's commitment to biological determinism while the latter would serve to critique it.[64] In fact, Phelps may have succumbed to readerly pressure against her better judgment, marrying off her New Woman doctor even at the risk of undercutting her political message.[65] This was certainly the case for Annie Nathan Meyer. In her letter to *The Bookman*, Meyer laments that her editor Jeanette Gilder "simply refused to recommend [*Helen Brent, M.D.*] to the firm she read for unless I wrote a happy ending" for readers.[66] Meyer buckled under pressure because she was young; *Helen Brent, M.D.* was her first publication. She further cites publisher influence as one of the reasons she resents Miss Kenton's criticism of her novel. Meyer claims that Harold's return to Helen at the close of the novel, which intimates not only reconciliation but also their future nuptials, "was not my own Harold at all, at least not the Harold of my first ending."[67] Even when a writer has the best of intentions, her narrative falls prey to patriarchy, which may ultimately affect her message. Nevertheless, readerly pressure may explain why so many women writers of medical fiction—Phelps, Meyer, and Gilman included—employ a marriage-or-career narrative that compromises their writerly intention with readerly expectations, removing the "or" in favor of "and." Readers do not give writers one option or the other because nineteenth-century culture would not give women one option or the other, regardless of their desires.

Or perhaps readers are only willing to digest the bitter medicine of a political message if the writer mixes sweet sugar in the form of a happy ending into the solution. After all, marriage of the New Man and New Woman is not a distinctive feature of feminist medical fiction. It also appears in belle époque novels. Rachel Mesch cites Marcelle Tinayre's *La rebelle* (1905) and Louise Marie Compain's *L'un vers l'autre* (1903) as quintessential fin de siècle French novels that highlight the role of the New Man in (re)constructing egalitarian marriage. Like feminist medical fiction, these *femmes nouvelles* resist legal oppression of women under the Naquet laws of 1884, which limited the conditions in which wives could petition for divorce, and Article 213 of the Civil Code, which dictated that wives must obey their husbands in exchange for protection.[68] However, Tinayre and Compain adopted fiction as their chosen platform for critique not because they feared censorship but because they recognized the role of culture in reform efforts. They knew that "changes to the Civil Code or divorce law do not directly transform these relationships," Mesch argues. "[T]he transformations follow instead from the process of questioning and discussion around proposed reform," and therefore they are "rooted in the social dynamics and pressures of the private sphere, rather than political forces."[69] Cultural narratives are powerful, which is why writers of feminist medical fiction employ the New Man figure as a guide through ideological conversion. At the same time, women writers were subject to narrative convention, reminds Cynthia J. Davis, who "suggest[s] that the conservatism may not lie in Phelps or even in the themes her narrative explores so much as in the formal concepts and conventions which filter and at least partially contain her narrative's radical elements."[70]

Marriage might in fact be a radical ending for readers of feminist medical fiction, since one of the (transatlantic) cultural narratives about female physicians casts their sex as neither male nor female but a kind of third sex.[71] From this vantage point, we might further consider the "trope of pairing a woman doctor and a male lawyer in the marriage plot" not simply as an act of reinforcing heteronormative hegemony, as Yao suggests, but also as a subversive means of drawing upon the power of these two "culturally symbolic authorities" to critique the biopolitics of medico-legal partnership.[72] As we saw in R_x 1, medicine and law were figuratively in bed with one another as lawmakers, politicians, and judges drew upon sexist medicine to justify their control over gendered social roles. Here, in feminist medical fiction, they are quite literally in (the marriage) bed with one another but for the purpose of sexual liberation rather than censorship. As a feature of both feminist medical fiction and belle époque fiction, the New Man balances form and politics by allowing the writer to end her narrative with the expected "happy ending" while also seeking to radically challenge her readers' worldview, which hinges on medical rationale for biologically determined social roles.

Narrative Affect in Disability Narratives

Ultimately, what defines Dr. Newcome and Mr. Yorke as fictional manifestations of the New Man is their commitment to the freedom of "woman" as a liberal subject, for they believe that women should be free from the physical and mental constraints society imposes upon their bodies. For 1912—much less 1882—this was a radical notion. Few women had the right to a higher education, and even fewer could successfully pursue a professional career as a physician.[73] Phelps and Gilman deploy the New Man to suture their narratives through marriage to the New Woman doctor, opening up a space for the New Woman doctor to continue her work as a physician and feminist activist. As Mitchell and Snyder might conclude, "the breach is healed and a disruptive anomaly"—in this case, the female physician—"is concealed before a more modest covering" of marriage to a New Man who grants her credibility within and beyond the narrative.[74] But the New Man does not wholly conceal the "anomaly" embodied in the character of the feminist physician. Nor would Phelps and Gilman want him to. The New Man draws us into the text toward the New Woman and her oppositional politics of medical theory and practice.

Phelps and Gilman know that gendered oppression cannot be healed through marriage, which is why they use a material-discursive device from within the medical institution—the prosthetic—and reform it for oppositional, feminist purposes.

Although Mitchell and Snyder imply that prosthesis of any kind, narrative or otherwise, indicates shame toward disability, I propose crip theorists reclaim prosthesis for positive ends. I embrace my prosthetics—my porcelain crowns and my antidepressants—not just for cultural reasons of disability "passing," but also for practical reasons of evading unnecessary pain. Like many women writers of medical fiction, including Phelps and Gilman, I welcome appropriate medical intervention because it allows people like myself with chronic pain to function productively in society. I was born with amelogenesis imperfecta, I struggle with chronic high-functioning anxiety, and as I highlight in R_x 1 in relation to Gilman's "The Yellow Wallpaper," I have a history of postpartum depression. These might be discrete diagnoses, but my embodied experience of physical impairment and mental illness eschews separate categories or the binaries of physical/mental, disability/impairment, social/material. Amelogenesis imperfecta is a condition in which one is born without enamel on one's teeth.[75] It is a rare condition that usually manifests with a percentage of missing enamel from either milk or adult teeth, or sometimes both. My condition is particularly "dire," or advanced, in that I had zero enamel on my milk teeth and still have zero enamel on my adult teeth; underneath my "prosthetics," or porcelain crowns, I have only dentin. Without crowns, people with amelogenesis imperfecta experience significant sensitivities to touch in terms of temperature and pressure. By contrast, chronic high-functioning anxiety and the emotional hypersensitivity that often comes along with it is not only more common, but also recognizable. Casual observers might recognize benign signs of it in my self-criticism, perfectionist tendencies, and obsessive-compulsive cleaning or organizing. Yet, during periods of intense stress, I am no longer "high-functioning" and suffer episodes of panic attack or depression.

My discrete socially constructed diagnoses complexly intertwine with my embodied experience of physical impairment (oral sensitivity to touch), which reveals how the somatic feeling of pain may result in the development of mental health conditions (shame, anxiety, and even depression when the former are left unmanaged), and alternatively, how mental illness (such as chronic high-functioning anxiety) may manifest with physical symptoms that are painful (such as panic attacks). Because of this entanglement in my embodied experience of disability, I promote a disability politics of crip affect that aligns with scholars such as Alison Kafer who welcome appropriate medical intervention, prosthesis, or cure.[76] Although disability activists rightly challenge the social and cultural frameworks that define a subject as disabled, such a positionality cannot ignore the embodied experience of pain and the desire to alleviate that feeling. As such, any narrative account of pain that I tell, write, or theorize must not only consider the conditions of environmental affect that alter my experience of normative stasis—changes in food or drink, sinus infection, pregnancy, personal or professional stress—but must also consider receptivity. How I tell the story will affect how the listener interprets my pain and the degree of medical intervention we negotiate as we move toward healing and away from trauma. Importantly, my pursuit of remedy, therapy, or prosthetic is compassionate. It is not just about managing my pain. It is also about evading displacement of my stress or trauma upon others, especially my friends, family, and students. People with disabilities are entangled in ongoing affective relationality such that David Mitchell and Sharon Snyder recently compiled a scholarly collection of essays on *The Matter of Disability*, which (finally!) theorize disability as material, as phenomenon, even as affect.

In the following two R_xs on Frances Ellen Watkins Harper's *Iola Leroy* (1892), Annie Nathan Meyer's *Helen Brent, M.D.* (1892), and Charlotte Perkins Gilman's *The Crux* (1911) and "The Vintage' (1916), I examine medical narratives of trauma and illness to theorize race, gender, and disability as affect using Karen Barad's theory of agential realism and the physical law of superposition as my framework. Here, I want to end by querying the efficacy of narrative prosthesis and crip affect: Does it work? Did it accomplish what writers of medical fiction intended when they deployed the New Man prosthetic as a means of being taken legitimately as contributors to medical discourse? Did readers engage in the practice of narrative medicine through reading? And if so, did they heed writerly (p)rescriptions for healing society from gendered oppression? Nineteenth-century book reviews of feminist medical fiction suggest that maybe the message was missed in translation. *The Atlantic Monthly*'s review of *Doctor Zay* compares Phelps's novel against Howells's *Doctor Breen's Practice*, even while acknowledging that "neither writer knew of the other's having written such a story until both novels were completed."[77] The reviewer succinctly summarizes the theme of *Doctor Zay* as a novel "in which Miss Phelps has worked out her ideas on some questions of professional and social life," and once again homes in on the marriage-or-career plot. Although this nods to her politics of gender, the reviewer elides Phelps's commentary on medical discourse. A much longer review of *Doctor Breen's Practice* observes Howells's critique of the social construction of gender, namely "how the crude, experimental, yet largely ethical elements of New England society have conspired to confine and torture the honest spirit of Dr. Breen."[78] Contemporary scholars are surprisingly less generous than nineteenth-century critics. Cynthia J. Davis read *Doctor Breen's Practice* as complicit in sexist medicine, while this particular nineteenth-century critic cautions against generalizing Dr. Breen's experience "as a class" of women physicians: "The perplexities which beset Dr. Breen are not paraded as triumphant obstacles to the practice of medicine by young women," the critic observes. "[T]hey are incidents in the life of one young woman, which throw a needed light upon her character and behavior."[79] In other words, the critic recognizes that not all young women are unfit for the field of professional medicine; rather, Dr. Breen's experience of trauma from lost love positions her as an individual who wrongly chose professional medicine as a method of personal healing. Such nuance seems unexpected for an 1882 reviewer.

Book reviews harness the potential for greater reception among a resistant audience, especially if they invite the reader into the work of feminist medical fiction with an air of hope toward the writer's politics. Yet they also leave writers vulnerable to what Rita Charon calls "narrative bad faith": an opportunity for the listener/reader to collect information and use the speaker/writer's words against the speaker/writer.[80] This kind of vulnerability is precisely what Judith Butler means in her Introduction to *Excitable Speech* "on linguistic vulnerability": Language threatens the body as much as it sustains it, and the very same words that encourage one can be used to harm another when deployed in a different context.[81] That disjuncture may in fact be the case with Edna Kenton's review of *Helen Brent, M.D.* in *The Bookman*, prompting Meyer to defend her narrative choices in a public forum. Whether these women writers of medical fiction were successful in converting late nineteenth- and early twentieth-century readers like Edna Kenton may not wholly matter for our purposes. We cannot change prior reactions, but we can learn how to read differently for future response. Reading for the New Man helps us learn to listen for the experiences of gendered oppression from the New Woman. It also teaches us more generally how to listen—and read—with empathy, of which the world can always use more. Charon warns listeners that learning empathy does not come easily; it requires a recursive practice of engaging in affective listening to the stories of others who are different from ourselves.[82] It may not occur within the span of a single story, or even a single novel, but perhaps a body of work such as medical fiction offers a good space for practice before engaging in narrative medicine in the real world.

Notes

1. Review of *Kitty's Choice: A Story of Berrytown*, *Godey's Lady's Book and Magazine* 88 (1874), 184, <https://babel.hathitrust.org/cgi/pt?id=pst.000020202385&view=1up&seq=176&q1=Berrytown> (accessed December 12, 2021).
2. Edna Kenton's review of *Helen Brent, M.D.* is titled "The Pap We Have Been Fed On VIII: 'Lady Doctresses' of Nineteenth Century Fiction," and appears in *The Bookman* 44 (1916), 280–7. Annie Nathan Meyer's letter to the editor of *The Bookman* was published in *The Bookman* 45 (1917), 548. Meyer expresses surprise that *Helen Brent, M.D.* still commands enough readerly attention for a book review some twenty-four years after its publication. That might speak to the book's longevity in the market, and yet, Ms. Kenton perhaps makes the same mistakes as readers twenty-four years earlier in her misunderstanding Meyer's use of gender satire.

3. Meyer, Letter to the Editor, 548; Meyer, *Helen Brent, M.D.*, 10.
4. Jeannette Gilder, Letter to Annie Nathan Meyer, March 29, 1892, Series MS-7: Annie Nathan Meyer Papers, Box 1, Folder 1, The Jacob Marcus Rader Center of the American Jewish Archives. See also, Review of *A Country Doctor* by Sarah Orne Jewett, *The Dial* (1884), 66; and Kristin Swenson's *Medical Women and Victorian Fiction*. In her letter to Annie Nathan Meyer, which discusses the title of what would become *Helen Brent, M.D.*, editor Jeanette Gilder refers to Meyer's novel as a "story with a purpose." Her usage of the phrase suggests that it was a common phrase among the literary market. Indeed, it may even have been the name of a genre of books. Gilder cautions against a heavy-handed title such as *Problems*, since "stories with a purpose are not branded as such in the titles." Gilder is not the only member of the literary market who uses this phrase to denote a genre of fiction. A review of Sarah Orne Jewett's *A Country Doctor* (1884) also uses the phrase to characterize Jewett's medical novel: "It belongs to the class of novels with a purpose," the reviewer points out. "[T]he purpose in the present case being to serve as a plea for the adoption of the medical profession by women." The reviewer finds Jewett mostly successful in achieving her purpose, albeit "a little obtrusive towards the end of the story—a very little indeed." As a genre, "stories with a purpose" seem to be defined by what Kristin Swenson would call their "self-consciously political" tone, in that the work of fiction presents an argument for social or political reform apropos to the author's own period. Today, scholars might categorize these fictional texts as "political fiction" or "social reform fiction," and yet they are a key feature of both medical fiction and utopian fiction.
5. One 1892 reviewer deigns to reference this medical narrative only to dismiss it, for the book "is readily readable" "in spite of a good deal of obstetrical and pathological allusion." See "Recent Fiction: *Helen Brent, M.D.*," *The Critic* 543.16 (1892), 30–1, <http://babel.hathitrust.org/cgi/pt?id=mdp.39015047773554;view=1up;seq=34> (accessed December 12, 2021).
6. Judith Butler, *Excitable Speech: A Politics of the Performative* (New York and London: Routledge, 1997), 40.
7. Karen Barad, *Meeting the Universe Halfway: Quantum Physics and the Entanglement of Matter and Meaning* (Durham, NC and London: Duke University Press, 2007), 280.
8. Jane F. Thrailkill, *Affecting Fictions: Mind, Body, and Emotion in American Literary Realism* (Cambridge, MA: Harvard University Press, 2007), 2.
9. Laura Otis, *Banned Emotions: How Metaphors Can Shape What People Feel* (Oxford: Oxford University Press, 2019), 3, 6–7. Otis eschews "affect" in favor of "emotion" because she seeks to emphasize the cultural construction and social impact of hierarchizing emotions. As a literary historian, she is interested in the history of emotions, especially how individual experiences of emotion and cultural representations of emotion shape one another. However, like affect theorist and literary historian Kyla Schuller, I find cultural and social constructionist approaches limiting. Nineteenth-century scientists and writers hierarchized feelings based on their negative and positive valence just as much as we do in the twenty-first century. This hierarchy, or what Schuller calls a "taxonomy of feeling," is a social construction itself that evolves from biopolitical efforts to control women, people of color, and people

with disabilities. *Feeling* motivates the construction of a hierarchy or taxonomy. As a form of relata, emotions—which are both material subjects and the product of material entanglements of mind, body, and environment—pre-exist the relating and co-constitute the cultural milieu within which they exist.
10. Weingarten, *Abortion in the American Imagination*, 48.
11. Werbel, *Lust on Trial*, 299–300. Women often committed suicide rather than face the public or private shame of giving birth as an unwed mother, confessing to pre-marital sex, or risking commitment to an asylum for masturbation, among similar vices. Werbel notes that one of the most common methods of suicide among young women was drinking carbonic acid. In fact, McGurk's, a saloon located in the Bowery, was referred to as "Suicide Hall" because of the many female suicides that occurred here in its alleyway. Unsurprisingly, Comstock publicly responded to these suicides with victim-blaming.
12. Horowitz, *Rereading Sex*, 23–5. Horowitz offers a thorough history of the Comstock Law, its origins, and those individuals convicted under federal law in chapters 18 and 19 of her book.
13. United States v. Bennett 24 Fed. Cas. 1093, No. 14,571 (S.D.N.Y. 1879), <https://law.resource.org/pub/us/case/reporter/F.Cas/0024.f.cas/0024.f.cas.1093.pdf> (accessed December 12, 2021).
14. It is worth pointing out that Mel Y. Chen discusses injurious speech in the first chapter of *Animacies*. Like Butler, Chen finds that "Insults, shaming language, slurs, and injurious speech can be thought of as tools of objectification" (30), but because they also rely on the animacy hierarchy for meaning-making within a specific culture, injurious speech also retains the potential for reanimation and empowerment. In fact, we see this in Dr. Armstrong's attempt to slander Dr. York. His use of injurious speech relies upon a commitment to the adult > nonadult or adult > child ladder of the animacy hierarchy (see Chen 26). Yet Dr. York's youthfulness and Dr. Newcome's experience of caring for an audience of children as a pediatrician offers them as space for reclamation and reanimation toward the end of the novel. They find a creative solution to establish Dr. York's reputation as a female physician amid a skeptical public: by merging their practices, a move which quite literally re-animates the child and the infantilized woman, given that this recalibration places a population of children and women at the center of their medical practice.
15. Butler, *Excitable Speech*, 4.
16. Ibid. 4.
17. Ibid. 137–8.
18. Naomi Mandel, *Against the Unspeakable: Complicity, the Holocaust, and Slavery in America* (Charlottesville and London: University of Virginia Press, 2006), 209.
19. Charon, *Narrative Medicine*, 5, 12, her emphasis.
20. Ibid. 33. Rita Charon describes this intersubjective relationship as a tension characteristic of all storytelling endeavors: "The tensions inherent in the relationship—writer/reader, teller/listener, analyst/analysand, patient/doctor—are exactly the tensions that *produce* the intersubjective connections and duties of the text and that clarify, through contradiction, that which the reader owes the writer or the teller owes the listener" (53, her emphasis). Narrative medicine should be as much a part

of mental health and the humanities as Charon encourages it for internal medicine and the hard sciences.
21. Ibid. 33.
22. Alicia Puglionesi summarizes most succinctly the impact of Comstockian censorship on women's health: "Comstock's crusade has been interpreted by feminists as actively opposed to women's rights and particularly to reproductive control; although recent scholarship has sought to modify that view, the Comstock Laws had an indisputable limiting impact on the lives and freedoms of women" (469). Horowitz presents a more complex representation of nineteenth-century discourses about sexual health. Prior to the passing of the Comstock Law, women shared knowledge through a kind of oral tradition, as "sisters, schoolmates, friends, and coworkers in the shop passed down girl culture" among themselves (441). Yet they also shared information in print culture, even if such vernacular education adopted euphemistic language, post-Comstock. Indeed, Puglionesi, Horowitz, and Janice Wood all find evidence of sex education among a female readership in popular subscription periodicals such as *Search Lights on Health*, *Dr. Foote's Health Monthly*, and the *Washington Alpha*, among others. However, scholars miss a key reason why the anti-Comstock movement is—and should be—considered a form of feminist politics: Medical knowledge was less accessible to women than it was to men. See Janice Wood, "Prescription for a Periodical: Medicine, Sex, and Obscenity in the Nineteenth Century, As Told in 'Dr. Foote's Health Monthly,'" *American Periodicals* 18, no. 1 (2008), 26–44.
23. See Mitchell and Snyder, *Narrative Prosthesis*. At its most basic and broad definition, narrative prosthesis is a "perpetual discursive dependency upon disability" in storytelling, plot, or narrative structure (47). Mitchell and Snyder cast this practice in negative terms as a "crutch upon which literary narratives lean" for creating meaning in a story (49). Although I take their point that narratives represent disability with a negative taint in the form of a villainous character or as a plot device to be "fixed" or "cured," I take issue with defining prosthesis in negative terms. Some prosthetics are necessary for the body to perform productively.
24. Ibid. 15, 36, 119, 167–8. I understand Mitchell and Snyder's concept of "the language of prosthesis" as the way in which we use language to impose order upon the narrative, thereby making meaning of events. Charon makes the same observation about the role of narrative in clinical medicine: "The engine of narrative is its urge to make sense of why things happen," to help us "find or imagine a connection among things" such as why we are sick or how we might heal pain (48). Narrative is essential to diagnosis, the first step toward healing, because it seeks "to categorize [a] set of events, *in the effort to emplot it*" (50, her emphasis). Charon acquiesces that narrative "act[s] like a prosthetic device or a tool with which to get at the truth" (6), and yet it also opens up a space for patients to process their experiences, heal from their trauma, and share a language with practitioners as they work toward a plan for healing.
25. Mitchell and Snyder, *Narrative Prosthesis*, 30. To be fair, Mitchell and Snyder acknowledge a few exceptions to the rule. Virginia Woolf, for instance, was not empathetic toward persons with disabilities in spite of her own experience of illness.
26. Ibid. 163.

27. Ibid. 163.
28. Charon, *Narrative Medicine*, 6.
29. Ibid. 6.
30. Margaret D. Stetz, "The Late-Victorian 'New Man' and Neo-Victorian 'Neo-Man,'" *Victoriographies* 5, no. 2 (2015), 108, 112.
31. Philip Gibbs, *The New Man: A Portrait of the Latest Type* (London: Sir Isaac Pitman & Sons, Ltd., 1913), 5, <https://babel.hathitrust.org/cgi/pt?id=hvd.32044014280564&view=1up&seq=9> (accessed December 12, 2021).
32. Ibid. 75, 78.
33. Quite the contrary, Gibbs finds the "manhood" of the New Man "emasculated" (86): "The New Man's acquiescence in the emancipation of woman has upset the balance of human nature in which, after all, man should still be the lord and master" (87), Gibbs concludes. He specifically finds this state of character "most apparent in the United States," where men are subordinate to the New Woman to the point of domesticity (81).
34. Elizabeth Stuart Phelps, *Doctor Zay* (Lexington, KY: CreateSpace Independent Publishing Platform, 2013), 164. Hereafter referred to parenthetically in the body of the text.
35. Sarah Grand, "The New Aspect of the Woman Question," *The North American Review* 158 (1894), 270, <https://archive.org/details/jstor-25103291/page/n1/mode/2up?q=new+woman> (accessed December 12, 2021).
36. This story of Sarah Grand's coining the term "New Woman" appears in two of the most comprehensive scholarly studies of the New Woman: Martha H. Patterson's *Beyond the Gibson Girl: Reimagining the American New Woman, 1895–1915* (Urbana and Chicago: University of Illinois Press, 2008) and Charlotte J. Rich's *Transcending the New Woman: Multiethnic Narratives in the Progressive Era* (Columbia: University of Missouri Press, 2009). There is some debate over whether the New Woman existed prior to 1894 when Sarah Grand coins the term "New Woman." I agree with cultural historian Carroll Smith-Rosenberg, who chalks up this discrepancy to the emergence of "generations" of the New Woman whose image was refined over a fifty-year period from the 1870s to the 1910s.
37. Grand, "The New Aspect of the Woman Question," 273.
38. Ibid. 272.
39. Davis, *Bodily and Narrative Forms*, 89–97. One of the reasons I did not include Phelps's *Doctor Zay* in the previous R_x alongside Louisa May Alcott and Rebecca Harding Davis is because Phelps does not theorize the environment as an agential healer. Instead, she draws upon the New Man in a more self-consciously political way than Alcott, Davis, or other contemporary writers of feminist medical fiction who deploy the New Man in their narrative. Cynthia J. Davis offers an excellent reading of Phelps's *Doctor Zay* as a response to both Edward H. Clarke's *Sex in Education* and William Dean Howells's *Doctor Breen's Practice* (1881), one that I do not seek to replicate here.
40. Davis, *Bodily and Narrative Forms*, 116.
41. Tim Morris, "Professional Ethics and Professional Erotics in Elizabeth Stuart Phelps's *Doctor Zay*," *Studies in American Fiction* 21 (1993), 141. I am actually

indebted to Tim Morris for introducing me to both Phelps's *Doctor Zay* and Charlotte Perkins Gilman's *The Crux* during my dissertating years. Although Tim Morris was not a member of my dissertation committee, he generously provided suggestions for reading and helpful conversation post-reading.

42. Lyman Tower Sargent's "The Three Faces of Utopianism Revisited" is often quoted when defining the concept of utopia. Sargent calls utopianism "social dreaming," a dream that inherently requires "a vision of a better future," whether it appears in the form of fiction, theory, political essay, or intentional community (27). In order for us to see the vision of where we want to go, we must ascertain where we are currently. Thus, utopianism "serves as a mirror of contemporary society, pointing to strengths and weaknesses" in the form of critique (27). Ruth Levitas agrees, though she summarizes utopianism as the "education of desire," which not only involves "a criticism of existing conditions" but also "the pursuit of a better way" (221). I would be remiss if I did not include Ken Roemer's definition of utopianism, especially since he emphasizes the role of audience and reader response. Roemer defines utopian writing in terms of contrasts "between what is and what should be" (74).
43. Davis, *Bodily and Narrative Forms*, 114.
44. Chris Ferns, *Narrating Utopia: Ideology, Gender, Form in Utopian Literature* (Liverpool: Liverpool University Press, 1999), 13–15, 27.
45. Ibid. 4, 9; See also Kenneth Roemer, *Utopian Audiences*, 27–9. Roemer emphasizes the role of narrative conventions and the framing of utopian texts in converting readers to the writer's social or political worldview. In the nineteenth century, readers were strongly affected by the presence of a romance narrative—as in the case of Julian West's courting of Edith Leete in Edward Bellamy's *Looking Backward* (1887) or the triple marriages in Charlotte Perkins Gilman's *Herland* (1915)—a point of fact which may offer some context as to why so many works of medical fiction contain a marriage-or-career plot.
46. Ferns, *Narrating Utopia*, 186.
47. Ibid. 179, 190–1.
48. Charlotte Perkins Gilman, "With Her in Ourland," *The Forerunner* 7, no. 12 (1916), 322, <https://babel.hathitrust.org/cgi/pt?id=osu.32435031112535&view=1up&seq=330> (accessed December 12, 2021).
49. Swenson, *Medical Women and Victorian Fiction*, 125.
50. Rich, *Transcending the New Woman*, 17.
51. Xtine Yao, *Disaffected: The Cultural Politics of Unfeeling in Nineteenth-Century America* (Durham, NC and London: Duke University Press, 2021), 111, 115, 129. Dr. Zay may, in fact, be queer, as she confesses to Mr. Yorke that she felt desire for an unnamed woman: "I wanted her," she says, but she ultimately suppresses her queer desire either for the sake of conforming to social convention, or focusing on her professional ambitions, or both (Phelps 164; Yao 133).
52. As readers well know, Mr. Waldo Yorke is the patient of Dr. Zay in Phelps's novel. Mr. Yorke suffers multiple injuries as a result of a carriage accident in which his buggy is overturned. Although I acknowledge Mr. Yorke as the traditional patient, I also read Dr. Zay as suffering from the psychological trauma of cultural narratives that cast the female body within the context of disability when the female

body does not perform within culturally prescribed gender roles. As we see in R_x 1, the body of the professional woman falls within the context of Edward H. Clarke's closed-body theory and as such is vulnerable to S. Weir Mitchell's pathology of hysteria, meaning that sexist medicine reads Dr. Zay as disabled by performing within her chosen career of medicine. Dr. Zay may not be the patient of this novel, but she does not suffer any less than Rose Campbell or Dr. Maria Haynes Muller, and in fact would be considered a patient under the care of Clarke or Mitchell.

53. Charon also discusses acceptance of identity without judgment as a goal of narrative medicine. Storytelling is a vulnerable act because it requires the speaker to reveal "aspects of the self closest to the skin" (78). Over time, the speaker and listener gain trust in one another such that the speaker feels safe "par[ing] away the optional layers—if you will—occupation, habits, even history and culture—to *get to the core of who [they] are*" (78, my emphasis). Dr. Zay may not have the language of narrative medicine at her disposal, but she is impressed by Mr. Yorke's ability to see past her occupation and love her for who she is, her core self.

54. Charon, *Narrative Medicine*, 99. Narrative medicine not only requires the practitioner-listener to develop listening skills over time, but also the patient-speaker needs space to gain the practitioner-listener's trust over multiple conversations.

55. Ibid. 177.

56. Ibid. 178; Phelps, *Doctor Zay*, 107. Charon claims that even before she began theorizing and practicing narrative medicine, she noticed that the doctor had replaced the priest or confessor who hears the patient-supplicant's most vulnerable thoughts, fears, and perhaps even sins. Culturally, this transition may have occurred during the nineteenth century with the growing professionalization of medicine. After all, Michel Foucault makes this same observation in *The History of Sexuality, Vol. 1*, calling medicine a "confessional science," albeit derisively (59, 63). Indeed, Dr. Zay comments, "the clergy have a poor [advantage] beside us" because doctors wield power over the patient's life or death. As our culture increasingly recognizes the power of professional medicine, doctors "stand at an eternal confession" (Phelps 107), playing what Donna Haraway might call the "god-trick." Doctors are everywhere and nowhere at once, determining our fate because of their advanced knowledge, and we, as patients, must confess all behaviors that might help doctors diagnose and heal our conditions. Charon speaks more to this biopower and its abuse in her chapter on bioethics.

57. Regina Morantz-Sanchez, *Sympathy and Science: Women Physicians in American Medicine* (Oxford: Oxford University Press, 2000), 5; see also Davis, *Bodily and Narrative Forms*, 21. Morantz-Sanchez explains that women physicians believed that "[t]hey alone could combine sympathy and science—the hard and soft sides of medical practice" as their "ethos" in the profession because of their unique position as nurturers in the role of wife and mother (5).

58. Charon, *Narrative Medicine*, 99.

59. Charlotte Perkins Gilman, *Mag-Marjorie and Won Over* (Forest Hills, NY: Ironweed Press, Inc., 1999), 141. Hereafter referred to parenthetically in the body of the text.

60. "Materia medica" was defined during the nineteenth century as a tool for restoring health to the sick. In the twenty-first century, we might call it a collection of

pharmaceutical knowledge that was passed down both orally and textually in the form of volumes titled *Materia Medica*. These volumes or manuals were commonly associated with homeopathy, as they alphabetically laid out a series of clinical diagnoses with a brief description of the condition underneath the clinical term, and a detailed recommendation for treatment or cure in the homeopathic tradition. A number of independent presses that published texts on homeopathic therapy produced *Materia Medica*. This medical textual culture aligns with Dr. Zay, who practices homeopathic medicine and keeps volumes of *Materia Medica* in her office.

61. Stephanie Peebles Tavera, "Her Body, *Herland*: Reproductive Health and Dis/topian Satire," *Utopian Studies* 29, no. 1 (2018), 11–15. Charles Darwin's cousin Frances Galton coined the term "eugenics" in 1883. The term translates to "good in stock," and is derived from the Greek prefix "eu" for "good" and the Greek word "genetai" for "coming into being" or "growing." As part of the late nineteenth- and early twentieth-century medical establishment, eugenics provided a scientific rationale for social hygiene, which eventually developed into sex education. Eugenics functioned as a form of social Darwinism, or Darwinian evolutionary principles applied to human growth and development. It flourished in America under Galton's concept of "positive eugenics," which emphasized sexual selection for a marriage partner and good hygiene to prevent the heredity of undesirable characteristics usually associated with race or disability. This came to a halt when Nazism adopted a "negative eugenics" approach of genocide, infanticide, and euthanasia of Jews, Catholics, homosexuals, and people with disabilities. In R_x 3, I discuss black eugenics in relation to Frances Ellen Watkins Harper's *Iola Leroy* (1892), while in R_x 4, I examine Gilman's support for eugenic marriage as a key teaching of sex education in *The Crux* (1911) and "The Vintage" (1916).
62. Charlotte Perkins Gilman, *The Crux* (Durham, NC and London: Duke University Press, 2003), 139.
63. Davis, *Bodily and Narrative Forms*, 99; see also Peter Brooks, *Reading for the Plot: Design and Intention in Narrative* (New York: Vintage, 1985), 94. Narratologist Peter Brooks claims that, like our lives, we make sense of our novels retrospectively from the vantage point of its conclusion. In her application of Brooks's claim to *Doctor Zay* and *Doctor Breen's Practice*, Davis interprets at least Howells's courtship plot as suggesting "heterosexual coupling as the narrative's cure-all" (211, n. 18). Davis concedes that Phelps may have succumbed to pressure.
64. Davis, *Bodily and Narrative Forms*, 119.
65. Ibid. 114–15.
66. Meyer, Letter to the Editor, 548.
67. Ibid. 548.
68. Rachel Mesch, "A New Man for the New Woman? Men, Marriage, and Feminism in the Belle Époque," *Historical Reflections* 38, no. 3 (2012), 87–8.
69. Ibid. 97.
70. Davis, *Bodily and Narrative Forms*, 115.
71. Richard von Krafft-Ebing, who was the foremost sexologist during the late nineteenth century, theorized the concept of the third sex. In so doing, Krafft-Ebing explicitly associates gender with sexuality, identifying this third sex as

the "Mannish Lesbian" who is cis-female but performs masculinity in terms of appearance or behavior. Historian Carroll Smith-Rosenberg claims that Krafft-Ebing wrote *Psychopathia Sexualis*, in which he theorizes the concept of the third sex and the Mannish Lesbian, as a response to the New Woman in fin de siècle American culture (272, 275).
72. Yao, *Disaffected*, 123.
73. Morantz-Sanchez, *Sympathy and Science*, 244–5. Morantz-Sanchez offers impressive statistics on the number of women practicing as regular physicians, the number of women enrolled in medical colleges, and the number of women physicians who were married. Her statistics help establish certain trends in terms of women in the medical profession during the nineteenth century. Morantz-Sanchez finds that the percentage of women in the medical profession overall averaged 4.8 to 5 percent during the 1890s at perhaps its highest capacity.
74. Mitchell and Snyder, *Narrative Prosthesis*, 164.
75. There are many research studies on children and adults with amelogenesis imperfecta, but one particular study published in the *Journal of the American Dental Association (JADA)* not only defines amelogenesis imperfecta, but also discusses the psychological and social impact of persons with amelogenesis imperfecta: K. D. Coffield, C. Phillips, M. Brady, M. W. Roberts, R. P. Strauss, and J. T. Wright, "The Pyschosocial Impact of Developmental Dental Defects in People with Hereditary Amelogenesis Imperfecta," *JADA* 136, no. 5 (2005), 620–30.
76. Kafer, *Feminist, Queer, Crip*, 7–8.
77. Review of *Doctor Zay*, *The Atlantic Monthly* 50 (1882), 432, <https://babel.hathitrust.org/cgi/pt?id=uiug.30112110809743;view=1up;seq=466m> (accessed December 12, 2021).
78. Review of *The Portrait of a Lady* and *Doctor Breen's Practice*, *The Atlantic Monthly* 49 (1882), 129, <https://babel.hathitrust.org/cgi/pt?id=coo.31924080787504;view=1up;seq=132> (accessed December 12, 2021).
79. Ibid.
80. Charon, *Narrative Medicine*, 77.
81. Butler, *Excitable Speech*, 5.
82. Charon, *Narrative Medicine*, 8.

R_x 3

KINETIC MEDICINE: SUPERPOSITION OF BLACK FEMALE SUBJECTIVITY BEFORE THE LAW

1892 was a banner year for feminist medical fiction. In January, Charlotte Perkins Gilman published "The Yellow Wallpaper" in *The New England Magazine*, exposing S. Weir Mitchell's rest cure as a fake therapy for a fake diagnosis of hysteria that masked a very real mental illness. Later that year, Annie Nathan Meyer debuted her first novel, *Helen Brent, M.D.*, with Cassell Publishing Company in New York. Not only was her titular protagonist the first gynecologist in a work of fiction, but Meyer scandalously defended sex education for women in the wake of a syphilis epidemic in New York City. Writer and orator Francis Ellen Watkins Harper rounded out the year with her publication of *Iola Leroy, or Shadows Uplifted*, which tells the story of a freeborn mixed-race woman sold into slavery after the death of her father. During the war, the titular heroine Iola Leroy is emancipated as contraband of war, serves as a Civil War nurse, and finds herself caught in a love triangle between a white physician and a Black physician. It is unclear why, nineteen years after the passing of the Comstock Law, women writers of medical fiction picked up the pace in production. Likely, the effect of censorship weighed on women writers, as they fought to be taken seriously as professionals and struggled against the "disability con" that places a burden of proof upon people with disabilities. Amy Werbel finds that by 1887—and specifically, after the arrest of Edmund Knoedler for displaying in his gallery photographic reproductions of paintings foregrounding the nude female body—Comstock began losing the war against obscenity even as he won some battles in court.¹ Comstock's attempts to convict his defendants for the production or distribution of obscenity in literature, drama, and art backfired as each subsequent court case led to greater publicity and higher volumes of sexually risqué material disseminating into American culture.²

Importantly, Comstock's personal arrest records, legal court records of obscenity cases, and historical examinations of the Comstock Law era exhibit a glaring absence of discourse concerning race. None of the legal cases that Werbel examines involve Black defendants. Indeed, Comstock's most high-profile convictions primarily implicate white middle- to upper-class men, as well as a handful of white women: Victoria Woodhull, Ezra Heywood, Edward Bliss Foote, D. M. Bennett, Thomas Eakins, Edmund Knoedler, and Margaret Sanger, among others. Unsurprisingly, Comstock was racist. In an August 1893 editorial of the *New York Recorder* on the World's Columbian Exposition, one reporter testified to Comstock's horrified reaction against the *danse du ventre*, or belly dancing, performances on the Midway.³ Although Comstock may have been responding per usual against the display of female bodies, we cannot discount the association of *danse du ventre* with Blackness, given that the exhibition itself staged the *danse du ventre* at the Streets of Cairo Theatre. This was not lost on Frederick Douglass, who decried that the scantily clad dancers misrepresented African culture and further entrenched already-held assumptions among white audiences of the inferiority of the Black race due to their "savage" nature.⁴ Comstock did not consider Black men and women subjects before the law. One early obscenity trial held in New York City exemplifies the medico-legal ideology underpinning his operations. In August 1842, Henry R. Robinson was indicted and convicted for selling obscene prints and books in the General Court of Sessions in New York under common law. The "obscene" texts in question were a series of prints titled "Practical Amalgamation" by Edward William Clay, which Robinson published in an effort to "shock audiences into opposition to anti-slavery reform."⁵ The surviving prints may or may not be read as explicitly suggestive of coition, at least to a twenty-first-century audience (see Figures 3.1 and 3.2), though the indictment describes one print of a (white) abolitionist man engaged "in an obscene, impudent and indecent posture with a negro woman."⁶

However, the courts were horrified by the title of the print series alone, "Practical Amalgamation," which is itself suggestive of sexual intercourse, as well as the depictions of African American men consorting, dancing, and marrying white women in mixed company. Figure 3.1 is, indeed, flirtatious in its depiction of two interracial couples, one of whom are perhaps suggestive of coition in their positioning as the white woman sits upon the lap of a Black man while kissing him. Comparatively, Figure 3.2, titled "The Wedding," represents a demure white woman whose eyes are cast downward while she holds hands with a Black man as they marry before a Black priest amid mixed company. The

Figure 3.1 *Practical Amalgamation* series, title unknown (1839). Lithograph print by Edward William Clay. Courtesy of the American Antiquarian Society.

Figure 3.2 *Practical Amalgamation* series, "The Wedding" (1839). Lithograph print by Edward William Clay. Courtesy of the American Antiquarian Society.

representation of this social amalgamation was enough to convict Robinson of obscenity. He had crossed a line. Even though he opines a pro-slavery position that abhors the indecency of racial mixing via sexual intercourse, which was a favorable position with the courts, Robinson nevertheless disseminated a controversial ideal into the cultural imagination.[7] (It is worth noting, however, that he neither paid a fine nor served jail time.) Amalgamation was not only against the law in many states but also akin to bestiality, given the unsettled debates over the evolution of the Black race throughout the long nineteenth century. Whether Comstock chose to avoid directly engaging in medico-legal discourse about race, or whether he simply did not consider Black bodies subjects before the law and therefore worth the effort of attention, the act of censorship affects the Black community and public perceptions of race, Blackness, and Black subjectivity. Comstock selectively censored art, literature, and drama to promote the stereotype of black (hyper)sexuality already being promulgated by racist medicine. In other words, what Comstock did not censor—and why—is just as telling and just as narratively affective in the American cultural imagination as what he did censor. Black women writers of medical fiction indirectly engage obscenity law in their narratives as they rescript cultural stereotypes of the Black female body underpinning racist medico-legal precedents such as antimiscegenation law and the one-drop rule.

In R_x 1, I examine the "materiality of language" in Louisa May Alcott's *Eight Cousins* (1875), Charlotte Perkins Gilman's "The Yellow Wallpaper" (1892), and Rebecca Harding Davis's *Kitty's Choice: A Story of Berrytown* (1873) through the linguistic concept of animacy and against the rhetoric of disability in nineteenth-century medico-legal discourse that seeks to de-animate the female body. In the ultimate act of de-animacy, Anthony Comstock strove to erase the female body from discourse, medical or otherwise, through legal censorship, but it did not work as women writers of medical fiction carefully opposed censorship and rescripted the narrative by distancing sex from the most socially debilitating illness of the period, hysteria. Women writers of medical fiction know that language is affective, and they deploy the power of animacy to "crip medicine," theorizing the agential environment as a key factor in health. In R_x 2, I examine the affective nature of narrative alongside Elizabeth Stuart Phelps and Charlotte Perkins Gilman, who teach their readers to listen affectively so that they might heal society from the trauma of gendered oppression. Phelps invents the concept of the New Man as a counterpart to the New Woman, and both ideals work to rescript patriarchal medical narratives that not only insist on animacy hierarchies but also deploy animacy hierarchies to oppress women, people with disabilities, and, as we shall see in this R_x, people of color. The New Man as a narrative prosthetic device does not mask disability or gender—rather he highlights both vectors of identity as complexly intertwined in medico-legal narratives of oppression under obscenity law. In this R_x, I examine the medico-legal discourse animating Frances Ellen Watkins Harper's *Iola Leroy, or Shadows Uplifted* (1892), which draws upon medical metaphors to offer the national body a path toward healing from the trauma of slavery and the Civil War. If narrative is affective, and Comstockian censorship fails to expurgate false cultural narratives of Black sexuality, then women writers of medical fiction must do the work of rescripting cultural stereotypes that oppress them.

Scholarship has long observed that Watkins Harper's Iola Leroy not only performs modesty to undermine the cultural stereotype of the hypersexual black female body, but is wholly ladylike as evidence of Black women's parity with white women.[8] Watkins Harper exposes the sexual violence threatening the Black female body as a reproducing (read: breeding) subject in the slave system. Historians corroborate the sexual trauma of slavery alongside Watkins Harper's medical novel, as well as the trauma of medical experimentation on Black female slaves for gynecological and obstetrical research. Yet, with the exception of Xtine Yao, few scholars situate Watkins Harper's one-off medical novel *Iola Leroy* within the larger medico-legal discourse operative in 1892 society,[9] which is significant given how animality in racial science not only dovetails with the objectives of legislation such as anti-amalgamation law but also works to perpetuate cultural narratives of biological determinism that collapse race with disability. Twenty-first-century theoretical discourses are still contending with this collapse, as posthumanist and new materialist theorists hesitate to engage conversations about race while scholars in Black disability studies continually adopt an outdated social constructionist framework because of their skepticism toward a materialist approach that risks essentializing race by locating it within the body. In her own theorizing of race at a dignified distance from the body of Iola Leroy, Watkins Harper offers a space for a (new) materialist reading of race as defined by affective relationality emerging from the superposition or entanglements of race, disability, and gender in an ongoing process of kinship. In other words, Watkins Harper's medical metaphors teach us to consider race, disability, and gender as manifestations of affective relationships that are irreducible to social constructs or material bodies. Defining subjectivity as affect may further aid contemporary theorists as our nation continues to grapple with the trauma of scientific and legal racism in the wake of police brutality.

Quantum Race and Racial Superposition

Racial and sexual biopower appears crystallized in the medicalization of the Black female body, not least because of the pervasive influence of race science on medical practice. The contemporary legal system further underscored race science as an authority on social behavior. Twenty-first-century theorists are still contending with the culture of trauma left in the wake of these material-discursive formations. Kyla Schuller narrates the "backstory" of nineteenth-century biopower in *The Biopolitics of Feeling: Race, Sex, and Science in the Nineteenth Century*, which describes how the deployment of binary sex and gender fragments race. Gender and sex "are variegations of race and effects of racial biopower," Schuller observes.[10] Her theory of race as affect does not wholly account for the role of disability, which historians and literary theorists identify as co-constituting race and gender in nineteenth-century science. Nevertheless, Schuller figures race as "a palimpsestic process in which impressions layer upon one another over the life span of the individual and the evolutionary time of race," which opens a space for disability as one of many layers in the process.[11] Schuller's theory of race as palimpsest functions as a useful metaphor akin to the principle of superposition from quantum physics, which I will invoke in my theorizing of race. Yet I offer (p)rescription as a differential model for theorizing the superposition of race, gender, and disability, as well as for describing the formation of race, of gender, and of disability as phenomenon, because I wish to draw out how Watkins Harper engages medico-legal discourse to imagine ways of healing the national body. I also posit an underlying consideration of how (p)rescription invokes the legacy of gender, race, and disability inequalities in our own healthcare system in the wake of recent conversations about the trauma of police brutality on survivors and their families, the racial and ethnic disparities of the COVID-19 pandemic, and increasing awareness of the mental health impact of the pandemic and of quarantine.

Theories of race and gender that account for disability often rely upon a social constructionist approach that disavows the theoretical apparatus as a component in the interpretive process of analyzing phenomena. Case in point: Disability theorist Ellen Samuels advances a useful apparatus she terms "fantasies of identification," which she employs as a framework for understanding how medico-legal discourses simultaneously construct cultural narratives of race, gender, and disability. Samuels observes that each of these identities not only appear inseparable from one another in their biopolitical function, but also further occupy a "state of perpetual tension between physical and linguistic means of identification."[12] Samuels confirms the materiality of language à la Mel Y. Chen operative in fantasies of bodily identity, which society attempts to mark and measure as a form of epistemological and biopolitical control deployed through the joint authorities of medicine and law. Yet her social constructionist approach tries to capture the process of superposition—of the narratological formation of fantasies of identification—as it develops through the nineteenth and twentieth centuries. She cannot wholly accomplish this objective since the "fantasy" apparatus marks this material-discursive process linearly as "a tension figured by race, mediated through disability, and often inscribed into contested bodies."[13] Samuels observes race, gender, and disability as affect, engaged and engaging in an ongoing process of signification, though she does not characterize the formation of race, gender, or disability in precisely those words.

Consequently, theorists must account for the apparatus itself as a component in the interpretive process. As Karen Barad points out in her theory of agential realism derived from the work of Niels Bohr, superposition or entanglement is an ongoing process in which two or more phenomena, or "waves," overlap: "the amplitude of one wave is added to the amplitude of the other wave, and the result is a wave with their combined amplitude."[14] Importantly, the result of the combined waves—whether of light, water, or identity categories—is *not* a mixture but a solution.[15] Any attempt to observe, measure, or interpret this ongoing process fails in its attempt because the product of analysis is the after-effects of entanglement. "When we observe a system" such as American patriarchal medicine, legal proceedings, or slavery, the ongoing process "ceases to be in a superposition."[16] What we are observing is affect. Barad resigns herself to the impossibility of observing any system—physical, social, or political—in process, as "it seems only to account for what happens to the wave function *between* measurements, and does not seem to describe *the abrupt transition that appears to take place as a result of a measurement*" or observation.[17] All we can observe are snapshots in time rather than the complete ongoing material entanglement itself.

Cristin Ellis right(ful)ly discerns the skepticism posthumanists and new materialists exhibit toward examinations of race in material-discursive phenomena. In *Antebellum Posthuman: Race and Materiality in the Mid-Nineteenth Century*, Ellis precisely targets animality and speciological discourse of the human as the primary reason for posthumanism's suspicion of materiality. No matter how fervently posthumanists insist that all humans are animals, there simply is no "getting over it" among racial minorities who have been cast as bestial in American cultural narratives of race.[18] Ellis initially responds with a categorical differentiation that almost casts posthumanism as yet another social constructivist offshoot: "The human, in short, is an ideology masquerading as a species," she opines.[19] She ultimately proposes a "decolonized posthumanism" à la Sylvia Wynter that promises to be liberatory in its emphasis on primordial relationality—even tribalism—over categorical differentiation among bodies and species, the latter of which appears to be a holdover from liberal humanism.[20] But what are we liberating to/from? We cannot wholly liberate ourselves from our bodies and the material networks necessary for sustaining those bodies regardless of how we rhetorically repackage identity. Nor should we desire to liberate ourselves from the social milieu that provides access to resources necessary for engaging in material networks. What we need is systemic and institutional reform that leads to greater access to resources among marginalized communities, not wholesale liberation from systems and institutions through their eradication.

Because posthumanism, new materialism, and social constructivism have deep roots in liberal humanism, and those roots have been deployed for alternatively racist or antiracist ends over the course of the nineteenth through twenty-first centuries, all three theoretical fields are limited in the cause of social justice and cultural inclusivity. On the one hand, as Schuller emphasizes, "[f]eminist 'new' materialisms generally insist that they are overturning long-standing Cartesian dualisms that contrast active mind with inert matter," but they are not actually accomplishing this work because (1) new materialism is not new and (2) materiality was deployed by nineteenth-century scientists for sexist and racist means.[21] This point has been evocative of the sexist medico-legal discourse of Edward H. Clarke, S. Weir Mitchell, and Anthony Comstock, as well as in the feminist medical fiction of Charlotte Perkins Gilman, Louisa May Alcott, and Elizabeth Stuart Phelps. Ellis further explicates how the racist science discourse of Samuel George Morton, Samuel Cartwright, Josiah Nott and George Glidden, and Louis Agassiz was deployed to justify slavery, while the anti-slavery literature of Frederick Douglass, Henry David Thoreau, and Walt Whitman adopts scientific principles that animate matter for liberating Black bodies.[22] Yet the ability to liberate using materiality rhetoric is not only limited because of the problem of proximity to animality and bestiality, but also because any attempt to measure race is always already a representation of affect since material entanglements are ongoing long after measurement, observation, and analysis.

A more rigorous account of biopolitics for both the nineteenth century and today must attend to race, gender, and disability as affective products and catalysts of material-discursive processes. I agree with social constructionists who assert that race is "entirely real," especially "in its import and impact on racialized bodies."[23] Yet I must rescript this statement of fact to theorize race as affectively real in the way that individuals, communities, and systems read race socially and materially within a specific system before engaging with raced, gendered, and disabled bodies based upon that reading. I am not the first theorist to posit race as affective. In his essay from *Material Feminisms* titled "How Real Is Race?" Michael Hames-Garcia makes a similar move in his assertion of race as phenomenon. Like my own theorizing of race as superposition, or affect(ive), Hames-Garcia draws upon the work of Karen Barad as a productive point of departure for describing how both the social construction of race and the material reality of race work to produce affect through the complex interactions of history, economics, law, and human bodily differences. Taking flight from biological classification disavows the very real physical matter of race in the form of both outward differences and inward genetic markers, which are not only observable, but also readable, and therefore, vulnerable to interpretation within specific social and cultural contexts: "To put it bluntly," Hames-Garcia exhibits, "how can I understand my ease at hailing a taxicab in New York City or Washington, D.C., in the face of countless stories from black friends about having to walk forty blocks without having one stop?"[24] This works on a level of racialized kinship, too: How else can I (as a white Anglo-Celtic-Scandinavian woman) understand my repeated detainment and interrogation at major US airports when returning from abroad with my husband, who is an immigrant from Mexico, a naturalized citizen of the United States, and very visibly a person of color with Indigenous and Black ancestry?

The social constructions of race, ethnicity, nationality, gender, and disability are useful for interpreting these experiences of discrimination, but they are limited because they do not account for how physical biological manifestations of race (and gender and disability) generate an affective response from an audience based upon the ways that said audience interprets bodily difference within a specific social context. Hames-Garcia summarizes that "what race is and how it functions results from the interaction of social ideologies of race with visible human difference," indicating the necessity of a cooperative framework between social constructionism and new materialism (or material feminisms).[25] I want to push on Hames-Garcia's use of "results from," as well as his nod to the work of Barad in describing the "causal role of matter in the formation of racial meanings and phenomena."[26] To restate Hames-Garcia using the language of quantum physics: Race is a product of the superposition of social ideologies of race and biological manifestations of race. Yet even this is too simple a formulation. To further complicate matters, social ideologies of race are created through the superposition of social systems including but not limited to history, economics, law, and medicine, while biological manifestations of race are created through the superposition of organic systems such as inherited chromosomes from each parent, cellular replication, and the release of chemical hormones. This is the wave (upon wave upon wave) function Barad describes. What we read is the amplitude of these waves, post-entanglement. All of these entanglements "leave different traces,"[27] whether visible or invisible, on individual bodies and on the socially informed reader of the body, who first experiences a sensorial impression before registering an emotional impression that generates response. Because the results of these entanglements and the traces they leave follow the laws of physics and yet are agential, we must describe race as neither determined nor random.[28] This indeterminacy does not preclude our ability to read race. On the contrary, we read race intuitively all the time. What we must be critically aware of is that what we are reading is affect. When we attempt to observe or "read" the ongoing processes that create race, which remain in continuous motion regardless of our efforts to observe them singularly in time, we must acknowledge that what we actually observe are the results—the after-effects—of superposition. Race is a moving target.

Iola Leroy Before the Law

Understanding race as superposition reframes our interpretation of the medico-legal discourses at work in Frances Ellen Watkins Harper's *Iola Leroy*, not least because the legal fiction of anti-amalgamation law depends upon race science for authority and enforcement. Iola Leroy struggles to choose a spouse in the context of anti-amalgamation law debates and Reconstruction-era social anxieties of racial mixing, to which Anthony Comstock adversely—and perversely—contributed in his refusal to censor or even denounce stereotypes of Black sexuality. This social context impresses upon Iola Leroy as she struggles with her own racial identity, since the biopolitics of marriage and eugenics dictate that she must marry a person of color as a mixed-race woman. Although Iola Leroy does ultimately declare her love for the mixed-race physician Dr. Frank Latimer, Watkins Harper uses the narrative as an opportunity to explore methods of racial uplift in which Black eugenics and caretaking, or nursing, function significantly. Watkins Harper opens up a space for us to read race, gender, and disability as affective because she struggles with fantasies of measurement, finding that neither physical bodies nor social constructionist interpretations of bodily measurements can do the work of race formation for mixed-race subjects like Iola Leroy, Harry Leroy, and Dr. Latimer. Their identities emerge from the superposition of medico-legal discourses, kinship ties, and Black nursing or doctoring.

Scholars have long read *Iola Leroy* as a kind of rescription that resists or rewrites racist cultural narratives of Black subjectivity. Hazel Carby reads *Iola Leroy* as engaged in political conversations about the status of "the Negro" alongside Black intelligentsia such as W. E. B. Du Bois. This rhetorical move includes a rejection of the belief in black inheritance of ignorance as espoused by anti-black suffrage writers and editors like Henry W. Grady, editor of the *Atlanta Constitution*.[29] Importantly for Hazel Carby, the mulatta functions as a "narrative device of mediation" who exposes the social construction of white privilege and Black lack of privilege given that Iola Leroy only has access to an elite education under her father's protection.[30] Bridgitte Fielder expands Carby's analysis of the mulatta as a "vehicle for an exploration of the relationship between races" through a reading of woman-centered kinfulness.[31] Iola Leroy has an "excess of kin," yet she defines herself in relationship to her biological mother, even refusing to marry until she has found her lost maternal figure.[32] In part, this privileging of the matriarchal Black family emerges because the plantation-master fathers did not typically recognize their mixed-race children, though this is emphatically not the case with Iola. On the other hand, woman-centered kinfulness implicates Iola herself as responsible for reproducing Blackness in her role as future mother and "the moral center" of both the nuclear family and the novel.[33] Several scholars locate Watkins Harper's *Iola Leroy* in conversations about Black female sexuality. Although Hazel Carby characterizes Iola as sexually repressed, Kyla Schuller rejects this reading in favor of an interpretation that foregrounds Watkins Harper's "black respectability politics" as a counternarrative to the race science myth of black female hypersexuality.[34] Cynthia J. Davis similarly finds Watkins Harper responding to race scientists Dr. Samuel George Morton, William Benjamin Smith, and even our notorious Dr. S. Weir Mitchell. Watkins Harper rejects the comparative anatomy of Dr. Morton, refuses the inferiority and weakness of "panmixia," or amalgamation, and denies the "anaesthetic capacity" of black bodies that simultaneously justifies medical experimentation on and the rape of Black women.[35]

Iola Leroy dramatizes Watkins Harper's argument for reproductive justice, or more specifically, Black female body autonomy in the face of sexual exploitation during and after slavery. She was in good company. Watkins Harper might have been echoing Mary Gove Nichols's and Paulina Wright Davis's early anatomy lectures, in which Nichols and Davis affirm that the systematic raping of slave women's bodies serves as necessary evidence for reproductive rights and body autonomy among all women.[36] Sarah Mapps Douglass made similar arguments on the lecture circuit as a "pioneering health activist" who "focused on disseminating information about anatomy, health, and hygiene to black women and young girls" as well as lecturing before "mixed audiences" on the specific sexual trauma women faced as slaves.[37] Britt Rusert, in fact, links the "politics of respectability" characteristic of Douglass's lectures on Black anatomy and physiology with the sentimentalism of Black women writers like Frances Ellen Watkins Harper.[38] Given that Watkins Harper was herself a renowned orator by the time she published Iola Leroy, it makes sense she would cite orators like Nichols, Wright, and Douglass.[39] Beyond the influence of the lecture circuit, Koritha Mitchell identifies three primary literary genres at play in *Iola Leroy*: sentimental romance, slave narratives, and plantation fiction.[40] However, it is important that we also consider *Iola Leroy* a work of medical fiction, not least because, as Yao points out, *Iola Leroy* may very well be the only work of nineteenth-century medical fiction written by a Black woman.[41] And that fact is essential. Watkins Harper could have engaged in medico-legal discourse through oration, like her peers, but she explicitly chose not to. Moreover, she chose to publish *Iola Leroy* as a bound book rather than serialize it in the *Christian Recorder* as she had her prior three novels. "Watkins Harper clearly hoped to reach the broadest possible audience while maintaining a community-centered perspective," Mitchell explains of the author's venue and genre decisions for this her fourth book.[42] Mitchell further speculates on Watkins Harper's authorial intent when Mitchell considers the similarities between *Iola Leroy* and Louisa May Alcott's "My Contraband" (1863).[43] Watkins Harper considers herself part of the *conversazione* on par with Alcott and her contemporaries,⁴⁴ as should we, for Watkins Harper provides a necessary perspective on the health of the Black community and the intersectional implications of gender, race, and disability for medico-legal discourses of Black women's health as only Watkins Harper could do.

In *Iola Leroy*, Watkins Harper offers an imaginative performance of Black women's respectability politics that carefully and meticulously disproves medical justification for legal disenfranchisement of women of color, one faulty rationale at a time. Following the tradition of woman-authored medical fiction during the Age of Comstock, *Iola Leroy* articulates a feminist politics of the body, but one that focuses specifically on the Black female body. In the course of her oeuvre, Schuller twice characterizes the feminist politics of Watkins Harper, drawing upon *Iola Leroy* as a point of departure in *The Biopolitics of Feeling* and a series of speeches and poems in *The Trouble with White Women*. On the one hand, Schuller argues that Watkins Harper deploys black respectability politics in *Iola Leroy* by couching a eugenic argument in the form of a sentimental novel.⁴⁵ Meanwhile her speeches, such as "We Are All Bound Up Together" (1866), originate intersectional feminism while simultaneously rejecting the white feminism of the mainstream women's suffrage movement led by Elizabeth Cady Stanton and Susan B. Anthony. Of course, these are not mutually exclusive politics. Only when Black women gain citizenship, suffrage, and body autonomy in a post-bellum world will they truly be free to control their reproductivity for the health of the Black community. *Iola Leroy* truly articulates an "embodied feminism" that "wasn't afraid of bodies."⁴⁶ Central to Watkins Harper's intersectional feminism is the work of disproving the hegemonic medico-legal theory that Black women are capable of impressing others yet being themselves unimpressible.⁴⁷

In fact, from Watkins Harper's perspective, Black women are just as impressible as their white counterparts, and more significantly, their children were impressible during pregnancy and after birth such that Black women are cautioned to choose spouses carefully so as to stimulate racial progress.⁴⁸ From this vantage point, Watkins Harper has more in common with feminist eugenicist Charlotte Perkins Gilman than scholars willingly avow, for both Watkins Harper and Gilman defend eugenic marriage (in the form of spousal choice) and "voluntary motherhood" as foundational to the future of race health. ⁴⁹ Eugenics emerged as a field of pseudo-science and social science during the late nineteenth and early twentieth centuries, when Charles Darwin's cousin Frances Galton coined the term "eugenics" in 1883.⁵⁰ The term itself means "good in stock," and is derived from the Greek prefix "eu" for "good" and the Greek word "genetai" for "coming into being" or "growing," but this translates to a practice of applying Darwinian evolutionary principles to human growth and development. In America, Galton's concept of "positive eugenics" flourished as a form of public health initiatives such as voluntarily choosing a marriage partner based on heredity or even legally requiring a clean bill of health from marriage applicants before obtaining a marriage certificate. The goal of such practices was to prevent genetic inheritance of undesirable characteristics associated with Blackness or disability among the next generation. Of course, eugenic practices are inherently racist and ableist.

And yet Schuller argues that Watkins Harper reclaims—or, as I might say, (p)rescribes—eugenic principles for Black race health and the politics of racial uplift, allowing her to "transform sexuality from an alleged site of Black slavery into a source of racial modernization for women" of color, and especially Black mothers.[51] Galton certainly did not have Black motherhood in mind when he theorized eugenics as the foundation of Social Darwinism. And yet, perhaps the supposed ridiculousness of reclaiming eugenics for racial uplift is Watkins Harper's point. By adopting a mad Black approach akin to satire, Watkins Harper exposes the slipperiness between ir/rationality, or the logical and illogical. Her juxtaposition of the Black female body to animality is so severe that the comparison appears certifiably mad. How can readers take the comparative anatomy of racial science seriously after such madness? "Madness becomes the place to engage because racism adheres to a peculiar kind of rationality, predicated on the long history of the Enlightenment and its material effects," Therí Alyce Pickens explains of her theorizing mad Blackness.[52] This "peculiar kind of rationality" is why nineteenth-century writers and scientists can deploy materiality for alternatively racist or antiracist purposes. It is logical from their worldview. Thus, when Watkins Harper reports a conversation among the slaves in which Tom Anderson overhears the slave master bragging, "'he meant to break her in,'" the reader is expected to be horrified that a Black woman might be compared to a horse.[53] This is, of course, coded language for rape. We are told that Master Tom "had tried in vain to drag her down to his low level of sin and shame" on more than one occasion, yet Iola successfully resists his sexual advances (88). Tom and Robert furiously work together to save Iola from slavery by acquiring a position for her as a Civil War nurse for a Black regiment. Even the (white) general of the regiment is horrified that such a beautiful woman as Iola could be treated "as chattel, with no power to protect herself from the highest insults that lawless brutality could inflict upon innocent and defenseless womanhood" (88).

Yet it isn't lawless. On the contrary, the law sanctions Master Tom's attempts at rape because the law does not recognize Black women like Iola Leroy as subjects before the law. As Andrea Stone explains of *Missouri v. Celia, a slave* (1855) and Harriet Jacobs's *Incidents in the Life of a Slave Girl* (1861), legal recourse for rape victims did not exist: Just as it was legally impossible for a husband to rape his wife, turning the concept of "marital rape" into an oxymoron, it was also legally impossible for a master to rape or "trespass on" his own property. Neither a husband nor a slave master would turn himself in for rape, and a female victim of rape could not report because she was not recognized by law as a subject with rights.[54] This same legal principle underlies the threat of sexual violence in *Iola Leroy*, a threat that becomes more heightened in the context of medical fiction. Medico-legal discourse uses the rhetoric of animality—such as comparing a Black woman to a horse—to dehumanize and objectify the subject, thereby justifying her abuse. Cary Wolfe theorizes animal subjectivity within a legal framework, lamenting that the reason animals do not have rights and protection under United States law is because legalities act as a cultural frame of reference for "who's in and who's out."[55] Animals are not subjects before the law in multiple valences: They are not "before the law" in the sense of being subjects "prior to the moment when the law, in all its contingency and immanence, enacts its originary violence."[56] Nor are they "before the law" "in the sense of standing before judgement," since the animal does not exist in the eyes of the law as a subject that can experience violence as a victim of crime.[57] The lack of subjectivity within a legal framework transforms the subject into an object by rhetorically de-animating the noun and relegating it into the grammatical space of a direct object as a commodity upon which the law passively acts.[58]

On the other hand, Wolfe observes that the legal framework for what makes a subject worthy of defense not only hinges upon linguistic affect but also implicates material affect in the aftermath of legal vulnerability: Lives that are not "grievable" do not count as human lives, and only human lives merit legal protection. Wolfe points out the hypocrisy of this on multiple levels, for not only do humans grieve nonhuman animal companions, but also nonhuman animals such as elephants and great apes grieve the loss of their own familial and tribal members.[59] And yet, Wolfe's assessment of how nonhuman animals are disavowed as subjects before the law within a twenty-first-century legal framework elucidates why Black men and women were not considered subjects before the law within a nineteenth-century legal framework. Even humans who are animalized are vulnerable before the law, as in the case of Jews during the Holocaust. Subjectivity hinges on how our culture historically and continually characterizes nonhuman animals, as well as how certain classes of humanity are characterized in relationship to animality.[60] Since race scientists categorize Blackness as akin to animality, and then doubly characterize nonhuman animals and Black men and women as unimpressible, nineteenth-century medico-legal discourses are bound to disavow Black men and women as subjects before the law in every sense of the phrase that Wolfe explicates. White cisheteropatriarchy, as Pickens terms the system, does not consider Black lives "grievable."

Watkins Harper exposes the falsity of this implicit cultural narrative by representing Black slaves nurturing and grieving one another in the wake of a violent war. As Tom Anderson suffers from blood loss in the aftermath of a scouting mission gone wrong, Captain Sybil insists he be given over to

Iola Leroy's care. "'If good nursing can win him back to life,'" Captain Sybil declares, then Tom "'shall not want for any care or pains that she can bestow,'" since Iola is repeatedly considered a "natural" healer and nurse (97). Iola recognizes that it is too late for Tom, but even in hospice, "her presence was a balm to his wounds" (97), and this explicitly involves grieving Tom's life both during and after his passing. Not coincidentally, Watkins Harper narrates, Iola "tenderly" "wiped the death damps from his dusky brow, and *imprinted* upon it a farewell kiss" (98, my emphasis). Black bodies can be imprinted, and they are imprinted with care and "affection" (98), signifying Black lives as grievable. After Dr. Grisham pronounces Tom dead, Iola releases "a flood of tears" brought upon by "the anguish of her heart" (98). Even before Tom's death, the reader observes Black slaves nursing one another. One slave, called Aunt Katie, is whipped for coming late to work in the field, yet Katie was late because she stopped to tend her husband, who was ill. She had earlier lost her baby, whom she left dead in the cabin because she had to milk the cows or risk violent punishment. When Aunt Katie returns to the cabin, "some one had been to her cabin an' took'd de pore chile away an' put it in de groun'" (80). "Pore Katie" didn't have a chance to grieve her lost baby or her lost husband, yet Uncle Daniel's story about his wife counters the cultural narrative that Black bodies are not grievable subjects. Like Tom Anderson, Katie's baby is a grievable subject, and each of these medical interventions in the narrative functions as an opportunity for impressing upon readers the fact of the impressibilty and subjectivity of Black bodies.

These episodes of Black nursing on the plantation and on the battlefield recall Koritha Mitchell's celebration of homemade citizenship as a form of belonging alternative to legal civic inclusion. The Law of the land might fail to recognize Black community, but Black men and women created a sense of belonging through empathetic caregiving all the same. And their success usually incited "know-your-place" aggression and violence.[61] Deirdre Cooper Owens corroborates Hollis Robbins's claim that "Iola Leroy is perhaps best appreciated as a sociological novel," for Watkins Harper represents plantation nursing as accurately as she represents the events of the Civil War.[62] Historians regularly recount the story of J. Marion Sims's medical experiments on the bodies of Black slave women in pursuit of a surgical cure for the vesicovaginal fistula. This oft-told story rightly villainizes Sims, the so-called Father of Gynecology.[63] Yet it also victimizes Black slave women as "silent bodies on operating tables," when, in fact, they contributed as active agents in a variety of medical roles as Sims's surgical assistants, as midwives to white and Black women alike, and as plantation nurses.[64] Owens finds evidence among several African American Works Progress Administration interviews of white owners and doctors not only deferring to the medical authority of Black women slaves, but also stealing their folk healing remedies as their own.[65] Plagiarism may be the sincerest form of flattery but it is still a kind of violence. Owens's findings from the WPA slave narratives and slave management journals contribute a more empowering perspective to the history of American gynecology as enslaved women exercise some agency in their role as plantation nurse. "As much as they could, enslaved black women planned and aborted pregnancies, engaged in sexual relationships with men they chose to love, and passed on medical knowledge to their loved ones despite the threat of physical punishment and retaliation by doctors and slave masters," Owens summarizes.[66]

Because Watkins Harper was well read, and because *Iola Leroy* functions as a kind of sociological novel informed by ethnography, we might read Watkins Harper's choice of profession for Iola Leroy as a way of deliberately shifting the cultural narrative of Black women's oppression under slavery. Yao agrees, as she speculates Iola will follow in the footsteps of Rebecca Lee Davis Crumper and Rebecca J. Cole to become the next Black woman physician, meanwhile rejecting the racist science of J. Marion Sims in her performance of Black communal nursing.[67] As first plantation nurse and then Civil War nurse, Iola corroborates the WPA slave narratives in which Black women disclose their own experiences of agency as plantation nurses and midwives. She further corroborates the vulnerability of Black female slaves whose "disclosure of sexual abuse" in the WPA slave narratives functions as "strong counternarratives to black women's supposed lasciviousness" and medically established hypersexuality.[68] Watkins Harper injects her own counternarrative into the sociopolitical unconscious through Iola Leroy's asexual and moral performance as a slave nurse and Civil War nurse, and this counternarrative undermines white cisheteropatriarchal cultural narratives of the Black female body on multiple levels. After all, if Black women are as animalistic as race science insists, then it should logically follow that white men's sexual abuse of Black women enacts bestiality, which is a moral sin. Robert, who we come to discover is Iola and Henry's uncle, succinctly highlights this contradiction with a rhetorical question: "'Isn't it funny,' said Robert, 'how these white folks look down on colored people, and then mix up with them?'" (81). Of course, it isn't "funny"; it's traumatic, even deadly, as Black women contend with the violence of the sexual act itself, as well as depression, repeated pregnancies, and in some cases, sexually transmitted diseases in the aftermath of rape.[69] In so many words, Watkins Harper exposes the irrationality of medico-legal discourse with the deadpan nature of Robert's question. This kind of mad Blackness amplifies the ridiculousness of legalized rape and the so-called medical evidence that sanctions it. It isn't "fun" or "funny" for the individual Black woman who is victimized, nor is it "fun" or "funny" for the communities that must contend with the traumatic aftereffects of this "mix up," including the "ten culled granchillen somewhar down in de lower kentry" that Ole Gundover's wife disavows at her death just as her son disowned them (81).

Robert's "black humor"—by which I mean both racialized humor and dark humor—recalls Mel Y. Chen's analysis of the queer animality and "black humor" of J. L. Austin's *How to Do Things with Words* (1962). Austin's series of lectures, given in 1955 at Harvard University, exemplifies the materiality of language as Austin performs language while lecturing on the performativity of oral speech itself. In one key demonstrative phrase, Austin jocularly suggests that excessive performativity—by which he means "over the top," or unnecessary—is akin to "mockery, like a marriage with a monkey."[70] Although Austin intends for his "black humor" to be heard as ridiculous, silly, or absurd, Chen opines that his phrasing betrays a cultural narrative of queer animality, which we may locate in late nineteenth-century political cartoons. "Arguably, African slaves first bore the epistemological weight of animalization," Chen observes, pointing to how pro-slavery political cartoonists render African slaves as laboring beasts in their collective effort to draw upon the authority of race science and its comparative anatomy approach to legitimize slavery.[71] One such political cartoon from an 1879 edition of *Harper's Weekly*, titled "The Civilization of Blaine," simultaneously infantilizes and simianizes an African slave against a white male politician in "a circuit of bodily intimacy" that "render[s] their relationship at once cross-racial, ambivalently cross-species, and queer."[72] Chen's analysis of "The Civilization of Blaine" recalls Amy Werbel's analysis of E. W. Clay's "Practical Amalgamation" print series, which we may recall the General Court of Sessions in New York City censored as "obscene." Both political caricatures were made in the service of upholding racist legislation, the former in protest against the Fifteenth Amendment (passed 1870) guaranteeing Black (male) suffrage and the latter in response to debates about repealing anti-miscegenation law. Both cultural depictions also rely upon a queer animality for conveying the rhetorical "horror" of amalgamation, whether politically or sexually, as they portray simianized Black men in a kind of intimate relationality with humanized white men or women.

The timeliness of this queer animality is key to understanding the capacious legacy of Comstock Law-era medico-legal discourse, not least because Comstock's crusade coincides with the development of race science, its commitment to comparative anatomy, and its deployment in upholding both anti-miscegenation law and black women's hypersexuality. Comstock actively promoted the cultural narrative of the "black rapist beast." Amanda Frisken explains that what Amy Werbel considers an omission in censorship bans was Comstock's way of actively courting the stereotype of black men as predators. During the 1870s, Comstock censored several periodicals guilty of publishing sexually explicit material, including but not limited to sporting news such as *The Days' Doings* and the *National Police Gazette*, yet he refused to censor interracial sexuality because of its "criminal" nature under anti-miscegenation law. Comstock notably censored the ankles of white women from public view, "but not the outlines or even frontal nudity of poor or racially distinct women," Frisken observes.[73] Moreover, as Comstock worked with editors to censor "obscene" or sexually suggestive visual and print material, he explicitly "erased white male rape" but permitted—even highlighted—depictions of black rapists.[74] "Representation of rape was apparently unproblematic if the alleged perpetrator was black, because it conformed to the post-Reconstruction political agenda of white supremacy," Frisken explains of Comstock's trend in censorship, or lack thereof.[75] Comstock's selective censorship practices must be considered within the context of anti-miscegenation law debates as they gained purchase in the 1840s, even prior to the Civil War, and reached their apex of intensity in the 1870s and 1880s. Although these debates resulted in the repeal of anti-miscegenation laws in eleven states, including Rhode Island (1881), Michigan (1883), and Ohio (1887), they reached a period of stasis that held until 1948. Ohio was the last state to repeal anti-miscegenation law during the nineteenth century and states would not revisit the legality of interracial marriage again until 1948, when California would repeal its anti-miscegenation law.[76]

Operating at the forefront of these political and social anxieties about amalgamation was queer animality, for even though J. L. Austin's exemplar of "marriage with a monkey" was meant as a joke demonstrative of ridiculousness, fear of animal relationality, and by extension, bestiality, motivates—even animates—anti-miscegenation law in the American cultural imagination from the 1840s through the 1960s. Simultaneously, Comstock and his cronies pushed the reality of white men's sexual abuse of Black women during and after slavery to the background in favor of the black rapist beast narrative in an effort to foreground an anti-miscegenation agenda. Amalgamation is cast off as ridiculous, and this ridiculousness acts as a detractor from the inherent contradiction of defending white rape while attacking interracial marriage. After all, if Black women are, by medico-legal definition, animals, then white male rape of Black females logically translates to bestiality, for amalgamation is akin to Austin's "marriage with a monkey." Yet white men would never admit to committing the sin of bestiality and further bemoan attempts to legalize interracial marriage. This is why Robert's question is not only explicitly rhetorical in its highlighting of the trauma of slavery but further implicitly critical of the medico-legal statures of late nineteenth-century anti-miscegenation law.

This is also why Watkins Harper adopts interracial marriage as her point of departure for exploring the complexities of mixed-race identity in *Iola Leroy*, which I situate squarely within a period of intense medico-legal debate about the ethics of amalgamation in an effort to highlight the complexities of Black female subjectivity before the law. However, we must also push back against this postmodernist and posthumanist commitment to rewriting—or rescripting—cultural narratives of animality, bestiality, and even Cary Wolfe's concept of "before the law" before we ourselves move forward with an analysis of Watkins Harper's critique of medico-legal discourse, and specifically the logic of anti-amalgamation and the law of hypodescent. One of the reasons critical race theorists like Sylvia Wynter are skeptical of the emancipatory promises of posthumanism is because theoretical concepts such as Wolfe's "before the law" risk oversimplifying issues of race and race-as-species by handing it off to the animal for resolution. Nineteenth-century biological and medical sciences already displaced issues of race onto the animal in the wake of Darwinian evolution: "Man was redefined by Darwin as a purely biological being whose origin, like that of all other species was sited in Evolution, with the human therefore existing in a life of pure continuity with all other organic forms of life."[77] For a population who scientists, lawmakers, and politicians already associated as "dysgenic or dysselected-by-Evolution conception" through its supposed close proximity with the animal, this redescription was unwelcome then and remains unwelcome in contemporary theories of race.[78] Wynter insists we must reinvent ourselves into our own ongoing existence, and she valorizes Franz Fanon's practice of "self-assertion" as central to the work of transforming liberal humanism from within rather than displacing the order of Man onto the nonhuman animal.[79]

Zakiyyah Iman Jackson similarly argues that posthumanism undercut its intervention into conversations about "the human" and liberal humanism's reliance upon Western notions of "Man" "when its scholars effectively sidestepped the analytical challenges posed by the category of race, colonialism, and slavery" by pursuing conversations of animality, bestiality, and race-as-species.[80] In adopting a Baradian approach to race as superposition, or race as phenomenon, I wish to confront the medico-legal discourse of selective censorship under Comstock law by highlighting how Watkins Harper must make a sort of substitution in the language of her narrative by distancing herself from the rhetoric of animality and adopting the language of impressibility, or affect. Unlike other women writers of medical fiction who are white, Watkins Harper cannot directly address or challenge the scientific rhetoric underpinning and rationalizing anti-amalgamation law. Neither can she insert her body into the narrative, for fear its performativity will reinscribe the myth of black female hypersexuality. Instead, Watkins Harper must appeal to the logic of anti-amalgamation, exposing the irrationality of medico-legal discourses of animality underpinning anti-amalgamation law for antiracist ends. Admittedly, Wolfe's *Before the Law* sets the grounds for analyzing this narratological substitution.[81] But, whereas Wolfe assumes whiteness as the natural point of origin for critiquing the Law of the land (Comstock law, anti-amalgamation) and the law of nature (law of hypodescent), Watkins Harper wholly challenges whiteness as the point of origin for both the Law and the law.

From Kinship to Kinetic

Nineteenth-century race science was smitten with measuring. Dr. Samuel George Morton measured the skulls of multiple people from a variety of races, ethnicities, and nationalities, carefully cataloging his observations in *Crania Americana* (1839).[82] From skulls, race science moved to pelvises, where Moritz Weber was among the first to posit that Black women give birth effortlessly because of their oblong pelvises, which he claims resemble those of orangutans.[83] Race scientists even measured breasts and clitorises in a turn toward sexist science.[84] Anne Fausto-Sterling and Ellen Samuels independently document American medicine's continued commitment to measurement as a form of authoritative data for regulating bodies, a trend which Samuels calls "biocertification."[85] Although Samuels examines blood quantum as a growing marker of biocertification, and specifically indigenous tribal membership during the late twentieth and early twenty-first centuries, it is worth noting that attempts to measure "blood" began as early as the 1790s with the cultural adoption of hypodescent, or the "one-drop rule."[86] Unlike blood quantum, the one-drop rule did not actually measure physical blood samples for genetic material, since the scientific method of drawing blood for dye to test and analyze did not yet exist. The one-drop rule depended upon a visible assessment of facial appearance, and especially skin color, or knowledge of an individual's genealogy. If an individual appears Black based upon social markers such as the configuration of hair, nose width, lip size, or shade of melanin, then the individual must be Black and function in society as a member of the Black race.[87] Similarly, if an individual was white passing but was believed to have an ancestor, whether a parent or grandparent, who identified as Black, then the individual must also be Black and function in society as a member of the Black race.[88] Classification was deceptively simple, since the one-drop rule was a zero-sum game.

Even though the law of hypodescent was not legally enforced until the 1830s, historian Winthrop D. Jordan argues that the social enforcement of the one-drop rule assumed greater influence and staying power. Indeed, Jordan argues that the one-drop rule still operates today, often for empowering purposes to celebrate "firsts" or moments of breaking the "glass ceiling," such as the first black Miss America or the successes of Halle Berry, Colin Powell, and Tiger Woods.[89] This is in part because of the medical authority backing the social enforcement of the one-drop rule, especially in its conflation of raciation as speciation. Medical science further gave the authoritative impression of measuring blood—or at least some*thing* biological—in its use of numerical language for quantifying and classifying race: quadroon, octoroon, mulatto/a. Samuels rightly considers the one-drop rule as operating under the fantasy of marking, citing historical scholarship on hypodescent in Virginia as evidence.[90] Under the fantasy of marking, nineteenth-century medico-legal discourse figures Blackness as an oversized birthmark, blemish, or imprint, and therefore a kind of physical disability.[91] Actual bodily markings such as scars or moles might also be used to identify lost family members, as during the trials of Salome Muller,[92] as well as in Iola Leroy's identification of both her mother and her brother during the post-war reunion (158, 163). Since the rhetoric of the one-drop rule gains import under the fantasy of measurement, while the embodied performance of the one-drop rule affects audiences through the fantasy of marking, we might consider the law of hypodescent as blurring the lines between each theoretical apparatus. In other words, the law of hypodescent is both a fantasy of measurement and a fantasy of marking. The former affects linguistically, while the latter affects socially. This implicates each theoretical apparatus in the ongoing process of superposition, thereby highlighting the simultaneous formation of race and disability as affective.

When we attend to the effect of the law of hypodescent on kinship, then race-, disability-, and gender-as-affect emerge from the ongoing process of superposition, since the individuals we choose as family define our personal and community identity through material proximity. In *Relative Races: Genealogies of Interracial Kinship in Nineteenth-Century America*, Bridgitte Fielder theorizes the process of race-making as a product of relationality, but specifically the relationality of family ties. For Fielder, race is constructed directionally and defined by proximity and intimacy: "through non-biological relations of adoption, 'horizontal' relations of sexual kinship, and 'backwards' genealogies of racial reflection from children to parents or 'circular' relations by which race is constructed and reconstructed *ad infinitum*."[93] For nineteenth-century audiences, marriage may be arguably the most provocative form of race-making through kinship because one not only chooses to identify as raced through spousal relationality, it is also assumed that married couples will further reproduce race through their biological offspring. Fielder traces a narratological trend across newspaper accounts of Mary King, a white woman who eloped with a Black male professor. In her comparison of the anti-amalgamation rhetoric of "The Mary Rescue" with the anti-amalgamation imagery of Edward William Clay's "Practical Amalgamation" series, especially "The Wedding" (see Figure 3.2), Fielder finds the law of hypodescent permeating artistic production during the 1840s and 1850s.[94] A white woman's proximity to Blackness threatens her purity, especially since the union will produce "mixed" children. For newspaper editors, writers, and caricaturists, the only logical response is to reject Black advances; those women who welcome the advances of Black men must be either mentally ill or impressible due to youth.[95] Notably, both rationalizations for interracial marriage implicate disability and gender, which indicates that the process of race production coincides with the process of disability and gender production.

Fielder rightly characterizes the process of race-making as a product of relationality. Yet her social constructionist approach not only places the onus on human interventions but also accounts for only one form of relationality that is emphatically human. Race is as much a product of material relationality as it is a product of (human) social and cultural constructions, but because it is difficult to witness affective (nonhuman) entanglements in process, we often disavow their agency. Kinship is certainly material in its bodily entanglement. But what about the other kinds of kin with which we find ourselves entangled? Schuller accounts for a much broader network of bodies in the race-making process, especially textual bodies, since many nineteenth-century writers, including Frances Ellen Watkins Harper, recognize writing as affective. Schuller's emphasis on the role of textuality characterizes race as "a palimpsestic process in which impressions layer upon one another over the life span of the individual and the evolutionary time of race."[96] Palimpsest is a kind of superposition. Both processes capture how time collapses in the moment of measurement or observation, as well as describing how bodies continually engage in complex forms of relationality. Traces fade, but never fully erase. It is the longevity of affect that I wish to account for in my theory of race as superposition, because the futurity of affect is not only indeterminate but also, significantly, emerges from specific intra-actions that we must acknowledge to engage responsibly in the ongoing process of race-making. The medico-legal discourse of anti-amalgamation law, the Comstock Law, and the law of hypodescent that animates anti-amalgamation law and the Comstock Law offer a specific framework for reading race in *Iola Leroy* because the decisions characters make regarding marriage and children have the capacity to affect cultural narratives of Black subjectivity generations after its publication.

The making of Iola Leroy's subjectivity as a Black woman began long before her birth. Because all "phenomena are ontologically primitive relations," and are therefore "relations without preexisting relata,"[97] race is always already made (as is disability and gender). Yet race is constantly re-made through superposition, or material-discursive entanglements such as kinship. Eugene Leroy could likely predict how his cousin Alfred Lorraine would react to the news of Eugene's engagement to Marie, a former slave. The reader could likely predict Alfred's reaction, too, especially after Watkins Harper describes Alfred's upbringing as the son of a wealthy Southern planter and a Northern mother whose "executive ability" neither allowed "shirking nor dawdling" among the slaves (104). Alfred takes no truck with suffragists and abolitionists. He exhibits precisely the "racial feeling" that Watkins Harper seeks to reform through the Black respectability politics of characters like Iola Leroy (137). Alfred's "racial feeling" is directly informed by the law of hypodescent, an aesthetic Alfred likely encountered across multiple cultural texts that not only impressed him but which he further invokes in the creation of his own text: his spoken argument deployed to impress Eugene not to marry Marie. "'One drop of negro blood in her veins curses all the rest,'" Alfred pronounces, citing anti-amalgamation rhetoric and eugenic logic as he defends the right of society "'to guard the purity of its blood'" (106). Alfred draws upon medico-legal discourse that simultaneously appeals to the fantasy of measurement and the fantasy of marking, which already exist in superposition, just as medicine and law already exist in superposition as they concern the manifestation of race, disability, and gender. What we read as "socially constructed" race in Watkins Harper's *Iola Leroy* is actually the after-effects of race during a specific moment in time of superposition captured through the act of "measurement" or observation.

Although Alfred is long-affected by medico-legal discourse and convinced of its authority, Alfred's own discourse fails to affect Eugene, who moves forward with his marriage to Marie regardless of Alfred's objections. Barad's theory of agential realism accounts for why Alfred's discourse fails: "Intra-actions are not the result of human interventions; rather 'humans' themselves emerge through specific intra-actions."[98] Eugene admits his knowledge of anti-amalgamation law and the law of hypodescent, for he laments, "'both law and public opinion debar me from following the inclination of my heart'" (106). Yet the specific intra-actions that produce Eugene's character—his education, (lack of) familial upbringing, social environment, genetic constitution—likely resist Alfred's material impressions just as the specific intra-actions that produce Alfred's character convince Alfred of the immorality of amalgamation. Specificity is key here: It is only under these conditions that Eugene marries Marie and sires three mixed-race children, Harry, Iola, and Gracie. Because Alfred's discourse impresses Alfred more than it impresses Eugene, Alfred convinces himself to personally intervene in the Leroy estate after Eugene's untimely death from yellow fever. Alfred does not simply make race by citing medico-legal discourse such as the law of hypodescent. Nor does Eugene only make race through the act of interracial marriage and the creation of kinship ties. In the case of Alfred, Black subjectivity is re-made as "an alien race" that threatens to contaminate the "pure" blood of the white race (106), while amalgamation is re-made as the product of mental illness in Alfred's declaring Eugene "mad" enough to be committed to an "insane asylum" (110). Similarly, Eugene might have once experienced a compatible "racial feeling," but after his encounter with Marie, who acts as a "faithful and devoted nurse" during a near-death experience, Eugene remakes race first as "pity" and then as "love" as a result of compassionate care (108). People are indeed hard to hate up close. But, unlike Brené Brown, Watkins Harper does not necessarily recommend moving in closer, or at least not so close that the next generation risks re-making the trauma of the previous generation.[99]

Watkins Harper further opens up a space for reading the superposition of race, gender, and disability as affect in *Iola Leroy* as Iola is deeply preoccupied with choosing kinship and community ties—as well as an appropriate eugenic marriage partner—because she cannot risk reproducing the trauma of interracial marriage that she experienced as a child. Blackness cannot be measured or quantified, in spite of legal attempts to do so in the form of anti-miscegenation law, the law of hypodescent, and even to varying degrees, the Comstock Law.

Because it cannot be measured or quantified, Iola must choose her kinship and community ties based on how she reads her own identity as an affective agent. Iola identifies as a future mother whose work as a child-bearer and caretaker is to "direct the future evolution of the race" for Black uplift.[100] Her material identity informs her social identity, moving her to choose the mixed-race Dr. Frank Latimer as spouse, not least because she "understands her own maternity to be racialized as Black."[101] Iola must also choose a mixed-race or Black partner because a same-race marriage opens up a space for personal, community, and generational healing. In twice rejecting the marriage proposal of Dr. Gresham, a white physician for whom she works, Iola invokes the trauma of amalgamation within the specific context of racially prejudiced post-war America. The first time Iola rejects Dr. Gresham, she invokes the materiality of race as defined by medico-legal discourse and especially the law of hypodescent: "'Doctor,' she said, and a faint flush rose to her cheek, 'suppose we should marry, and little children in after years should nestle to our arms, and one of them show unmistakable signs of color, would you be satisfied?'" (141). This is a trauma Iola has already personally experienced. And even if the answer is yes, as in the case of Iola's own father, the answer would likely be no among Dr. Gresham's family and the larger community within which they live. Thus, when Dr. Gresham persists, Iola must further appeal to the social construction, or interpretation, of race based upon the fantasy of measurement: "'Would they be willing to ignore all the traditions of my blood?'" Iola asks, invoking the rhetoric of anti-amalgamation (141). Iola answers for Dr. Gresham, absolving him of potential "embarrassment": "'New England is not free from racial prejudice,'" she declares (141), and thus, she cannot expect Dr. Gresham's immediate family, much less the larger community, to accept their union or future children. After all, racially ambiguous children are precisely the "result from such a marriage" that proponents of anti-amalgamation law strove to avoid (141).

Watkins Harper recognizes that the physical laws of heredity can only guide the likely outcomes of biological formation among offspring. Our posterity, whether biological or adoptive, is indeterminate because all causal relationships are indeterminate in ongoing social and material negotiations. As Barad would say, the nature of wave-particle duality indicates that although we can predict the likeliness of an outcome because the wave follows a general physical law, we cannot know how specific particles will react under a specific set of conditions.[102] Iola and Dr. Gresham's children will be Black because the general law of hypodescent wholesale follows the condition of the mother. Yet Iola cannot know the specific conditions under which her future children will be born and raised: whether her future children will show "unmistakable" signs of color, whether they will be white-passing, whether social ideologies will shift toward greater inclusivity of interracial marriages and mixed-race children, or whether Dr. Gresham's immediate family and the New England community will welcome their interracial family, among other values. It's not just that there are too many possible generalizable outcomes to predict a specific likely effect, but that the values themselves are in a state of flux even before the hypothetical marriage of Iola and Dr. Gresham. Such is the nature of indeterminacy.

One fact of determinate value that Iola can know is that her children will be read socially as Black, and because they will be Black, she may be able to control some of the indeterminate values influencing their well-being. Iola invokes the trauma of shame or "'veil of concealment,'" which she not only has personally experienced in the wake of her father's death but also has "'too much self-respect to enter'" now that she knows she is mixed-race (141). In the immediate aftermath of Eugene Leroy's death, teenage Iola discovers for the first time that she is a Black woman and "burst[s] into a paroxysm of tears succeeded by peals of hysterical laughter" as she grapples with the news of her father's death, her parents' invalidated marriage, her mother's invalidated manumission, and her own remanding into slavery (134). This trauma upon trauma upon trauma upon trauma leaves Iola vulnerable because she never fully reconciles with her prior experiences of trauma before being exposed to new threats of trauma in the form of sexual violence and the violence of civil war. Watkins Harper narrates that Marie always knew "this silence was oppressive" (117). Nevertheless, Marie must remain complicit in concealing the truth of Iola's identity because her husband Eugene believes the "painful knowledge" of racial identity is too much for his children to bear (118). It is unspeakable. In trauma studies, the concept of "the unspeakable" refers to a rhetorical device that invokes "the limits of language, comprehension, representation" while simultaneously deferring "toward atrocity, horror, trauma, and pain."[103] The unspeakable silences victims in its assumption that the pain of trauma is too much for survivors to bear, much less articulate through the act of narrative. It masquerades as an ethical practice that purportedly respects the memory of the victims. Yet, in many cases, invoking the unspeakable is an act of self-preservation on the part of the speaker; it denotes the limits of the speaker's willingness to engage in discourse, not necessarily the limits of language itself. But what is unspeakable for Eugene Leroy? Is it amalgamation? The knowledge that his children are mixed-race? His marriage to a woman of color and former slave? Perhaps what is actually unspeakable for Eugene Leroy is his complicity in the slave system and his forced complicity of his wife Marie, against her will, a kind of dual complicity for which he judges himself guilty of violence, especially since that very system later enslaves his daughter Iola.

In *Against the Unspeakable: Complicity, the Holocaust, and Slavery in America*, Naomi Mandel meditates on complicity as a domain that preconditions identity, ethics, and accountability. Importantly, Mandel finds complicity does not equal culpability. Complicity describes the condition of participating in a system one does not endorse, of being in relation to it even while despising it.[104] Admittedly, this is a "gray area" for multiple reasons: Complicity neither accuses nor excuses the subject implicated in the system; rather, complicity holds the subject accountable for reforming the system from within,[105] which is precisely the objective that Sylvia Wynter advances in her critique of liberal humanism. In the act of acknowledging personal complicity in a system for oppression, the subject must form his identity in relation to the system, and this very act of identity-formation requires an articulation of difference: Do I fit in? The answer—yes, no, and why—thereby opens up a space for productively opposing the system that elides the conditions of difference that define the subject's identity. In the case of the Leroys, Marie acknowledges her forced complicity in a system that oppresses their kin, but it is Eugene who is ultimately responsible for behaving (un)ethically toward his children. His failure to act leaves the children vulnerable to the evil actions of Alfred Lorraine, and because Eugene specifically cannot rectify the situation during his lifetime, Eugene slides from complicity to culpability as the reader judges him for his inaction.

Mandel, however, extends complicity beyond personal relationships. In her study of the unspeakable in narratives about suffering, and specifically the Holocaust and American slavery, Mandel argues that we are all complicit in contemporary systems of oppression such as anti-Semitism and racism because we are touched by them: "To assume that one could be in any kind of relation to evil and not be touched by it is to vastly underestimate the nature of evil."[106] We are enmeshed, entangled. We breathe racist air. Watkins Harper knew this, as Iola laments that the long reach of slavery poisons society because "'the spirit which animated it still lives'" (206), and will continue to live until we shift our cultural narratives of race. Complicity, then, is not the issue. As Mandel insists, and I agree, complicity "should not be avoided" because it forces us to not only confront the evils of our society, but speak about them and against them. Trauma persists when we silence victims. Although some psychologists argue that "talk therapy" or the "talking cure" risks retraumatizing victims through the act of telling their story, trauma studies scholars not only document a "need to tell" trend among writers of trauma but also suggest that art serves as a safe space for writers to work through and heal from their trauma.[107] Rita Charon agrees, for not only does the practice of narrative medicine position storytelling as *the* essential activity for guiding patients toward healing but, Charon boldly claims, the act of sharing a story allows for the sharing of the storyteller's burden among speaker and listener, and "[o]nce shared, the suffering is lessened."[108] However, we must have "genuine intersubjectivity," or we risk harming the speaker-victim.[109] Citing the same large-scale traumatic events as Mandel and Deborah M. Horvitz, including the Holocaust, the Vietnam War, and genocide in Rwanda, Charon argues for the value of narrative medicine even among trauma survivors, given that both oral historians and trauma studies scholars document the act of storytelling as a method of healing. "What we can learn already from oral history and trauma studies is that the work of bearing witness does not do violence to the speaker, does not interfere in the telling, but rather is committed to active, respectful, confirming listening," Charon stresses.[110] The crux of healing lies not only in the telling, but also in the listening, for when we fail to listen affectively, only then do we risk retraumatizing survivors.

Nursing Narratives, Narrative Nursing

Might the act of reading about and listening to stories of trauma further aid audiences in the act of national healing as they gain knowledge about the experience of suffering? Watkins Harper seems to think so. She draws upon medical metaphors to describe the conditions of suffering in the wake of slavery, racist science, and the Civil War, while simultaneously offering a prescription for healing the nation from the trauma wrought by systemic violence. Captain Sybil rightly describes slavery as "a deadly cancer eating into the life of the nation" (150), and it is no mere coincidence that Eugene Leroy—a wealthy planter—catches yellow fever while his wife and child are spared. Watkins Harper explicitly titles Chapter 11 "The Plague and the Law" to implicate the medico-legal discourses upholding slavery as a kind of yellow fever, a contagious and deadly illness. Mixed-race women and children like Marie, Gracie, and Iola, whom society casts as diseased because of their Blackness, are literally kept safe from disease.[111] She cannot be the source of illness, as she was never ill herself.

Watkins Harper further highlights the hypocrisy of anti-amalgamation law and undermines the medical authority that legitimizes legal racism by couching discussions of anti-amalgamation law in collegial conversations among Black physicians and white physicians during a medical conference. Dr. Frank Latimer charges white Southern gentlemen like Dr. Latrobe with creating a law that they themselves violate for their own self-gain. If the blood of Black men and women is "tainted," Dr. Latimer accuses, it is because white men tainted it through sexual violence: "'[Y]ou Southerners began this absorption before the war,'" he condemns. "'I understand that in one decade the mixed bloods rose from one-ninth to one-eighth of the population and that as early as 1663 a law was passed in Maryland to prevent English women from intermarrying with slaves; and even now, your laws against miscegenation presuppose that you apprehend danger from that source'" (214–15). Watkins Harper, via Dr. Latimer, knows her history. Historian Winthrop D. Jordan corroborates this citation with the details of the case: In 1662, the Virginia House of Burgesses prohibited sexual intercourse between (presumably white) Christians and Black men or women, and Maryland followed suit two years later.[112] America is a nation built not only upon legal racism, but also the fantasy of anti-amalgamation, as though laws could prevent interracial sex. As though anyone were actually of a "pure" race. The so-called "danger" that white Southern men "apprehend" from amalgamation is purely self-reflexive: White Southern men and their laws against miscegenation are the "source" of danger and disease, not the Black race. If Dr. Latimer sounds angry, he should, because as a mixed-race man, he is literally an "illegal" person, as his mixed-race identity emerges from the violation of anti-amalgamation law and further proves its ineffectiveness. Like Eugene, Dr. Latrobe isn't just complicit in post-slavery racial oppression; he is culpable, and perhaps more so.

And if this has a ring of familiarity to our own twenty-first-century politics, it should, because describing a person as "illegal" before the law repudiates their life as "grievable," justifying violence against them. I am directly invoking the politically charged false logic of "illegal" persons from twentieth- and twenty-first-century discourses about "illegal immigrants." As the wife of a formerly illegal immigrant, I would be remiss if I failed to point out how the concept of "illegal" persons as it is and has been deployed among the conservative right in the United States has its roots in anti-amalgamation law and the law of hypodescent. Ironically, my husband and I have violated these so-called laws of nature (and their ancestral, historical laws of the land) many times over, as we married while he was still an "illegal" immigrant, had a child together prior to his consular processing (for which I sponsored him), and raised that child, who is a mixed-race first-generation American on his patrilineal side. I empathize with Dr. Latimer when he charges Dr. Latrobe with inciting violence through the use of injurious speech that maligns mixed-race children with "illegal" status, thereby stigmatizing them as a "danger" to society. My own son shares a kinship with Dr. Latimer. Certainly, the stakes are lower for my husband, my child, and myself as individuals, and for our family as a relational unit, than perhaps they were for late nineteenth-century readers who identified with Iola and Dr. Latimer, or Iola and Dr. Gresham, as well as the children that might result from either union. Yet, even in twenty-first-century America, injurious speech affects: To be "illegal" in twenty-first-century America is to have limited employment options, to be disqualified from college scholarship or grants, to fear being "discovered" every time you drive your car to the grocery store because you cannot (or should not) legally have a driver's license, to pay hundreds of dollars in fees as an apology and in reparation for entering the country illegally, to undergo an invasive years-long interview process during consular processing, and ultimately to be forcibly separated from your family as a result of "voluntary" deportation until a decision is made (hopefully in your favor) post-consular processing.

This is the shared reality of being an "illegal" immigrant in twenty-first-century America and the (now adult) "illegal" progeny of amalgamation in nineteenth-century America: You are not a subject before the law. Iola may well be acting the prophet when she declares, "'Slavery . . . is dead, but the spirit which *animated* it still lives; and I think that a reckless disregard for human life is more the outgrowth of slavery than any actual hatred of the negro'" (206, my emphasis). One of the reasons why the spirit which animates slavery lives on in the twenty-first century is because animate language from nineteenth-century medico-legal discourse still energizes twenty-first-century cultural narratives of Blackness, and especially the alignment of Blackness with animality, hypersexuality, and disability or disease. Race is affective not only because it is an ongoing material process, but also because it is the product of an energetic exchange on an emotional, corporeal, and tactile level. Race is embodied kinship and it's *kin*etic. But if race is affective, then racism needs an affective remedy. Watkins Harper offers such a remedy in the form of communal nursing, or more broadly, empathetic caretaking: She imagines ongoing community caregiving as an act of empathy that simultaneously breaches racial divides and heals nationwide trauma. In the third act of the novel, after a hate crime abruptly ends her career as a schoolteacher, Iola Leroy returns to the profession of nursing. Her first patient is a young fifteen-year-old (white) girl named Daisy Cloten, whose mother characterizes Iola's bedside manner as "tender, loving sympathy" (203). In a speech thanking Iola for her service, Mrs. Cloten connects the singular practice of Iola's nursing her daughter with the communal practice of nursing the nation, which allows Watkins Harper to emphasize spiritual care—and especially empathy—alongside physical care. Only "[w]hen we have learned to treat men according to the complexion of their souls, and not the color of their skins, we will have given our best contribution towards the solution" of racism (203). While I will admit her colorblind approach is problematic, I take Mrs. Cloten's larger point: Nursing without empathy is not a healing practice.

Watkins Harper more fully articulates her theory of empathetic caretaking using the rhetoric of spirituality. As with many slave narratives, including Martin Delany's *Blake, or The Huts* (1859), Watkins Harper differentiates between the religion of the oppressors and true Christianity. As Aunt Linda aphorizes, "'I larn'd my 'ology at de foot ob de cross,'" utterly rejecting the suggestion of Robert that she learn theology so she can preach (175). Iola agrees, declaring, "'the moral aspect of the nation would be changed if it would learn at the same cross to subordinate the spirit of caste to the spirit of Christ'" (175). Iola often functions as a spokesperson for Frances Ellen Watkins Harper, but especially in this moment as she echoes the "Note" following the novel proper, in which Watkins Harper claims that her purpose for writing *Iola Leroy* is to "awaken in the hearts of our countrymen a strong sense of justice and a more Christ-like humanity" toward the oppressed (251). Cynthia J. Davis reminds readers that it is this kind of spirituality rhetoric that earns Watkins Harper criticism for sentimentality and (unrealistic) idealism even today.[113] And yet, when we consider Watkins Harper's spirituality from the broader perspective of medical fiction or the nursing narrative,[114] her invocation of the love of Christ as central to nationality actually conveys a commitment to empathy as a practice of caretaking à la Rita Charon's narrative medicine. Watkins Harper identified as a Christian, and she emphatically believed that moral Christianity should be central to national identity, but in the context of medical fiction, and especially a nursing narrative, Watkins Harper's emphasis on selfless love and "the spirit of Christ" stands in for empathy rather than Christian spirituality as an antidote to the shame that selective censorship of the Black female body engineers.

Although literary critics and theorists often assign negative valences to biopolitics, eugenics, and nationalist agendas, Schuller argues that the biopolitics of touch, of impressibility, and of sensation in *Iola Leroy* adopt a positive valence in their emphasis on racial uplift and Black women's empowerment. Watkins Harper not only had to render Black pain in detail, she had to render Black *trauma* in detail. Her emphasis on a nationalist agenda for healing Black trauma simultaneously disproves medico-legal discourse that hinges on Black insensibility to pain, and renders Black lives grievable. In a way, Watkins Harper is an early activist for Black Lives Matter, because Black lives do *matter*. And they matter not least because Black lives are material. Black lives matter because they affect and effect. Admittedly, Watkins Harper's nationalist agenda threatens to generalize the Black experience of trauma in fin de siècle America, given that the act of generalization itself threatens to erase the specific experiences of survivors.[115] And yet Watkins Harper meets scale with scale: Race scientists were already generalizing the experience of pain among Black bodies, while racist politicians threatened to generalize the trauma of slavery by referring to its nearly "sixty million and more" victims as collective property and currency in an economic system.[116] Even now, over 150 years later, politicians continually threaten to generalize slavery through the broad-strokes way it is taught in the American grade school system (and especially in my home state of Texas). Watkins Harper bears witness to the specific experiences of Black women by contextualizing their pain within the specific medico-legal discourses that de-animate and objectify Black women as property before the law, eliding their subjectivity with the full rights that representation entails. Although her nationalist agenda for healing involves community caregiving, she is specific about what that caregiving entails: empathy.

Notes

1. Werbel, *Lust on Trial*, 203. Werbel offers a full discussion of the Edmund Knoedler case on pages 190–203.
2. Ibid. 205, 232. Bottom line: Sex sells.
3. Ibid. 239. The article to which Werbel refers is "Anthony is Shocked," which was originally published in the *New York Recorder*, but was reprinted several times including in the August 13, 1893 edition of the *Sunday Globe*.

4. Ibid. 238.
5. Horowitz, *Rereading Sex*, 214. Bridgitte Fielder also briefly discusses this series of prints as evidence of her claim that "anti-amalgamation literature depends upon the construction of both Black male sexuality and white female racism" in disseminating a rhetoric of fear of the black rapist beast (63). Clearly, this cultural narrative pervaded multiple forms of artistic expression including fiction and visual art.
6. Quoted in Horowitz, *Rereading Sex*, 214. Horowitz takes this passage to mean that the either now-lost or non-existent print from the series depicts a white male and Black female engaged in sexual activity, since the description "constitute[s] the legal euphemism used for an image of a heterosexual couple engaged in coition."
7. Horowitz, *Rereading Sex*, 214–15.
8. Hollis Robbins, Introduction, *Iola Leroy, or Shadows Uplifted* by Frances Ellen Watkins Harper (London: Penguin Books, 2010), xix, xxvii. Following the practice of women of color scholars, especially Koritha Mitchell and Xtine Yao, I refer to the author of Iola Leroy as "Watkins Harper" to emphasize her role as a public figure prior to her marriage and her writing *Iola Leroy*.
9. Yao's recent book *Disaffected* discusses Watkins Harper's *Iola Leroy* alongside two black woman physicians, Rebecca Lee Davis Crumper and Rebecca J. Cole. This important context elucidates how Iola Leroy models the objective passionlessness of Crumper and Cole as a means of distancing herself from the emotional weight of racist medicine upon the Black community (158), as well as taking Iola seriously as a medical professional who specializes in Black women's health whether as a nurse or future physician (145, 169).
10. Schuller, *The Biopolitics of Feeling*, 17.
11. Ibid. 93.
12. Ellen Samuels, *Fantasies of Identification: Disability, Gender, Race* (New York: New York University Press, 2014), 17.
13. Ibid. 17.
14. Barad, *Meeting the Universe Halfway*, 255.
15. Barad explains that the result of superposition is not a mixture of particles but an interference pattern. These are different things, as mixtures produce a homogeneous solution in which one subject wholly dissolves into another subject. Interference patterns, such as those produced by the which-slit experiment, do not create a solution of any kind. On the contrary, some particles will be sorted out of the product of the experiment (*Meeting the Universe Halfway* 268). If we apply this to our theorization of race as superposition, or race as phenomenon, then "amalgamation" is a misnomer because "amalgamation" means "mixture," and the product of genetic inheritance in any individual is not evenly distributed from both parents or sets of grandparents. However, I will use the rhetoric of amalgamation because of its prevalence in nineteenth-century studies scholarship.
16. Barad, *Meeting the Universe Halfway*, 280.
17. Ibid. 281. Her emphasis.
18. Ellis, *Antebellum Posthuman*, 140. Ellis is citing Christopher Peterson, who points out that posthumanists somehow expect scholars of color to simply "get over" the fact that all humans are animals. Ellis astutely recognizes that posthumanists may

not fully understand critical race theory's resistance to posthumanism as posthumanists' emphasis on the nonhuman risks eliding a history of human inequality that relies upon the rhetoric of animality for its authority (140, 142). But this is only part of the issue. Critical race theorists like Sylvia Wynter and Zakiyyah Iman Jackson are critical of posthumanism's continued reliance upon liberal humanism, a tradition that is itself entangled in colonial ideologies of race. Ellis rightly critiques both critical race theory and posthumanism for their commitment to the liberal human subject, which threatens to collapse both fields back into humanist hierarchies.

19. Ibid. 144.
20. Ibid. 159.
21. Schuller, *The Biopolitics of Feeling*, 25.
22. One aspect of my analysis that may be considered conspicuously missing: I take the animality of race science as fact, and as such, I do not recount the history of comparative anatomy in race science. In part, I adopt this pretense because there are many excellent scholarly texts that recount this history, including Londa Schiebinger's *Nature's Body*, Harriet A. Washington's *Medical Apartheid*, Cristin Ellis's *Antebellum Posthuman*, and Bridgitte Fielder's *Relative Races*. Another reason that I do not recount this history is because, unlike Louisa May Alcott and Charlotte Perkins Gilman, who *do* respond directly to Edward H. Clarke and S. Weir Mitchell respectively, Frances Ellen Watkins Harper does not directly respond to race scientists Samuel George Morton, Samuel Cartwright, Josiah Nott and George Glidden, and Louis Agassiz, among others, in her medical novel *Iola Leroy*. I read her as responding to anti-amalgamation law, the law of hypo-descent, and by extension of the two, the Comstock Law.
23. Bridgitte Fielder, *Relative Races: Genealogies of Interracial Kinship in Nineteenth-Century America* (Durham, NC and London: Duke University Press, 2020), 5.
24. Hames-Garcia, "How Real Is Race?" 325.
25. Ibid. 324.
26. Ibid. 325.
27. Barad, *Meeting the Universe Halfway*, 265.
28. Race is indeterminate, and therefore irreducible to biology because of its indeterminacy. Another way of saying this is: Race cannot be reduced to biological determinism because we cannot predict the results of ongoing material processes that produce race. Case in point: We know that all human offspring have twenty-three pairs of chromosomes, derived in equal amounts from each parent. This is a physical law of nature. However, there is no way to predict which proteins and the codes they carry will be passed on from each parent. We can determine probable outcomes, but no one outcome is guaranteed (Barad 265). Understanding race as superposition aligns with Schuller's characterization of race and sex during the nineteenth century as sociobiologically indeterminate. On the one hand, the construction of race follows predictable social rules and physical laws of nature, yet the results of multiple entanglements remain unpredictable and ongoing. There are probable outcomes based on observation or experience, which allows Hames-Garcia to suggest that his ability to hail a cab is easier than his Black friends' because taxi drivers judge potential clientele negatively based upon

visible racial markers. It is also why I can suggest that being detained and questioned at US airports is a xenophobic move that results from my traveling with an immigrant spouse within a country grappling with its own historically and politically informed social anxiety about undocumented immigration. However, these social and biological conditions are not fixed even if there are cues for likely interpretation.

29. Hazel Carby, *Reconstructing Womanhood: The Emergence of the Afro-American Woman Novelist* (Oxford: Oxford University Press, 1987), 85, 92–4.
30. Ibid. 89.
31. Ibid. 89.
32. Fiedler, *Relative Races*, 130.
33. Ibid. 140. Although most scholars agree that Watkins Harper does not exclusively appeal to an audience of white women for *Iola Leroy*, Hollis Robbins characterizes Iola as performing white womanhood to gain acceptance among Watkins Harper's readership. Some scholars have even criticized Watkins Harper for this conspicuous portrayal of whiteness. Yet it is worth noting that, as the "moral center of the novel" (Robbins, Introduction, xxvii), Iola performs white female domesticity akin to novelistic counterparts such as Rose Campbell, Dr. Zay, and Dr. Helen Brent, as well as among other non-medical women such as Marmee of *Little Women*, or even feminized non-women such as Dr. Alec Campbell of *Eight Cousins*. Perhaps we might read this as part of a trend in medical fiction bent on gaining authority for the protagonist, who must walk a fine line between gender-appropriate and professional behavior.
34. Carby, *Reconstructing Womanhood*, 80; Schuller, *The Biopolitics of Feeling*, 85, 84.
35. Davis, *Bodily and Narrative Forms*, 158–60. Historians Deidre Cooper Owens and Harriet A. Washington contextualize Cynthia J. Davis's findings that nineteenth-century medico-legal discourse legitimizes the rape of Black women. Owens and Washington alternately explain that white men rationalized their sexual abuse of Black women by indicating the lack of subjectivity among Black women before the law. "As the personal property of the master, black women had no social or legal protection," Washington explains. "They could not legally be raped" (45). Owens agrees, adding that the bodies of Black women were read presumptuously among white men as perpetually available and always willing (68). However, the reason that Black women were read as perpetually available and always willing is because several prominent nineteenth-century medical practitioners, researchers, and writers use comparative anatomy to establish Black women as hypersexual in a manner akin to primates.
36. Lisa Tetrault, *The Myth of Seneca Falls: Memory and the Women's Suffrage Movement, 1848–1898* (Chapel Hill: University of North Carolina Press, 2014), 5; see also Britt Rusert, *Fugitive Science: Empiricism and Freedom in Early African American Culture* (New York: New York University Press, 2017), 202.
37. Rusert, *Fugitive Science*, 198, 187, 203.
38. Ibid. 199.
39. Yao, *Disaffected*, 156, 163.
40. Koritha Mitchell, Introduction to *Iola Leroy; Or Shadows Uplifted* (Ontario: Broadview Press, 2018), 32.

41. Yao, *Disaffected*, 154.
42. Mitchell, Introduction, 49.
43. Mitchell, Introduction, 36.
44. For definition and use of *conversazione*, see Mitchell, Introduction, 31.
45. Schuller, *The Biopolitics of Feeling*, 85.
46. Kyla Schuller, *The Trouble with White Women: A Counterhistory of Feminism* (New York: Bold Type Books, 2021), 21, 34.
47. Schuller, *The Biopolitics of Feeling*, 10–14. Schuller explains in her introduction that this was a common belief among race scientists. To be unimpressible signifies objectification, since an unimpressible body is characteristically inert, overly malleable, and benumbed to pain. The belief that Black women were unimpressible may have been why physicians like Dr. J. Marion Sims refused anesthesia to Black female slaves like Lucy, Anarcha, and Betsy, on whom he experimented over a period of four years.
48. Ibid. 88.
49. See Tavera's "Her Body, *Herland*." Tavera argues that Gilman adopts a comparative anatomy approach for disseminating sexual hygiene, or sex education, discourse in *Herland* (1915). Gilman compares Herlander reproduction with hymenopteran (or aphid) reproduction to help her female readers imagine what body autonomy might guarantee: access to birth control, marriage equality, and personal and generational health. For Gilman, a feminist eugenic approach to sex education means describing the white female body in terms of aphids rather than flowers, while for Watkins Harper, a black eugenics approach means distancing animality from the Black female body altogether.
50. There are many good historical and literary studies of eugenics, including: Angelique Richardson's *Love and Eugenics in the Late Nineteenth Century: Rational Reproduction and the New Woman* (Oxford: Oxford University Press, 2003); Wendy Kline's *Building a Better Race: Gender, Sexuality, and Eugenics from the Turn of the Century to the Baby Boom* (Berkeley: University of California Press, 2001); Lois A. Cuddy's and Claire M. Roche's *Evolution and Eugenics in American Literature and Culture, 1880–1940* (Lewisburg, PA: Bucknell University Press, 2003), and Kimberly A. Hamlin's *From Eve to Evolution: Darwin, Science, and Women's Rights in Gilded Age America* (Chicago: University of Chicago Press, 2014). Eugenic principles as practiced by supporters of the eugenics movement seemingly adopt the Great Chain of Being and the animacy hierarchy as a point of reference for determining "good stock." Of course, this means that the eugenics movement considered the best "stock" middle-to-upper-class white men and women with sound mental and physical health. Charlotte Perkins Gilman was an outspoken advocate for the eugenics movement, a point of pride for which contemporary scholars harshly criticize her. I discuss Gilman's specific eugenic beliefs in R_x 4 alongside scholarly criticism of those eugenic beliefs, but it is important to acknowledge that historian Mary Ziegler terms feminist activism on behalf of the eugenics movement "eugenic feminism." Although this sounds like a contradiction in terms, Ziegler claims it was not for women like Gilman, and, I would add, Watkins Harper. Eugenic feminists imagined that the formerly "private" sphere of motherhood would become part and parcel of

the public sphere itself through scientific principles including eugenic science, and this was a liberatory move for them and their sex. For more on Ziegler's concept of eugenic feminism, see Mary Ziegler, "Eugenic Feminism: Mental Hygiene, the Women's Movement, and the Campaign for Eugenic Legal Reform, 1900–1935," *Harvard Journal of Law & Gender* 31, no. 1 (2008): 211–35.
51. Schuller, *The Biopolitics of Feeling*, 90.
52. Theri Alyce Pickens, *Black Madness::Mad Blackness* (Durham, NC and London: Duke University Press, 2019), 14.
53. Frances Ellen Watkins Harper, *Iola Leroy, or Shadows Uplifted* (1892), ed. Koritha Mitchell (Ontario: Broadview Press, 2018), 88. Hereafter referred to in the body of the text.
54. Andrea Stone, *Black Well-Being: Health and Selfhood in Antebellum Black Literature* (Gainesville: University of Florida Press, 2016), 123–4. Stone even argues that fear of reporting among victims persists today in the twenty-first century because of this cultural trend of refusing to recognize women as subjects with a right to legal recourse.
55. Cary Wolfe, *Before the Law: Humans and Other Animals in a Biopolitical Frame* (Chicago and London: The University of Chicago Press, 2013), 8.
56. Ibid. 8–9.
57. Ibid. 9.
58. Chen, *Animacies*, 45, 53. Chen explains this as the principle of subordination, which is both characterized by sentence structure and a linguistic hierarchy of animacy.
59. Cary Wolfe, *Before the Law*, 18.
60. Ibid. 44–9. I take Wolfe's point that humans and nonhuman animals are both left vulnerable by the law because they are not considered "grievable." Yet I take issue with the term "animal holocaust" for a couple of reasons. First, as Naomi Mandel explains, "holocaust" derives from the Greek for "sacrifice by fire" (40). Sacrifice invokes a sacred act of offering a slaughtered animal to God, but the kind of "animal holocaust" that Wolfe invokes is profane rather than sacred. Moreover, Mandel details the tensions in Holocaust studies of using the word "Holocaust" for genocide of the Jews during World War II. Many scholars and survivors prefer the word "Shoah" because of its Hebrew origins and sacred tenor (40). The term "Holocaust" is often employed for a post-Holocaust world and a non-survivor audience. It is a word that helps us try to make sense of the senseless massacre, and yet it is often used to invoke a horrific event that is unspeakable (42). If the term "holocaust," capitalized or otherwise, is contentious even in relationship to the genocide of Jews during World War II, it is even more contentious in the context of factory farming, and therefore I am uncomfortable invoking it in the latter context. Later in this R_x, I will return to Naomi Mandel's concept of the unspeakable from *Against the Unspeakable*.
61. Koritha Mitchell, *From Slave Cabins to the White House: Homemade Citizenship in African American Culture* (Urbana: University of Illinois Press, 2020), 6, 22.
62. Robbins, Introduction, xxiii. Watkins Harper bolsters the realism of her narrative by "dramatiz[ing] the benefits of reading newspapers and keeping current of political and cultural affairs" (xxxi). Watkins Harper was herself well read, as evidenced by

accurate references to Fort Sumter, Bull Run, and the infamous Union general "Beast" Butler, all of which are referenced in the narrative.
63. Many historians have told variations of the story of how J. Marion Sims surgically experimented on Black female slaves before marketing the surgery to white women patients. Others have also recounted how he began the Women's Hospital in New York City, the first US hospital to specialize in gynecology. Both of these histories are steeped in racist practices. For a fully contextualized history of these events, I recommend Deborah Kuhn McGregor's *From Midwives to Medicine: The Birth of American Gynecology* (New Brunswick, NJ: Rutgers University Press, 1998), Deirdre Cooper Owens's *Medical Bondage: Race, Gender, and the Origins of American Gynecology* (Athens: University of Georgia Press, 2017), and Harriet A. Washington's *Medical Apartheid*.
64. Owens, *Medical Bondage*, 46.
65. Ibid. 45. In one particular episode, plantation nurse and slave Mildred Graves embarrassed not one but two white male attending physicians of Mrs. Leake when Graves successfully delivered Mrs. Leake's baby after both physicians declared that mother and infant would die in childbirth (Owens 65). They did not.
66. Ibid. 61.
67. Yao, *Disaffected*, 169, 166–7.
68. Owens, *Medical Bondage*, 49.
69. Ibid. 49.
70. Chen, *Animacies*, 94.
71. Ibid. 111.
72. Ibid. 114.
73. Frisken, "Obscenity, Free Speech, and 'Sporting News' in 1870s America," 558–9.
74. Ibid. 562.
75. Ibid. 564.
76. Fielder, *Relative Races*, 201–5. Anti-miscegenation law was fully and finally struck down with the Supreme Court Case *Loving v. Virginia*, 388 U.S. 1, a civil rights case that lifted the ban on interracial marriage in the United States.
77. Sylvia Wynter, "Unsettling the Coloniality of Being/Power/Truth/Freedom: Towards the Human, After Man, It's Overrepresentation—An Argument," *The New Centennial Review* 3, no. 3 (2003), 314.
78. Ibid. 325.
79. Ibid. 330.
80. Zakiyyah Iman Jackson, "Animal: New Directions in the Theorization of Race and Posthumanism," *Feminist Studies* 39, no. 3 (2013), 671.
81. Although Wolfe primarily derives his theory of "before the law" from Jacques Derrida's essay "Before the Law" (1992), the title of which was itself derived from Franz Kafka's parable *Before the Law* (1915), Wolfe nods to Judith Butler's own theorizing of the law as an apparatus for constructing identity with the appearance of a determined and fixed entity when, in fact, it isn't. In *Before the Law*, Wolfe cites Butler's *Precarious Life: The Powers of Mourning and Violence* (2004), which explores how post-9/11 American culture determines which lives are grief-worthy. However, Butler explored the implications of "before the law"

and its role in constructing grieveable subjects as early as *Gender Trouble: Feminism and the Subversion of Identity* (New York and London: Routledge, 2006 [1990]) and "Imitation and Gender Insubordination," from *The Lesbian and Gay Studies Reader* (New York and London: Routledge, 1993). In *Gender Trouble*, Butler observes how juridical power "produces" "a subject before the law" and then "conceals" other(ed) subjects "in order to invoke that discursive formation," i.e. the law itself, "as a naturalized foundational premise that subsequently legitimates that law's own regulatory hegemony (*Gender Trouble* 3, 11). And so, we are once again back to Michel Foucault, as Butler considers the production of subjects before the law as a form of biopower. Butler perhaps makes her point more explicit in "Imitation and Gender Insubordination" when she describes how oppression functions through the act of suppression, censorship, or prohibition: "Here it becomes important to recognize that oppression works not merely through acts of overt prohibition, but covertly, through the constitution of viable subjects and through the corollary constitution of a domain of unviable (un)subjects—objects we might call them—who are neither named nor prohibited within the economy of the law" (312). Names, as words, matter because they affect and effect, calling us into and out of being.
82. Fielder, *Relative Races*, 11, 246 n. 19. Londa Schiebinger takes this history back even further into the eighteenth century, where she identifies Petrus Camper as the father of craniometry. In 1792, Camper published a study of evolutionary race in which he was "one of the first to suggest that skull measurements could illuminate the natural relationship among apes, Negroes, and Europeans" (149). Morton builds upon the work of Camper in *Crania Americana*.
83. Schiebinger, *Nature's Body*, 158.
84. Ibid. 65, 91, 164.
85. Anne Fausto-Sterling, *Sexing the Body: Gender Politics and the Construction of Sexuality* (New York: Perseus Books, 2000); see also Samuels, *Fantasies of Identification*, 17–18. Fausto-Sterling especially critiques our continued reliance upon measuring hormones to accomplish the work of sex differentiation (193).
86. Winthrop D. Jordan, "Historical Origins of the One-Drop Rule in the United States," *Journal of Critical Mixed Race Studies* 1, no. 1 (2014), 104, <https://escholarship.org/uc/item/91g761b3> (accessed December 12, 2021).
87. Ibid. 101.
88. Ibid. 99. Note the phrase "believed to have," since physical proof of genealogical descent was not necessary to determine Blackness.
89. Ibid. 101.
90. Samuels, *Fantasies of Identification*, 91.
91. Ibid. 87.
92. Ibid. 94.
93. Fielder, *Relative Races*, 4.
94. Ibid. 63.
95. Ibid. 63. In the 1790s, Dr. Benjamin Rush also began disseminating the belief that blackness is contagious through sexual relations (39), giving further medical authority to anti-amalgamation law and social behavior of same-race marriages.

96. Schuller, *The Biopolitics of Feeling*, 93.
97. Barad, *Meeting the University Halfway*, 139.
98. Ibid. 352.
99. One of Brené Brown's kitschy—and catchy—phrases is "People are hard to Hate Close Up. Move in." It is, in fact, the title of one of her chapters from *Braving the Wilderness: The Quest for True Belonging and the Courage to Stand Alone* (New York: Random House, 2017). What Brown means by this phrase is that individuals develop hate for specific populations of people based upon the stereotype created by cultural narratives and disseminated by various forms of popular media. When we actually meet someone who belongs within a population that is the object of our hate, we struggle to hate the individual because they perform a nuanced perspective of the population rather than the expected stereotype. Brown even argues that the rhetoric of hate is actually a reflection of our own integrity, or lack thereof: "When we reduce Muslim people to terrorists or Mexicans to 'illegals' or police officers to pigs, it says nothing at all about the people we're attacking," Brown explains of the inefficacy of stereotypes in the formation of community identities. "It does, however, say volumes about who we are and the degree to which we're operating in our integrity" (75–6). I am not sure Watkins Harper would agree with this position, though she might, depending upon the degree of engagement between members of would-be opposing communities, as in the case of Dr. Latrobe and Dr. Latimer.
100. Schuller, *The Biopolitics of Feeling*, 86.
101. Fielder, *Relative Races*, 140.
102. Barad, *Meeting the University Halfway*, 265.
103. Mandel, *Against the Unspeakable*, 4.
104. Ibid. 214.
105. Ibid. 216. In vernacular terms, "gray area" denotes an ill-defined situation or condition for an existing set of rules. Mandel defines it as a structure that creates the conditions of complicity when a community loses the limits that define them as a population and must reconstruct the bonds of community through complicity. I am invoking both meanings in my use of the phrase "gray area," since the recognition of one's complicity in a system automatically creates a sense of loss of identity, which thereby requires a reconstruction of identity based upon newfound information and a newly configured relationship to the system itself.
106. Ibid. 214.
107. Deborah M. Horvitz, *Literary Trauma: Sadism, Memory, and Sexual Violence in American Women's Fiction* (Albany: SUNY Press, 2000), 18–19.
108. Charon, *Narrative Medicine*, 33.
109. Ibid. 33.
110. Ibid. 180.
111. Cynthia J. Davis contextualizes Iola Leroy in relationship to medical discourse on "panmixia," which pseudoscientists such as William Benjamin Smith posit as a disease that weakens the constitution of the body because of black blood in white bodies, but also serves as a "deadly enemy" to the south and its way of life (159, 166). The cultural narrative of amalgamation-as-disease likely existed prior

to and during the time that Watkins Harper wrote *Iola Leroy*, though it is worth pointing out that Smith did not coin the term "panmixia," or theorize its etiology, until 1905 with the publication of his clearly eugenic book, *The Color Line: A Brief in Behalf of the Unborn.*
112. Jordan, "Historical Origins of the One-Drop Rule in the United States," 112.
113. Davis, *Bodily and Narrative Forms*, 169.
114. Marlowe Daly-Galeano defines the nursing narrative as a genre of literature that is characterized prominently by the representation of acts of nursing. Louisa May Alcott founded the genre of the nursing narrative when she wrote and published *Hospital Sketches*, a collection of loosely autobiographical stories about her experience as a nurse during the Civil War. Daly-Galeano claims that the nursing narrative draws upon generic conventions from travel writing, journalistic reporting, the sentimental novel, and the American prose romance (à la Hawthorne) in the creation of a wholly new genre, all of which certainly characterize Watkins Harper's writing style in *Iola Leroy*.
115. Mandel, *Against the Unspeakable*, 19.
116. Ibid. 170, 248, n. 2. Historians agree that 15 to 20 million people is a more realistic estimate of slave victims. Since we cannot know the precise number, I invoke Toni Morrison's dedication of *Beloved* to the "sixty million and more" as a rhetorical strategy of emphasizing scale.

R$_x$ 4

AFFECTIVE FEAR: VULNERABILITY AND RISK IN ANTI-VD CAMPAIGN COUNTERNARRATIVES

Sexual energies coalesced around New York City circa 1913 as Charlotte Perkins Gilman once again took Comstockery to task in the wake of the Anti-Venereal Disease Campaign, which opined a new risk to impressi(ona)ble youth who suffered under a "conspiracy of silence" created by a culture of censorship. Comstock knew he was losing the war against obscenity. His conviction rate during the last three years of his life and reign fell from 76 percent to 40 percent. Only forty-five defendants served jail time between 1912 and 1915.[1] Comstock, therefore, adopted a different tactic in enforcing censorship law: He strove to destroy the obscene text rather than punish the obscene writer, publisher, bookseller, or distributor.[2] Yet the damage was done. Threat of shame from search and seizure alone was debilitating, much less the process of prosecution, regardless of whether conviction was imminent.[3] Comstock made shame commonplace in sexual hygiene discourse. Supporters and activists on behalf of the Anti-VD Campaign capitalized on fear rhetoric and the culture of shame to justify the need for public sex education programs in the military, the school system, or hospitals and health clinics. Evidence of their public health education tactics are perhaps best encapsulated in the deluge of Anti-VD Campaign films produced during the 1910s: *Damaged Goods* (1914), *The Black Stork* (1915), *Open Your Eyes* (1919), *The Solitary Sin* (1919), *Fit to Win* (1919), *Wild Oats* (1919), *End of the Road* (1919), and *The Gift of Life* (1920), among many, many others. The first of these American sex hygiene films, the now-lost film *Damaged Goods*, established the tone and message of the campaign itself. The film became a cultural icon, a kind of pulp fiction film or "cult classic."[4]

Itself an adaptation from a theatrical play, *Damaged Goods* became so popular that Upton Sinclair collaborated with the original playwright, Eugene Brieux, to adapt the play/film into a novel of the same name.[5] Even Charlotte Perkins Gilman and Annie Nathan Meyer knew of the film and the play (and possibly the novel), and they explicitly write against its seduction narrative, which victimizes young male syphilitics and vilifies their young female sexual partners. During a period of censorship in America, the syphilis scare sanctioned sex education as a public health initiative yet the etiology of medical discourse located syphilis in the sensualized female body, and especially the body of the prostitute. Authors of feminist medical fiction would not accept this narrative designating women as responsible for the venereal disease epidemic. Annie Nathan Meyer insists in her novel *Helen Brent, M.D.* (1892) that diseases are themselves unsexed, and neither woman nor man is responsible for their dissemination. She instead implicates a lack of comprehensive sex education and the white male censors responsible for the cultural "conspiracy of silence" in allowing this "social evil" to spread. Charlotte Perkins Gilman makes a similar argument in *The Crux* (1911) and "The Vintage" (1916). Unlike that of Meyer, "the crux" of Gilman's argument does not center on individual women, their reproductive rights, or their personal access to sex education. Gilman offers a eugenic argument on behalf of sex education for collective womanhood and race health, since she feared venereal diseases were hereditary and would diminish (white) race health over several generations.

In this R_x, I argue that Meyer's *Helen Brent, M.D.* and Gilman's *The Crux* and "The Vintage" engage in a counter-campaign against the Anti-VD Campaign that explicitly promotes "a woman's right to know" about her sexual health, or what we might today call "informed consent." Their efforts work to rescript the popular Anti-VD Campaign seduction narrative originating from the independently produced film *Damaged Goods*, which represents venereal disease as a rationale for implementing public sex education programs. Because the film was co-opted by government departments for institutionalized sex education, federal endorsement of the film suggests a broader public endorsement beyond Comstockian censorship of medicalized sex education. Meyer's and Gilman's medical fiction reacts to and deviates from this public endorsement and its socially accepted narrative, which blames women—and especially prostitutes—for the spread of syphilis and gonorrhea. Instead of the military, Meyer opts for hospitals and clinics as her method for deploying sex education. Gilman does not specify a preferred location, at least not in *The Crux* or "The Vintage."[6] Nevertheless, both Gilman and Meyer emphasize open communication in doctor-patient relations in a manner that prefigures Rita Charon's practice of narrative medicine, and they further adopt venereal disease as their point of departure for justifying public sex education.

Although Gilman and Meyer engage in an emerging discourse at the fin de siècle concerning "a woman's right to know," their work derives from that of their predecessors and specifically from Louisa May Alcott, who articulates an early version of this call for sex education among young women when Rose Campbell declares, "'I intend to know what kills me if I can.'" As we might recall from R_x 1 of this book, Rose then proceeds to study the hip joints of her manikin during Uncle Alec's human physiology course.[7] Meyer similarly echoes calls for the right to what we might call informed consent, using a phrase that recalls the popular rallying cry among women phrenologists of "know thyself."[8] Dr. Helen Brent, who is a gynecologist—*not* a phrenologist—tells her protégé Lotus Bayley that her reason for becoming a doctor "is to make all women find themselves . . . their complete, rounded selves,"[9] and specifically, their corporeal selves, so that they know what threats to their health exist in the built environment. Gilman reprises this call in *The Crux* when she diagnoses ignorance from censorship as the contemporary cultural illness of the day. Using Grandmother Pettigrew as her spokesperson, Gilman highlights how a fear of impressibility among young women creates the conditions for health vulnerabilities to the very population responsible for race health. "'[W]e bring up girls to think it is not proper to know anything about the worst before them,'" Grandmother Pettigrew explains to her granddaughter Vivian, citing syphilis and gonorrhea as two of the "worst" threats lying in wait for unmarried women.[10] Yet Grandmother Pettigrew—and by extension Gilman—argues, "[T]he young girls are precisely the ones *to* know!" (139, her emphasis).

Although Meyer and Gilman rightly call for informed consent in the wake of sexist medicine, their emphasis on class and race respectively raises questions about how medical science and sex education implicate disability in theories of the female body. During the yellow fever epidemic of 1793, medical practitioners insisted that African Americans were immune to yellow fever, a falsity that resulted in greater exposure, vulnerability, and death among Black Americans.[11] Similarly, the cultural narrative surrounding the 1918 Spanish flu epidemic in the United States conflated the spread of the flu with soldiers coming home from the war, such that medical health experts described the virus as a new invader from abroad.[12] The syphilis epidemic informing Gilman's *The Crux* further coincides with the end of World War I and the Spanish flu epidemic, yet the cultural narrative surrounding syphilis identified women as responsible for its spread.[13] Our current global pandemic is no different. If anything, the 2020 COVID-19 pandemic echoes the cultural narratives of the yellow fever, Spanish flu, and syphilis epidemics in the United States, reminding us that we have yet to confront—let alone resolve—a centuries-long history of racism, xenophobia, and misogyny. Worse, the popularity of *Damaged Goods* led to a deluge of Anti-VD Campaign films that produced racist and classist variations on the traditional sexist seduction narrative popularized by *Damaged Goods*.

One such propagandist film produced under the guise of public health initiatives is *The Black Stork* (1915), which historians Martin S. Pernick and Harriet A. Washington consider a key cultural production that not only perpetuates the narrative of black hypersexuality but also actively de-animates Black bodies, in a rhetorical move that legitimizes later medical experimentation on Black bodies in the form of the Tuskegee Syphilis Study and the Norplant Depo-Provera Trials. Keeping this historical framework in mind, I revisit *The Crux* as a site of eugenic imaginative experimentation in which Gilman's marginal(ized) characters Jeanne Jeaune and her son Theophile perform race and queer affect in ways that crip/queer Gilman's (p)rescriptions through the lens of Black medico-sexual history. The outbreak narrative of *The Crux*, and of the broader Anti-VD Campaign within which it engages, exposes disability as affect—as engaging in the ongoing process of superposition—alongside race. New materialist critiques of the 1980s HIV/AIDS epidemic find that narratives of contagion emerge from a misunderstanding of how immune systems work.[14] On the one hand, such misunderstandings rhetorically dis-place specific communities in kinship with—or in proximity to—the perceived origins of the disease. This is yet another version of de-animacy à la Mel Y. Chen. On the other hand, this displacement creates narrative tension, for while people outside the gay and lesbian community narrate the experience of illness in terms of disability or debility, as alternatively "crippling," "toxic," or "dying from within," those within the medical community—including immunologists, volunteers, and hotline workers—discuss illness as a space for community-building, for bringing marginalized groups together.[15] Priscilla Wald describes the dissonance of outbreak narratives in terms of contagion and communicability: "people literally and figuratively bump[] up against each other," communicating and spreading diseases, as well as cultural ideas about diseases.[16]

How we tell the story of illness matters. In this R_x, I tell a different story of disability and the female body, one that not only challenges the rhetoric of fear and disability in our narratives of sexuality, sexual hygiene, and sex education but also posits narrative and disability as affective agents capable of shifting medical discourse toward greater inclusivity. I first provide a historical context for the Anti-Venereal Disease (Anti-VD) Campaign, which emerged from the social hygiene movement and propelled institutional sex education in the wake of Comstockian censorship. This historical context serves to elucidate how Meyer and Gilman rescript the Anti-VD Campaign seduction narrative popularized by *Damaged Goods* in their works of medical fiction *Helen Brent, M.D.* and *The Crux* and "The Vintage," respectively. Using crip affect, I then rescript the marginal(ized) characters of color Jeanne Jeaune and Theophile from Gilman's *The Crux* alongside historical critiques of *The Black Stork* to articulate my own critique of eugenic marriage, a program which Gilman not only supported but which gained legal authority in several states. Tracing the seduction narrative through Anti-VD Campaign films and counternarratives of "a woman's right to know" in medical fiction exposes fear as the operative rhetorical device affecting subjectivity at the fin de siècle. And yet, if the COVID-19 pandemic has taught us anything, it's that affective fear continually works on us, shaping our beliefs, behaviors, and public actions in the wake of an unknown future.

Cripping the Anti-VD Campaign Seduction Narrative

During the 1913–14 academic year, the first public institutionalized sex education program was implemented in Chicago secondary schools. Ella Flagg Young, superintendent of Chicago schools, appointed a Committee on Sex Hygiene, which designed a course of three "personal purity" lectures to be conducted by outside male physicians at each of Chicago's twenty-one high schools. Girls and boys were taught in separate classrooms and subjects included physiology, venereal disease prevention, and moral hygiene practices such as "continence, cleanliness, and clean thoughts."[17] The program was shut down due to religious opposition (predominately led by the Catholic community) and published excerpts from physicians' talks were prohibited under Comstock law.[18] Sex education, however, resurfaced in popular discourse during World War I. Fearing soldiers would return from abroad with untold "foreign" diseases, in 1917 US Secretary of War Newton Baker founded the Commission on Training Camp Activities (CTCA) as a means of combating venereal diseases.[19] This required program was implemented for new army recruits during basic combat training and, like the failed Chicago public school sex education program, it focused extensively on physiology and venereal disease prevention. As Jeffrey P. Moran observes, "the training camps made it clear that the young soldier was not the same as the young civilian," and thus military sex educators were far more explicit about sexual intercourse and the dangers of venereal disease. CTCA instructors "did not shrink from displaying the most grotesque consequences of syphilis and gonorrhea."[20]

From its formal organization, American sex education programs—not simply "health" and "disease"—have been framed within a military context. However, this framework also strongly relies upon fear rhetoric and scare tactics. Emily Martin finds such rhetorical strategies still at work in contemporary American immunology discourse, which indicates that a cultural or political unconscious from early twentieth-century sex education theory informs our concepts of bodies, health, and disease well into the twenty-first century. In her "Historical Overview," Martin does, in fact, attribute military imagery to early twentieth-century bacteriology: "This notion [of defense] was clearly already present in imagery from the early decades of the century," as early as a 1918 medical text, *The Primer of Sanitation and Physiology* by J. W. Ritchie. In this "primer," Ritchie depicts the body as a "castle of health" in which "[t]he two outer defenses," or curtain walls, "'[k]eep germs from being spread about,' and '[g]uard the gateways by which they enter the body,'" Martin explicates.[21] She compares Ritchie's rhetoric with a 1955 article from *Life*, "Science Moves in on Viruses" by R. Coughlan, which "shows the body as a seamless whole, its surface besieged by germs of all sorts, some drilling away with drill bits, and some slain and marked by the victory flags of effective vaccines."[22] Significantly, in the illustration accompanying Coughlan's article, the physical body of a woman replaces the castle itself, but metaphors of "invasion," "defense," and "victory" remain.

If we believe contemporary medicine has moved beyond such metaphors, Martin finds we must reevaluate—and complicate—our rhetorical strategies, for "the metaphor of warfare against an external enemy" dominates cultural narratives of immunology in popular media and allopathic medicine.[23] Martin teases out these metaphors in articles from *Reader's Digest*, *Time*, and *US News*; two major film productions, *The Fantastic Voyage* (1966) and *The Immortal* (1970–71); science teaching films for grade school, middle school, high school, and college audiences; articles from academic journals such as *Immunology Today*; and interviews with several scientists and medical professionals currently practicing in the field. Her anthropological work is comprehensive, covering a variety of texts from the 1950s through the 1990s, yet she ultimately pronounces this dominant military metaphor limiting regardless of period. It reinforces a binary model of self/non-self as well as, I might add, disabled/able-bodied, black/white, and female/male, since the invading subject is often cast in terms of gender, race, and class.[24] Macrophages responsible for "cleaning up dirt and debris, including 'dead bodies,'" are labeled "housekeepers" and are thereby raced or feminized, while microphages become "big, primitive garbage collectors," "a cleanup crew," or "roving scavengers," thereby adopting a lower-class position.[25] There are even heterosexual narratives in which a body's T cells are cast as "a brawny, brutal he-man" and a suitable partner for mature, "upper-class female" B cells, which together must (re)produce antibodies against invading antigens.[26]

In spite of the Comstock Law, or perhaps because of it, social hygiene reformers sensed an acute need for implementing public sex education programs beyond military institutions as a means of preventing the spread of venereal disease. Syphilis and gonorrhea, specifically, were perceived as an epidemic threatening "race health," and prostitutes were considered uniquely responsible for their spread. Young men and women, by contrast, were innocent victims lured into their "social evil." This new spin on the popular seduction narrative appears in multiple sex hygiene films from the Progressive Era, including: *Damaged Goods* (1914), *The Black Stork* (1915), *Open Your Eyes* (1919), *The Solitary*

Sin (1919), *Fit to Win* (1919), *Wild Oats* (1919), *End of the Road* (1919), and *The Gift of Life* (1920). Even if we did not know the stock narrative of these films, the euphemistic titles alone are suggestive of a culture of shame, eugenics, and (re)productive futurity. Men and women are shamed for sowing their "wild oats," engaging in "the solitary sin" of masturbation, damaging the "goods" of reproduction and futurity, which are "the gift of life" in the form of children. Audiences are expected to "open their eyes" to the "damage" they will cause in spreading venereal disease among future generations. Although the primary intended audience was young men because of the impressibility of young women, eventually both parties became responsible for the perpetuity of good race health.

Sex hygiene films replace the Major Peter Sanford-type character from popular seduction narrative Hannah Webster Foster's *The Coquette* (1797) with a prostitute. Eliza Wharton—the innocent, naive victim type—appears in multiple characters from married couples to college boys or soldiers. Interestingly, most of these films place men in the victim role, not women, indicating pathologization of the female body within medical discourse. By the Comstock Law era, medical authorities had relocated the origins of venereal disease from female bodies generally to female prostitutes specifically.[27] Nevertheless, a female body—that of the prostitute—is implicated in this Anti-VD cultural narrative, a phenomenon Gilman reflects in her own counternarratives. Importantly, race and sexuality play a key role in the narrative, as both victim and villain are white and heterosexual. Andrea Stone suggests that Harriet Jacobs reworks aspects of the seduction narrative in *Incidents in the Life of a Slave Girl* (1861), effectively downplaying Mr. Sands' vice to grant Linda Brent greater autonomy over her own sexuality.[28] Yet, as we have seen in the previous R_x, because Black women were not subjects before the law they could not be cast as seducers nor as victims of seduction. The cultural narrative simply would not translate and the message would be lost on its audience, a point at which Gilman further hints in her own reworking of the seduction narrative through the character of Jeanne Jeaune. In fact, in the Anti-VD Campaign film *The Black Stork*, the original description of our protagonist Claude is one of a mixed-race man: Claude is the product of his (white) slave-owner grandfather and (Black) slave grandmother. In the 1927 remastered version, Claude's backstory is revised. He is now the grandson of a wealthy white man and his "unclean" white servant girl.[29] As we might recall from the previous R_x, anti-amalgamation laws were still in place in many states during this period of legal stasis between 1887 and 1948. Yet, for the sake of conveying a clear affective message that goads an audience toward eugenic marriage, Anti-VD Campaign films must specify the origin of the disease. Black bodies muddy the narrative because they were already culturally read as diseased—and therefore, contagious—due to their biological composition.

Every adaptation of *Damaged Goods*—whether play, novel, or film—appears to corroborate a unified narrative etiology for syphilis: the female prostitute. The first American sex hygiene film, *Damaged Goods*, was originally produced for the military in 1914, yet it became an independent cultural icon during the 1910s.[30] When the Mutual Film Corporation re-released it in 1915 for civilian audiences, it became a smash hit, generating $2 million in box-office revenue. Since the original film is lost, historians speculate that its plot follows that of Eugene Brieux's play *Damaged Goods*, which opened in New York City in 1913.[31] Scenes and captions from the herald, or movie poster, for the 1914 film provide further evidence that suggests the plot of the film closely followed the original play (see Figures 4.1 and 4.2).[32] The play, like the film, relates the story of a young man who contracts syphilis. Given his bourgeois status, he marries to collect a dowry, ignoring his physician's warning against marriage. He subsequently infects his wife and child, and although many reviewers considered the play a "medical sermon," it is unclear whether it resolved in the same manner as the film with the young man's suicide.[33] The film does, however, contain specific details that share in the predominant Anti-VD seduction narrative: "George Dupont [the male protagonist] was described as 'a young man of excellent home,' a lawyer by profession, who is set to marry 'a prominent social belle.' George gets syphilis from a 'street walker,'" or prostitute.[34]

Figure 4.1 Herald for *Damaged Goods* (1914), an American silent film starring Richard Bennett. The herald boasts the original Broadway cast.

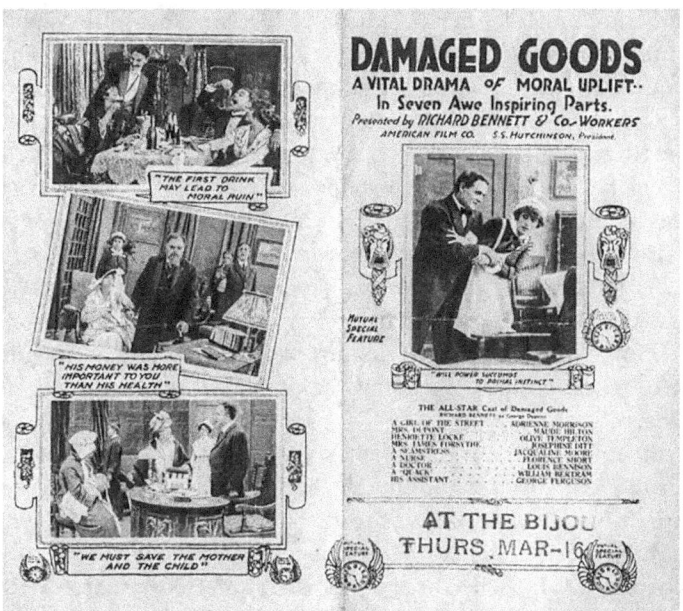

Figure 4.2 Herald for *Damaged Goods* (1914), featuring Richard Bennett in the starring role of George Dupont, who originated the role in the Broadway play. This herald contains the full cast listing.

Eric Schaefer and Annette Kuhn observe that, as in most Anti-VD Campaign films, prostitutes are identified as the principal cause of venereal disease.[35] Further, Schaefer claims, the narrative itself is cast within a gender and class conflict: "[V]enereal disease was seen as a malady of the Other inflicted on the bourgeoisie," the "Other" representing both gender and class.[36] In other words, using the culturally dominant military rhetoric of immunology, the male body is invaded by a diseased female subject and is thereby feminized; his bourgeois status is invaded by that same subject's lower-class status, and his class status is thereby threatened. Historian Martin S. Pernick finds this narrative of contagion variously interpreted, at least among the literati of the period. Upton Sinclair and George Bernard Shaw interpret *Damaged Goods* as "blaming venereal disease on poverty and the class system, ignorance and traditional morality, not on the poor" or "the poor prostitute."[37] Sinclair and Shaw observe systemic injustice at play, not the pathologizing of a specific class or sex. Gilman emphatically disagrees, faulting prostitution for the communicability of syphilis in her own Anti-VD counternarrative, *The Crux*. She even specifically calls out three prostitutes by name: Coralie, Anastasia, and Estelle (103). Jeanne Jeaune, the former madam of a brothel who also suffers from syphilis and communicates her condition to her son Theophile, shames her former girls and their frequent patron Morton Elder to stop the spread of syphilis in their community through public health initiatives like sex education. Gilman does not allow the seduction narrative of *Damaged Goods* to play out in *The Crux*, no matter how hard Morton tries to kiss Vivian without her consent or force her declaration of love when she is not willing. Vivian is twice saved by a doctor. First, Dr. Richard Hale interrupts Morton's attempt to seduce Vivian when he stumbles upon them in the garden on his way to the boardinghouse; and then Dr. Jane Bellair discloses to Vivian her discovery that Morton is a syphilitic, while also giving her a brief sex education and confessing her own story and Jeanne Jeaune's story of acquiring syphilis. Gilman imagines the role of the doctor as essential to stopping the communicability of syphilis and the seduction narrative.

In her theatrical review of Brieux's *Damaged Goods*, published in *The Forerunner* (1913), Gilman admits that her desire to see the play came from a place of horrified curiosity: "I was told that 'Damaged Goods' was far more terrible than 'Ghosts,'" she confesses, opening her review with a comparison of the two plays.[38] Henrik Ibsen's *Ghosts* (1881) does deal with venereal disease. It is, in fact, one of the earliest works of fiction to address the subject, as the protagonist of the play, Helen Alving, debates whether to comply with her son Oswald's request for euthanasia over his suffering the late stages of syphilis. Gilman pronounces both plays "terrible" (though *Ghosts* is worse), not least because the subject is terrible, but also because none of the characters in *Damaged Goods* are sympathetic. "Two things presented themselves sharply," she criticizes of Brieux's drama. "[T]he naïve, unmitigated selfishness of every person appearing" in the play and the fact that "no one suggested warning the young women who confront this terrible danger when they marry."[39] Gilman consoles herself with the prospect of political awareness as she reasons that perhaps "it is a good thing to have the subject brought before" the public in the form of a popular drama, even in the flawed form of *Damaged Goods*. Yet she still fears the danger that this play poses to continuing the "conspiracy of silence" among women as well as the further dissemination of narratives that blame women for contagion. In contrast with Gilman's lengthier critique, Annie Nathan Meyer offers almost zero evaluation of *Damaged Goods* in her letter to the editor of *The Bookman*. In the selfsame critique of Edna Kenton's book review of *Helen Brent, M.D.*, Meyer offhandedly prides herself that her book on the syphilis outbreak narrative came before *Damaged Goods*. Yet she points out that her book was satirical, whereas *Damaged Goods* was not: "For all the satisfaction that I have taken in the fact that she has pointed out my story antedated Brieux's *Damaged Goods*, nevertheless it is a little trying to have such palpable satire as this entirely overlooked."[40]

Pernick characterizes both *Damaged Goods* and *The Black Stork* as melodrama meant to appeal to the logic of science through emotional rhetoric. Because we feel for George DuPont's multiple losses—the loss of his health, and eventually the loss of his life—we might then accept the logical premise of eugenic science, which tells us to vet our future spouse based on heredity so as to prevent recreating disease or disability. Gilman accepted the scientific premise, though she was moved more for DuPont's wife and child than DuPont himself. Meanwhile, Meyer prided herself on the fact that she got it right first before Brieux—or Gilman. In their versions of the Anti-VD Campaign seduction narrative, Gilman and Meyer shift their concern from the victimized bourgeois male to the victimized middle- to upper-class female. In "The Vintage," Howard Faulkner, a young doctor, witnesses his beloved Leslie Vauremont Barrington Montroy marry another man, Rodger Moore, a man Dr. Faulkner knows to be infected with syphilis, since Moore is Faulkner's patient. Gilman describes Leslie as "a girl of good family" from "one of our proudest Southern states" with "a string of family names" indicating her noblesse oblige.[41] Gilman essentially reenacts *Damaged Goods* with minor differences. Rodger Moore becomes George Dupont, a young bourgeois who marries "a prominent social belle," Leslie. Like George Dupont, Rodger Moore marries Leslie for her dowry. He, therefore, becomes responsible for diluting upper-class society by "invading" one of their own, an innocent, "pure" young woman with "blazing health" (297). He also causes his son to be born diseased—which Gilman recasts as "disabled" or "crippled"—and later, his wife's death. Like *Damaged Goods*, Gilman includes the protesting (male) physician, Dr. Howard Faulkner, who maintains doctor-patient confidentiality against his better judgment. Unlike *Damaged Goods*, Gilman implicates the husband foremost in Leslie's death and their son's disability, and recommends "masculine continence" just as she does in her critique of *Damaged Goods*.

In her 1916 gender reversal of the Anti-VD Campaign seduction narrative, Gilman deviates from the traditional narrative, which considered prostitutes responsible for the spread of venereal diseases. The female body does not—and cannot—deploy disease into American society, at least in this version of Gilman's narrative. Female bodies are, in fact, absent from her narrative, since Leslie dies and her body is literally absent from the text. She never even speaks. As a subject, Leslie haunts the text, but remains beyond it. Gilman instead concerns herself with Leslie the son, who must suffer as a "cripple" due to his father's poor decision-making. This focus invokes a eugenic narrative stemming from venereologist, social hygiene reformer, and early sex education theorist Prince Morrow, who differentiated among venereal diseases based upon their origins and impacts: "syphilis of the innocent," he proclaimed, denotes a condition in which innocent victims, namely women and children, acquire venereal disease through the husband/father's immoral behavior.[42] In "The Vintage," Gilman fictionalizes Morrow's "syphilis of the innocent" theory, pathologizing the heterosexual male body as responsible for originating venereal disease.

Gilman further plays off Morrow's "syphilis of the innocent" theory in *The Crux*, as well as imagining a plausible, albeit fictional scenario that legitimizes Morrow's political rallying cry for "a woman's right to know." But unlike Morrow, in her 1911 version of the Anti-VD Campaign seduction narrative, Gilman explicitly pathologizes the body of the female prostitute as communicably syphilitic. As she educates Vivian about sexually transmitted diseases, Grandma Pettigrew draws from Prince Morrow's work in venereology, insisting that "'Dr. Prince Morrow in New York, with that society of his—(I can never remember the name—makes me think of tooth-brushes) has done much'" for the cause of feminist sex education (139). The society Grandma Pettigrew cannot recall is the American Society for Sanitary and Moral Prophylaxis (ASSMP), which was an early sex hygiene organization dedicated to eradicating prostitution and venereal disease.[43] Vivian concedes that she knows of Morrow, but has not read him. In her ignorance, Vivian embodies Morrow's and Gilman's female innocent, and they locate this innocence in what Michel Foucault calls his "repressive hypothesis":

> "That's it!" responded her grandmother, tartly; "we bring up girls to think it is not proper to know anything about the worst before them. Proper!—Why my dear child, the young girls are precisely the ones *to* know! It's no use to tell a woman who has buried all her children—or wishes she had!—that it was all owing to her ignorance, and her husband's. You have to know beforehand if it's to do you any good." (139, Gilman's emphasis)

Morrow and Gilman assert a need for sex education in response to a "conspiracy of silence" emerging from a perceptibly "repressive" Victorian past. Of course, Foucault finds such a silence did not emerge from this "repressive hypothesis"; rather, we transformed sex into discourse and sanitized it through various methods of biopower, including Comstockian censorship. "There is not one but many silences," Foucault claims, and many local power relations at work.[44] In this instance alone, we find national government (the Comstock Law), sexist medicine, and family dynamics at work, contributing toward Vivian's ignorance.

Gilman's biopolitics depart from Morrow's as Gilman finds prostitutes responsible for originating venereal diseases.[45] Like George Dupont in *Damaged Goods*, Morton Elder contracts syphilis from a prostitute. Several prostitutes, in fact, for chef Jeanne Jeaune not only "'ha[s] heard of him since, many times, in such company,'" but can also identify three of the prostitutes by name: Coralie, Anastasia, and Estelle (104, 103). Morrow wrote in *Social Diseases and Marriage* that "[t]he prophylaxis of venereal diseases and the prevention of prostitution are indissolubly linked," and Gilman vehemently agreed.[46] She, in fact, advanced his position further, blaming prostitutes for the existence of syphilis. She opposed prostitution, even to the point of supporting national- and state-level eugenic sterilization laws, which required compulsory sterilization for "defectives" such as prostitutes.[47] Ironically, Gilman sets *The Crux* in fictional Carston, Colorado, a former mining town not unlike real-life Denver, which might not have survived without brothels![48] Gilman's rescription of the outbreak narrative should not wholly surprise us. Even though she implicates a group of women as (im)morally responsible for the spread of syphilis, the act of scapegoating a "fringe" or "foreign" community who is considered to be the originary host appears consistent with the genre of the outbreak narrative. If the outbreak narrative exposes human networks as increasingly elaborate and complex, then they also expose "the tragic consequences of human behavior" that is "amplified" by engaging in that web irresponsibly.[49] In other words, when one contracts a communicable disease, the signs and symptoms of the disease on the body are (mis)read as physical evidence of immoral behavior.[50] Gilman amplifies this logic by moralizing against prostitution and in defense of young women who suffer as innocent victims of their immoral male partners.

Gilman's campaign against prostitution not only undermines her long-held argument for financial independence among women; her outbreak narrative further contributes to the broader cultural narrative that pathologizes and stigmatizes the body of the prostitute. Gilman's baby utopia *Moving the Mountain* (1911), which many scholars take as a serious manifesto on her desired social reform procedures, further promotes sterilization among prostitutes and outlaws prostitution.[51] Gilman's rationale for sterilization harkens back to nineteenth-century gynecological discourses linking female mental disorders with normative sexuality. As Ben Barker-Benfield explains, "the psychologic origins of woman's mental disorders" were located in "sexual transgressions" of which "masturbation, contraception, abortion, orgasm," and of course, sexual desire and pleasure, were symptomatic.[52] Deviation from a normative sexual hypothesis designating women as naturally frigid or unarousable signified mental disorder, of which the prostitute appeared uniquely—and irredeemably—mentally disabled.[53] Gilman articulates this differently in her theory of "over-sexed" bodies. In her essay "Birth Control" (1915), Gilman defends birth control as one method for healing our "over-sexed" nation. More importantly for my purposes, Gilman defines "over-sexed" bodies as "thousands of generations of over-indulgence" in sexual pleasure which require "reputable physicians or other competent persons to teach proper methods of restriction."[54] She speaks of "over-sexed" bodies as unnatural given that other species, she observes, "only crave this indulgence for a brief annual period," as should humans, but our desires have gone awry, she concludes.[55] In *Moving the Mountain*, she speaks of the "over-sexed" body of the prostitute as a medical condition, or as "pathological—cases for medical treatment" and "perhaps surgical" treatment as well.[56]

Gilman affectively rescripts the dominant nineteenth-century gynecological narrative which defined "woman" by her body, specifically her uterus or ovaries, shifting the location of pathology to a different body entirely in the hopes of distancing normative (read: white, middle- to upper-class, heterosexual) women from disability rhetoric. Because Gilman defines woman by her normative race, class, and sexuality, the prostitute must be defined by her deviance from that normative sexuality. She reasons that prostitutes are "over-sexed," find pleasure in sexual intercourse, and are degraded to a lower economic class because their income is dependent upon oversexual performance; therefore, they must be mentally disabled. In *The Crux*, Gilman departs from the traditional Anti-VD Campaign seduction narrative by stopping the seduction narrative in its tracks and offering an alternate trajectory for our heroine, Vivian. Her (p)rescription transforms the traditional gendered and sexed narrative into a disability narrative. Gilman imagines that she is able to stop the seduction narrative from playing out in fiction—and hopefully, in cultural reality—by providing Vivian and her readers with a sex education via supporting characters Dr. Jane Bellair and Grandmother Pettigrew. Whereas *Damaged Goods* and "The Vintage" must end with disease, death, or both, precisely because the characters do not have adequate sex education, *The Crux* deploys sex education as a means of preventing disease or death. However hopeful Gilman appears in her maternalist approach to sex education,[57] her fear rhetoric suggests that disease and disability will always remain immanent: "They [gonorrhea and syphilis] are two of the most terrible diseases known to us; highly contagious, and in the case of syphilis, hereditary," Dr. Bellair educates her friend, Vivian. "You may have any number of still-born children, year after year. And every little marred dead face would remind you that you allowed it" (128, 130).

Stillborn children are not the only possible "consequence," as the chapter title invokes. Dr. Bellair claims Vivian might also bear "crippled children," "idiots," or "children born blind" (129): "Do you want a son like Theophile?" Dr. Bellair asks Vivian during her impassioned sermon (129). Theophile, Jeanne Jeaune's disabled son, serves as an omen for readers. He is initially introduced as "a boy of sixteen," and "not bright, but a willing worker" (67). He is alternately described as a "monkey" and "person of limited understanding," the latter indicating that Theophile suffers from intellectual disability (93, 94, 95). His mother, Jeanne, even identifies syphilis as responsible for Theophile's condition: "I married, and—*that* [syphilis] came to me! It made me a devil—for awhile. Tell her, doctor—if you must; tell her about my boy!" (104, her emphasis).

Much like Leslie in "The Vintage," who represents physical rather than intellectual disability, Theophile becomes the poster child for syphilis-induced disability, and Dr. Bellair does use Theophile in the sermon-like speech she gives Vivian against marrying Mortimer. Importantly, fear rhetoric marks the outbreak narrative, and by extension, the Anti-VD Campaign narrative which strives to stop the spread of syphilis, since Gilman's rationale in defense of eugenic marriage hinges on avoiding the communicability of disease and the perpetuity of disability not only in the present (re: innocent young women) but also amid future generations (re: unborn children).

In (p)rescribing the traditional Anti-VD Campaign seduction narrative, Gilman implicates disability in sex education, using it as an impetus for frightening her readers and Vivian from engaging in marriage or (pre)marital sexual relations without full knowledge of the potential partner's medical history. Although she defends a woman's right to autonomy over her own body, Gilman's eugenic feminist approach emphasizes race health rather than individual rights.[58] Echoing venereologist and sex education theorist Prince Morrow, Grandma Pettigrew insists that "[w]e can religiously rid the world of all these–'undesirable citizens' . . . by not marrying them," "them" being men diagnosed with syphilis. Yet the phrase "undesirable citizens" refers to intellectually and physically disabled children like Theophile and Leslie as much as it refers to potential partners like Morton. In this particular passage, Gilman draws from rhetorical strategies employed by the voluntary motherhood movement, which proclaimed as their primary platform the right of a woman to reject her husband's advances.[59] Gilman extends this concept of "voluntary motherhood" to marriage itself, insisting upon voluntary wifedom: A woman, she suggests, should have the right to choose her spouse, and further, she requires his full medical history in order to make a wise (read: eugenic) choice. Thus, like her short story "The Vintage," Gilman communicates a "medical sermon" that supports eugenic marriage, or a woman's right to choose her own partner, alongside "a woman's right to know," or gain a sex education, as a means of preventing undesirable children.[60]

Fear Campaigns, or (P)rescribing Shame in the Anti-VD Campaign Outbreak Narrative

Nineteen years before Charlotte Perkins Gilman defended sex education and "a woman's right to know" in *The Crux*, Annie Nathan Meyer offered her own defense of public sex education in *Helen Brent, M.D.*, which did not replay the specific seduction narrative of Anti-VD Campaign propaganda, since Meyer's novel was written before the social hygiene movement from which the Anti-VD Campaign emerged. Nevertheless, *Helen Brent, M.D.* does relay a seduction narrative à la Hannah Foster's *The Coquette*, and with each successful seduction, the seduced female dies a tragic Eliza-Wharton-like death. In *Helen Brent, M.D.*, the titular character, Dr. Helen Brent, witnesses a syphilis outbreak within upper-class New York City society, and the origins of the mini-epidemic are none other than New York City society's most eligible bachelor, Mortimer Stuart Verplank. Syphilis ravages three female bodies including an unnamed patient who visits Dr. Brent's clinic; Rose Bayley, Mortimer's fiancé and Dr. Brent's patient; and Louise Skidmore, the wife of Harold Skidmore, Dr. Brent's former lover. Mortimer, of course, adopts the role of Major Peter Sanford from Foster's *The Coquette*. Yet there are three "coquettes," or Eliza Whartons, in this narrative, and Meyer implicates all four individuals in their fates, not simply one or the other, Mortimer or his coquettes. Unlike *The Crux*, prostitutes do not make an appearance in *Helen Brent, M.D.*, and therefore are not involved in deploying syphilis. Since female bodies are not responsible for originating syphilis, Meyer wholly unmakes, and thereby, challenges, the dominant nineteenth-century medical narrative that considered the female body the origin and site of syphilis.

Given the timeliness of Gilman's *The Crux* and "The Vintage," I find reading both texts as Anti-VD Campaign seduction narratives useful for understanding how disability affect emerges through superposition with sex, class, and race in syphilis discourse. But Mortimer Stuart Verplank is not George Dupont, and his victims do not simply suffer from disease—rather, all three victims die. Meyer never wholly clarifies why she wrote her one-off medical novel *Helen Brent, M.D.* In her autobiography, *It's Been Fun* (1966), Meyer summarizes *Helen Brent, M.D.* as "the story of a woman who refused to give up her career for marriage" and a book that "handled with great frankness the theme of social evil," by which she means "venereal disease" or "syphilis."[61] Unlike Gilman, who wrote feminist medical fiction prolifically and returns to reproductive health themes in her nonfiction, Meyer never again returned to the subject of venereal disease. In her autobiography, Meyer does confess she had "an unpublished novel written about thirty-five years ago" that dealt with artificial insemination and I, personally, recovered a diary entry which sketches a feminist dystopian novel concerned with global infertility and reproductive technologies such as birth control.[62] However, *Helen Brent, M.D.* is Meyer's only published work of medical fiction, and she never again returns to the subject of syphilis, or even venereal disease.

How, then, do we contextualize Meyer's novel, which itself appears an anomaly within a late nineteenth-century historical context and within Meyer's personal canon? Was *Helen Brent, M.D.* "ahead of [its] time," as Meyer suggests in her autobiography? Was "the world . . . not ready to understand" her message?[63] Perhaps an autobiographical context might help uncover Meyer's purposes. Annie Nathan Meyer married pulmonologist Alfred Meyer in 1887, and together, the couple were active in New York City social hygiene reform movements. Alfred Meyer was perhaps most passionate about health education, particularly as a means of preventing tuberculosis. He also successfully reformed nurses' training at Mount Sinai Hospital, where he was employed as a pulmonologist. Meyer often joined her husband in his reform endeavors, and even once lectured at Mount Sinai Hospital's Nurses Training School upon her husband's request.[64] Her scrapbooks contain numerous clippings from articles on nurses' training, advances in medicine, and debates within the medical community. She was well informed in the field of medicine and developed strong opinions on medical ethics.[65] Although Alfred adopted tuberculosis as his primary public health advocacy, and Annie likely shared his concerns, *Helen Brent, M.D.* might be read as Annie Nathan Meyer's political manifesto for sex hygiene reform, and specifically syphilis.

Since she was heavily associated with and involved in hospital communities, Meyer certainly knew of J. Marion Sims's Women's Hospital in New York City, the first US hospital to specialize in gynecology.[66] In her scrapbooks, Meyer, in fact, has newspaper clippings on an article about T. Gaillard Thomas, a well-known gynecologist during the nineteenth century and protégé and colleague of the so-called "father of gynecology," J. Marion Sims, who worked at the Women's Hospital.[67] The fact Meyer kept this article does not necessarily indicate support for the racist, classist, and sexist practices Thomas and Sims were performing at the Women's Hospital. Gynecology gained legitimacy as a professional field of medicine through surgery, and Sims's Women's Hospital gained credibility by performing surgical procedures. Since these surgical procedures were highly experimental, and lower-class patients were often practiced on as guinea pigs, hospital floors were organized by social class and doctors treated patients based on their assigned social class.[68] Meyer was likely aware of this class-based hierarchical structure, and further, did not approve. In *Helen Brent, M.D.*, Brent encounters her first female patient suffering from syphilis while interviewing nurses. Dr. Brent is specifically searching for a wet nurse for one of her patients who is a new mother. The woman who enters does not fit Dr. Brent's or her patient's needs: Her baby has died, and her "sunken eyes" "told of present ill-health and misery" (40).

Yet Dr. Brent does not turn the "utterly wrecked" woman away, as did medical practitioners at three other hospitals (41). Instead, embodying the position of Good Samaritan, Dr. Brent takes her interviewee to the Root Memorial Hospital, where the unnamed woman becomes her patient. It is worth noting that Meyer is not clear about this unnamed woman's class status, though Meyer suggests she was a former member of upper-class New York City society. Upon her out-of-wedlock pregnancy, however, the unnamed patient quickly fell from grace, not unlike Eliza Wharton in Foster's *The Coquette*, and she is no longer received in society—or even in a hospital. Meyer describes her unnamed patient as a "girl" with "fair skin" and "pretty, soft, blond hair that told of former beauty" (40). Her "hollow cheeks" and "sunken eyes" betray her, and Dr. Brent imagines that the absent lover, Mortimer, "would have shrunk in horror and disgust from this poor, ruined woman" (40, 41). Because of "the cruelty of the social structure of morals" which "was brought before her [Dr. Brent] with particular violence" (41), this unnamed woman will not completely recover from her situation: "Here in the hospital," Dr. Brent reflects, "lay a woman whose future was utterly wrecked, whose physical condition was utterly ruined, who, if possibly spared to life, would have no future, no outlook, who would be shunned and pitied (that would be far too mild a word)" (41).

Dr. Brent offers empathy and provides healthcare where other medical practitioners and hospital personnel would not, indicating that Meyer held similar critical views toward New York City hospitals, and especially, Sims's Woman's Hospital. Earlier in the novel, when Dr. Brent first establishes the Root Memorial Hospital and College for Women, she pointedly contradicts the feminist Woman's Club and their vision for the hospital and college. The Woman's Club imagines the hospital and college as a veritable feminist utopia in which "the very best instruction could be obtained by women" and "not only the students, but all the instructors would be women" (28). Meyer rejects such an essentialist vision, insisting instead that her feminist physician "cared more for the development of humanity than for the development of woman, more for the progress of civilization than for the progress of a certain portion of it" (29). Although she acknowledges "[t]he Root Memorial was really founded to advance the medical education of women," Dr. Brent hires primarily male doctors and male professors, for she "preferred to have the best irrespective of sex" (25). Just as Dr. Brent does not discriminate against class among her patients, she also does not discriminate against gender or sex among her employees or administration (including the board of directors). Thus, Meyer imagines the hospital as a space for initiating social reform within institutions such as professional medicine and higher education—and it was. As Regina Morantz-Sanchez explains, several women's medical colleges were founded in association with women's hospitals much like Dr. Brent's Root Memorial Hospital and Women's College, and they did open a space for women's entrance into professional medicine.[69]

However, hospitals also served as a space for social hygiene reform, a point Meyer acknowledges in *Helen Brent, M.D.*, but which she extends beyond the hospital in her insistence upon sex education for women. Before the social hygiene movement and its Anti-VD Campaign, the conservative social purity movement called for "a single standard of morality for both sexes," namely that all sexes should remain celibate before marriage and chaste during marriage.[70] It was a "broad-based national movement" by the 1890s, and included many different stakeholders such as suffragists, temperance workers, and clergymen.[71] Consequently, these stakeholders articulated various goals, some contradictory, yet one unifying focal point during the 1890s was sex education. In fact, John D'Emilio and Estelle B. Freedman claim that the first public calls for sex education in the United States appear during the social purity movement:

"Women, they argued, must teach children about sex, lest they learn incorrectly from other sources," yet feminists quickly moved sex education beyond the privacy of the home.[72] As Deborah Kuhn McGregor explains, feminist health reformers found "female adolescents were ignorant of physiology and the biological cycle of reproduction," and in response, they began holding classes in hospitals and other public buildings as well as disseminating information so as to "make knowledge of sexuality and reproduction public and accessible."[73]

In writing *Helen Brent, M.D.*, Meyer publicly joined the social purity movement, articulating her own feminist approach toward sex education,[74] yet her approach focused heavily upon death as a scare tactic for encouraging celibacy or chastity. In 1909, German chemist Paul Ehrlich discovered Salvarsan, or the "magic bullet," a drug which treated but did not cure syphilis.[75] Ehrlich's "magic bullet" was a significant discovery, since during the 1890s, a syphilis diagnosis was considered a death sentence. Syphilis is an infection caused by a type of bacterial organism called *Spirochaeta pallida*, or more specifically, *Treponema pallidum*. As a class, spirochetes derived their name from their spiral shape. Nineteenth-century physicians were correct in their classification of syphilis as a sexually transmitted disease that can also be passed on congenitally from an infected mother to her child. The first signs of syphilis are chancre sores, followed by flu-like symptoms. Left untreated, syphilis develops further externally through skin growths and running sores, as well as internally in the form of bone decay and heart damage. In the final stages, syphilis causes significant neurological damage including blindness, paresis, paralysis, and finally, death.[76] But this degenerative condition did not progress as quickly as Gilman and Meyer suggest. Syphilis is a slow death that can take up to thirty years before running its course. Why, then, do Gilman and Meyer misrepresent the progression of the disease? In "The Vintage," Leslie passes away before her son's first birthday, while in *Helen Brent, M.D.*, Rose dies during the honeymoon phase of her marriage to Mortimer Stuart Verplank.

Perhaps Gilman and Meyer speed up the narrative—and the progression of disease in the narrative—to make their point that the stakes were high for female bodies. Upon discovering Mortimer Stuart Verplank's condition through consultation with the unnamed patient at her clinic, Dr. Brent immediately visits his future mother-in-law Mrs. Bayley to relay the news. But Dr. Brent is quickly dismissed: "'Now, my dear doctor,'" Mrs. Bayley retorts, "'you don't really think that I have thought a handsome young fellow with such an enormous fortune could very well have lived the life of a saint?'" (43). She further challenges the source of Dr. Brent's information based upon the patient's social class. "'How do we know that she really came from a respectable family in the country?'" Mrs. Bayley charges. And if that were not enough, because the young woman has fallen from stature, she must be no more than a "'wretched girl'" who "'is at this moment delirious with high fever,'" and therefore, confused about who or which sexual partner gave her syphilis (43–44). Mrs. Bayley either does not understand the stakes or simply does not care. She casts off Dr. Brent's warning, concluding that the girl is lying, and her daughter Rose Bayley is not at risk. The greater risk for Mrs. Bayley is calling off her daughter's high-society wedding, since such a move would "'make a public scandal which might *kill* her'" (44, my emphasis). This use of the word "kill" opens up a space for Dr. Brent—and Meyer—to emphasize what is really at stake, life and death. Rose Bayley dies, never knowing what killed her. Meyer further stresses death by describing both Helen Brent and Mrs. Bayley as murderers. Dr. Brent guilts herself, for "[w]hen Helen stood over Rose's body she felt like a murderer," but then turns toward Mrs. Bayley, grieving "[h]ow much more cause had the mother to feel" a murderer (48). Mrs. Bayley similarly blames herself as she "hysterically reiterated that she had killed her only child" (48). Her lament betrays her perverse commitment to class status at any cost. Mrs. Bayley actually has two biological daughters, Rose and Lotus. One dies from syphilis, while the other is disowned when she chooses to become Dr. Brent's protégé.

Like Gilman, Meyer uses Rose's death as evidence for "a woman's right to know." Rose certainly has much in common with Leslie, who dies under similar circumstances as a young bride ignorant of the threat of sexually transmitted disease. She appears to have less in common with Dr. Brent's unnamed patient beyond their shared sexual partner. Nevertheless, Meyer—via her representative Dr. Brent—refuses to judge a woman for her actions but judges society for its failure to provide women a proper sex education. In a strange and personal twist, Helen Brent discovers her former fiancé's now-wife having an affair with none other than Mortimer Stuart Verplank. Like Rose before her, Louise Skidmore contracts syphilis from Mortimer, and although Dr. Brent keeps her thoughts private from society, Meyer lets her readers in on Dr. Brent's internal turmoil: "God!" Dr. Brent thinks, "Was that man to enter her life again? Was he to cut down another flower? Was he still at large, feeding upon the purity, the innocence of the most beautiful, the most loveable women of society?" (87). Sexist medicine frequently compares women with flowers and to "cut down" a flower is to cause her death. Meyer plays on this not only in her word choice, but also in naming her first fated character Rose, who must die immediately in order for Meyer to make clear what risks exist for women who fail to gain a sex education.[77] Unlike Rose, Louise suffers from cycles of illness and recovery that will eventually result in death. She first gives birth to a stillborn child, and throughout her pregnancy and labor, Dr. Brent feels haunted by "[t]he details of Rose's death" which "were constantly before [her]" (97). Louise recovers slowly. But, because she knows Louise will never fully recover, Dr. Brent prescribes travel abroad for Harold and Louise as a way of encouraging them to make the most of Louise's time left. Harold, for his part, sends Louise to vacation alone in Europe until an important court case has concluded. Louise does not wait for Harold, but instead "runs off to Europe with the Heir of the Verplank Millions," a newspaper headline reads (107). In the final chapter of *Helen Brent, M.D.*, Helen receives a letter from Harold "postmarked Egypt," in which he apologizes for not listening to her, accepts his "punishment" of a deceased wife, and vows to return to her, "'knocking at [her] gates, a broken Harold . . . eyes lowered, kneeling in the dust'" in repentance (111, 112–13).

As we might recall from R_x 2, Meyer claims to loathe this ending of *Helen Brent, M.D.*, though she is unclear as to her reason for such intense dislike. Possibly, she dislikes the sexist and classist emphasis on moral marriage that the ending implies. Following nineteenth-century moral standards, Harold could only become Helen's lover once again, as he suggests in the postmarked letter, if his own wife has died. Meyer ends with reconciliation upon Louise's imminent death, a death that she repeatedly foreshadows in her linking the fates of Louise and Rose several times throughout her novel. Moral marriage is a recurring theme throughout *Helen Brent, M.D.*, as it was a recurring theme among social purity reformers, who insisted that the syphilis epidemic revealed a need for "marital sexuality." Social purity reformers "emphasized love and reproductive responsibility" in marital relationships, and even encouraged sex education for stronger marriages.[78] Instead of discouraging public sexual discourse, as did Anthony Comstock and his supporters, social purity reformers encourage it; yet they wanted to define the parameters for public sexual discourse within the context of heterosexual marriage. Through her fictional spokesperson Dr. Helen Brent, Meyer appears to articulate a similar argument. As Helen educates Harold, "marriage must be a state of higher duties to both man and woman; it is only when both sexes understand the responsibility which rests on each, it is only then that marriage can be truly ideal" (104). But was this aphorism Meyer's words, or was it filtered through her editor, Jeanette Gilder?

Meyer pedestals Kate and John Dunning as "relationship goals," we might say in the twenty-first century. Their marriage is the standard for all other marriages in the novel emphatically not because of their class status but because they do not divide labor based on gender: "The Dunnings were a marvelous couple," Meyer declares. "They were not well-to-do people," and they "did not share the prevailing theories of the division of duties in the family" (65–66). John Dunning cares for their infant boy, washes dishes, cleans the home, and holds down a job to which he regularly commutes. He supports his wife's decision to teach kindergarten, and does not care if he and his child must wear machine-made clothing because Kate is too busy to sew. For these reasons, Meyer twice declares John a "hero" and considers the Dunnings the marriage to emulate. Like Elizabeth Stuart Phelps, Meyer plays into the romance plot, leading readers to recognize the marriage-or-career narrative over and above her larger critique of patriarchal medical practices that leave women vulnerable to syphilis and death. But we as twenty-first-century scholars must not make the same mistake as Meyer's book reviewers, for one thing is certain: Meyer rejects the culture of shame that Anthony Comstock seeks to manufacture. Meyer blames neither men nor women for the spread of syphilis, though notably only her female characters die untimely deaths. If Mortimer suffers physically, Meyer does not tell us, because to draw attention to his suffering would undermine her rescription of the cultural narrative that designates women responsible for the spread of syphilis.

Meyer's point is that syphilis does not recognize sex or class. She makes her point in a manner that prefigures new materialist observations of the transcorporeal yet invisible nonhuman agent that "*do[es]* things—often unwelcome or unexpected things" regardless of sex, class, or even species.[79] The fact of transcorporeality does not indicate humans should not intervene in unwelcome processes. We should protect ourselves from such diseases, as Meyer and Gilman indicate. How we intervene matters, and the story we tell about disease and intervention matters, too. Meyer crips the female body itself, playing off our long-held cultural belief that "disease" means "system breakdown," and eventually, system *shut*down. In *No Magic Bullet: A Social History of Venereal Disease in the United States since 1880*, Allan M. Brandt claims that 1980s American cultural anxieties concerning the communicability of HIV/AIDS mirror late Victorian cultural anxieties concerning the communicability of syphilis.[80] Because a specific outcast social group, the homosexual community, was associated with HIV/AIDS, victims were stigmatized and discriminated against, Brandt explains. The same, however, was true of syphilis, for contraction not only suggested an association with the sex work community—either as a worker or a patron— but also exposed your (im)moral character as one who engages in premarital or extramarital sexual intercourse. It is worth echoing alongside Allan Brandt that "AIDS is not syphilis."[81] Nor did the cultural milieu create the same conditions for citizens within a risk society, even though death and shame were used as fear tactics for public health campaigns warning against the risk of sexually transmitted disease. Importantly, I must emphasize that Meyer does not actively contribute to this culture of shame. Rather—in a move that directly counters Comstock—she abjures it, even as she promotes fear of contagion among her readership.

Meyer admittedly buys into the notion of the body as a currency of health. Dr. Brent asserts that the reason she does not consider Mortimer Stuart Verplank "the handsomest man in New York" alongside her female peers is because "In her professional eyes, beauty meant health, and health was one of the last qualities with which Dr. Brent would have credited Mortimer Stuart Verplank" (39). Anthropologist and feminist theorist Emily Martin warns against using the immune system as a currency of health specifically because it promotes fear rhetoric, which not only engenders fear of a specific disease but also fear of individuals who suffer from that specific disease. Martin prescribes immune system thinking as an antidote to fear rhetoric and the currency of health underlining cultural narratives of contagion, since immune system thinking emphasizes networks and groups rather than solitude or otherness. Martin's prescription sounds an awful lot like the practice of narrative medicine, for as we may recall, Rita Charon claims that when we share the burden of suffering, the experience of suffering lessens for all. This kind of shared empathy can only happen through coalition-building.

Meyer doesn't quite get there, but she opens a space for the possibility of future immune system thinking among her readership as all three of these women—Rose, Louise, and the unnamed patient—share the burden of contagion from the same source: patriarchal society and the medico-legal discourse that upholds it. If only these three women had the time and the opportunity to share their stories of illness with one another, might they have saved one another from suffering? Might they have saved other women from a similar fate? Following the logic of narrative affect, this kind of coalition-building becomes our charge now as Meyer encourages all women to "find themselves," "their complete rounded selves" (61, 62). Dr. Brent, in fact, warns her protégé Lotus against "'mak[ing] the mistake which many women make and cry out blindly against men,'" for in her experience, "'women fail to understand'" one another "'much more than men do'" (60). Meyer demonstrates this lack of coalition among women when Dr. Brent chastises Mrs. Keith-Brew for publicly gossiping about Louise Skidmore's affair with Mortimer rather than privately intervening in Louise's affairs to protect her from public scandal—and from catching a deadly bacterial infection. Dr. Brent blames Mrs. Keith-Brew for Louise's illness as much as she blames Mortimer Stuart Verplank, for "'society, with its smiles and bows up to the last moment of endurance, only smooths the way down to the lowest pit of shame,'" thereby manufacturing shame through "'talk and gossip'" and "'secret sneers'" (109). Women are not only complicit in the conspiracy of silence surrounding syphilis—they are also complicit in the culture of shame that Comstock promotes through censorship and the unspeakability of the female body, especially the female body marked by illness, disease, or contagion.

Race-ing toward Crip Affect

If sex and class are unmistakably prominent in Gilman's and Meyer's Anti-VD Campaign counternarratives, which critique the cultural narrative of contagion in the female body, then race appears conspicuously absent in their works of medical fiction. Yet, in *Medical Apartheid: The Dark History of Medical Experimentation on Black Americans from Colonial Times to the Present*, Harriet A. Washington emphasizes the centrality of race to syphilis discourse and Anti-VD Campaign films. Indeed, *The Black Stork* adapts the outbreak narrative and seduction narrative of its predecessor *Damaged Goods* by opening with exposition that describes the story of a white, wealthy slave owner who is seduced by his Black female servant, resulting in the birth of a mixed-race child (our protagonist Claude) who carries a genetic taint, implied to be syphilis. It is no mistake that "the very first image" of the film following the title slide "is that of a black child": "In titling the film, [Harry J.] Haiselden was mindful of both the negative and the racial connotations of the word *black*," Washington elucidates, and of course, the "stork" of the title invokes reproductive health given that the mythological stork carries babies to would-be parents.[82] It is rhetorically implied that the "black stork" of the title mistakenly delivers an undesirable child who is marked by race and disability. Of course, these are not mutually exclusive identities, as both Washington and Ellen Samuels have independently pointed out: Nineteenth-century race scientists and medical practitioners equate Blackness with disability, as to be "marked" is to be "defective." We must make no mistake: *The Black Stork* is eugenic propaganda that promotes infanticide as an acceptable manner of eliminating the "genetically inferior."

Pernick highlights *The Black Stork* over *Damaged Goods* as the single most important Anti-VD Campaign film promoting a national eugenic agenda because of the longevity of its popularity among a movie-going public. I emphasize the affective nature of *Damaged Goods* for several reasons: It was the first film of its kind, and as such, it was a cultural phenomenon in and of itself that inspired the production of additional Anti-VD Campaign films including *The Black Stork*, as well as a host of adaptations like Upton Sinclair's novel *Damaged Goods* and George Bernard Shaw's preface to the republication of the screenplay. Additionally, we have evidence that Gilman saw the play live on stage in New York City, and that Meyer was at least familiar with the narrative as a cultural phenomenon. Even though we emphasize different Anti-VD Campaign films, Pernick at least agrees with their cultural significance, finding that narrative not only communicates but also is communicable: "Early motion pictures proved critically important in *communicating* to the lay public the tremendous medical and public health revolution of the turn of the century."[83] The infectious power of the Anti-VD Campaign outbreak narrative and seduction narrative rests in the ability of the film or novel to hold an audience's attention for a prolonged period, and then sway that impressionable audience toward or away from the writer's or producer's sociopolitical values.

Admittedly, the perpetual dissemination of the Anti-VD Campaign outbreak narrative and seduction narrative creates the conditions of longevity for specific cultural narratives such as the pathologization of the diseased female body, the shame of sexual intercourse, or the fear of contagion from a person who suffers from a sexually transmitted disease, whether that disease is syphilis or HIV/AIDS. On this count perhaps, *The Black Stork* succeeds, for *The Black Stork* was not only popular enough to receive a retouch in 1927 with a new prologue and ending, but also became a key feature of road shows from 1927 to 1942. This timeline overlaps with the onset of the Tuskegee Syphilis Study in 1933, which allows historian Harriet A. Washington to make the claim that its cultural narrative of black hypersexuality further legitimized medical experimentation among Black bodies in the aftermath of slavery. *The Black Stork* differs from the outbreak narrative and seduction narrative of its predecessor *Damaged Goods* in two key ways: *The Black Stork* conflates race and disability, and it conveys a message of either eugenic marriage as a form of prevention or alternatively support for infanticide of the diseased offspring of syphilitic parents. After Claude proposes to his beloved Anne, the ghost of his grandfather visits him three times to offer him visions of the future should he marry Anne and have children with her. One vision predicts Claude and Anne's ill son will attempt to kill his mother, and then the doctor who saved him as an infant, as retribution for his suffering, while another vision imagines the sympathetic obstetrician—played by Dr. Harry J. Haiselden—as allowing the ill baby to die or be euthanized. Claude inexplicably disappears at the end of the film. Pernick imagines he either dies from syphilis, is tossed by Anne when she discovers the truth of his illness, or runs away from the burden and guilt of his disease. *The Black Stork* first and foremost supports the eugenic practices of Dr. Harry J. Haiselden who was involved in the film's production: clean marriage, voluntary motherhood, and infanticide. Yet we cannot ignore the racial implications of *The Black Stork*, not least because of the racial valence of the film's title. The film carries the (t)race of Blackness from the original 1915 narrative, regardless of whether the 1927 version revises Claude's racial heritage.

As an advocate for feminist eugenics and euthanasia, Charlotte Perkins Gilman may have sympathized with the position of Dr. Harry J. Haiselden, though she likely would have issues with *The Black Stork*'s clear and present failure to fault Claude or his grandfather for the communicability of syphilis. Gilman's racism and xenophobia are well documented in literary scholarship, especially as it concerns her utopian fiction *Herland* and *Moving the Mountain*. In fact, Alys Eve Weinbaum claims Gilman's eugenic propaganda in her utopian fiction most visibly highlights her racist convictions, while Stephanie Peebles Tavera argues that Gilman's eugenic agenda in *Herland* has implications for both race and disability.[84] And yet, because race co-evolves with disability throughout the long nineteenth century and is further a function of racial biopower,[85] when Gilman theorizes disability in *The Crux* she is also simultaneously theorizing race. Dana Seitler likewise perceives the racial undertones of *The Crux*, noting that although there are no obvious persons of color in the narrative, "the intense repetition of Vivian's white accessories"—her gown, her pearls, her scarf—"together with the emphasis on her white skin also seems to signal the racial requirements of this narrative."[86] On the one hand, Vivian's whiteness signals her "sexual purity and racial 'purity,'"[87] but I argue that it also signals her lack of disability because she avoids catching syphilis by choosing a eugenic spouse, Dr. Richard Hale. Vivian's juxtaposition to boardinghouse chef Jeanne Jeaune works to emphasize Vivian's whiteness against Jeanne's perceived Blackness, as Jeanne repeatedly watches Morton Elder attempt to seduce Vivian from the shadows of her kitchen behind the peephole in the swinging door. "Mrs. Jeaune would come no nearer," Gilman narrates, "but peered darkly upon them" from a distance (79), and again "Jeanne Jeaune watched him darkly with one hand on her lean chest" while Morton flirts with Vivian (86).

Like Vivian, Jeanne's darkness reflects her race and her status as disabled by syphilis. Dr. Hale describes her as ethnically French (67), which at the very least racially distinguishes her as "other." She is not one of them, because she is either an immigrant or the daughter of an immigrant, and because she is not white in her "dark" appearance. Similarly, Mrs. Pettigrew cannot be bothered to learn the pronunciation of Ms. Jeanne Jeaune's name (which should be pronounced "Zhahn Zhōne"), settling on calling her by an anglicized version of her last name instead, "Ms. Jones" (68). Grandma Pettigrew, in fact, signifies Jeanne's otherness when she exclaims, "'Johnny Jones! queer name for a woman!'" (67). Queer, indeed. Yet perhaps fitting for a woman of color who crips/queers medicine by insisting that Dr. Jane Bellair use Jeanne's personal experience of syphilis as evidence for the need of access to sex education among women and the informed consent of patients. In other words, Jeanne conforms to the normative standards of race, gender, and disability so her narrative might be useful for an act of medical intervention that promises to protect vulnerable women like herself and Vivian from exploitation. She pleads with Dr. Bellair to "'Tell her doctor—if you must'" about Jeanne's own personal experience of contracting syphilis and giving birth to a syphilitic son who exhibits signs of intellectual disability (104). Jeanne imagines the power of narrative affect emanating from her personal story of illness will influence Vivian to make an informed decision about marrying Morton. Similarly, Gilman imagines the power of narrative affect on readers as her melodramatic medical novel *The Crux* replays the exact same rhetorical function as the seduction narratives of *Damaged Goods* and *The Black Stork*, but with a difference of gender: Gilman uses Jeanne Jeaune and Dr. Jane Bellair to appeal to the logic of science through the emotional rhetoric of fear, and specifically, the fear of illness and of disability.

Jeanne's agency appears limited partly because Jeanne defers to Dr. Bellair for medical authority attesting to her embodied experience. She also fails to correct evidently racist behavior such as Grandma Pettigrew's mispronouncing her name, as well as hiding herself in the shadows of the kitchen because she is ashamed of her status as a working-class woman of color with a disabled son. Yet Jeanne is not passive. She exhibits a kind of "complex embodiment," as Tobin Seibers describes of disability identity. Gilman tells us that after another evening of games, dancing, and revelry, "Silence reigned at last in the [boarding]house. Nor for long, however" (103). Jeanne breaks the silence literally and figuratively when Dr. Bellair finds Jeanne tapping her fingers against Dr. Bellair's bedroom door and then begging her pardon for waking her, all the while insisting they must speak. "'You are a doctor, and you can make an end to it,'" Jeanne implores (103). And Dr. Bellair does make an end to Vivian and Morton's engagement by doing exactly what Jeanne cannot because of her lack of authority: tell her story of illness. Dr. Bellair actually tells both stories, hers and Jeanne's, as Dr. Bellair confesses to Vivian that she became a doctor to "save other women" once she herself discovered that she had caught gonorrhea from her husband: "'When I found I could not be a mother I determined to be a doctor, and save other women, if I could,'" Dr. Bellair explains to Vivian (128), once again invoking motherhood as the sine qua non reason for marriage. Jeanne may "regard" her son "as any other boy," and behave "fiercely watchful lest anyone offend her son" because of her love for him (95, 68), yet she also allows—even beseeches—Dr. Bellair to use her son as a poster child for syphilis and the consequences of non-eugenic marriage.[88]

Arguably, Jeanne (p)rescribes Gilman's eugenic approach as a kind of black eugenics that empowers women of color to make decisions that protect their personal and community health in a manner akin to Frances Ellen Watkins Harper. Even if deploying black eugenics at all—for racial empowerment or uplift—stigmatizes people with disabilities like her sixteen-year-old son Theophile, whom the women of the boardinghouse repeatedly infantilize in a manner that suggests children with intellectual disabilities are undesirable. Jeanne performs a kind of complex embodiment informed by her personal experience of syphilis and of raising a son with an intellectual disability in a culture that doubly marks them for the visible signs of illness and Blackness. Jeanne knows this, and we as readers know this because Jeanne "embodies the knowledge of what it means to be a disabled person" and a person of color in 1910s America.[89] "Disabled embodiment holds a different knowledge of society," Seibers explains of his theory of complex embodiment, "and this knowledge" is what "identifies" a person as disabled.[90] While Morton's Aunt Orella surmises that Morton's sore throat and cold sores might be "diphtheritic," Dr. Bellair suspects that he might be exhibiting the early symptoms of syphilis (90). Jeanne, however, already knows that Morton has syphilis, in part because of her personal experience of illness. Seibers accounts for both the role of the social environment and the role of materiality in signifying disability. He further describes this process of signification as "mutually transformative," for the social and physical environment manifests itself in the (human) body and the body reads and interprets both social and physical environments through specific contexts.[91] In other words, Seibers recognizes the social model of disability as a (new) materialist framework in its affective nature. If, in its most general definition, affect means to influence or change a subject, then Seiber's theory of complex embodiment recognizes the role of affect as his theory "teaches that disability is both *affected* by environments and *changed* by the diversity of bodies, resulting in specific knowledge about the ways that environment and bodies mutually transform one another."[92]

But what if the result is yet another catalyst for change? The result of Jeanne deploying her complex embodiment is a kind of familial intervention that sets in motion a series of events: Dr. Bellair's sex education talk with Vivian, Vivian's rejection of Morton's marriage proposal, Morton's shame and subsequent exile from the city of Carson, and Vivian's eugenic marriage to Dr. Richard Hale. Even though Gilman stops the Anti-VD Campaign seduction narrative in its tracks, she appears to propagate shame just like *The Black Stork*, *Damaged Goods*, and even Comstockian censorship before her. Joshua Kupetz theorizes this network of local and systemic actors as a "disability ecology," which as a model seeks to unite Tobin Seiber's theory of complex embodiment with Alison Kafer's political/relational model of disability. Kupetz critically accounts for the role of affect in his disability ecology model as he recognizes "the affective capacities" of medico-legal discourse in disability narratives like Richard Powers's novel *Gain* (1998), as well as the affective nature of narrative itself from which the reader makes meaning of the experience of disability. Disability truly is affective in Kupetz's account as "disability ecology extends this awareness" of the material effects of the built environment on bodies "to the social and ideational environment, investigating how attitudes, beliefs, and practices direct disabled people toward or away from possible futures."[93]

My theory of gender, race, and disability as affect—as an ongoing process of superposition—is akin to Kupetz's disability ecology model. I do not seek to untangle this Gordian knot of actors so much as describe the knot itself, whether as a network, as Kupetz describes, or as a wave-particle entity à la Karen Barad, because any attempt to untangle this ongoing process of superposition gives the impression of stability, of the subject of inquiry being measurable or observable. Instead, I follow these moving targets to capture how affective values of (bio)power and empowerment, dominance and superiority, and even shame and empathy become enmeshed in cultural narratives that draw upon the medical imagination and maintain a long reach in our medico-legal discourse and narrative tradition beyond the late nineteenth and early twentieth centuries. What is absent in this discourse is just as significant as what is present. *The Black Stork* tries to erase its racist connotations but leaves traces behind, not least because of the title. Gilman eschews describing Jeanne Jeaune as Black, yet alludes to Blackness in Jeanne's "dark" appearance and in her experience of micro-aggression and discrimination. Annie Nathan Meyer similarly does not address race in her medical novel *Helen Brent, M.D.* She imagines syphilitic contagion as a product of and threat to the middle- to upper-class women of New York City society. And yet literary historian Carla

Kaplan considers Meyer to be one of "[t]he most effective allies of the Harlem Renaissance" because Meyer's play *Black Souls* (1924) exposes the protection of white feelings as responsible for perpetuating racism, and especially, the lawless disciplinary practice of lynching.

In the Conclusion to this book, I discuss *Black Souls* alongside Angelina Weld Grimké's anti-lynching plays *Rachel* (1916) and *Mara* (c. 1920) to argue that the genre of the anti-lynching drama—a genre which Grimké founded—not only emerges in response to Margaret Sanger's birth control movement, but also initiates a political turn toward early reproductive justice among women writers of the post-Comstockian era. Meyer remains silent in *Helen Brent, M.D.* on the subject of race, perhaps to avoid criticism as a white woman who fears she has little to no authority to speak on the experience of Black sexuality at that moment in her life. Perhaps she also feared the subject of race might complicate her purpose of defending sex education for women. By 1924, some twenty-two years after the publication of *Helen Brent, M.D.*, and after developing a decades-long friendship with Zora Neale Hurston and George Schuyler, Meyer finally decides that to remain silent on the subject of race is to contribute to the problem of racism. I hope that the experience of writing *Helen Brent, M.D.* awakened her to the realization that fear produces shame just as it did for Rose Bayley, Louise Skidmore, and Dr. Brent's unnamed patient. Fear and shame ultimately lie at the crux of Charlotte Perkins Gilman's and Annie Nathan Meyer's medical novels. Although Gilman and Meyer package fear differently in an effort to equalize gender, their fear emanates from the same place as the Comstock Law, *Damaged Goods*, and *The Black Stork*: disability, disease, and chronic illness.

Notes

1. Werbel, *Lust on Trial*, 307.
2. Ibid. 178.
3. Ibid. 306.
4. Lost films are feature or short films that no longer exist in any studio archives, private collections, or public archives, and are, therefore, unviewable. The US Library of Congress maintains plot descriptions for some lost films such as *Damaged Goods* (1914). Additional knowledge concerning specific lost films usually arises from secondary sources such as documented first-person accounts, film posters, or stills.
5. Martin S. Pernick, *The Black Stork: Eugenics and the Death of "Defective" Babies in American Medicine and Motion Pictures Since 1915* (New York and Oxford: Oxford University Press, 1996), 146; see also Eric Schaefer, *"Bold! Daring! Shocking! True!": A History of Exploitation Films, 1919–1959* (Durham, NC: Duke University Press, 1999). *Damaged Goods* was first staged in 1913 in New York City. Because of its explicit content about sexual health, the *Medical Review of Reviews* produced the play to stave off public protests (Schaefer 20–1). It was such a hit that a special performance was arranged for President Woodrow Wilson in Washington,

DC (Schaefer 21). To understand the degree of popularity, contemporary scholars might think of it in these terms: *Damaged Goods* was the *Hamilton* of its day. Richard Bennett, the star of the theatrical play, also starred in the film production, the latter of which debuted late in 1914, a little over one year after the hit play made its debut. In the meantime, Upton Sinclair capitalized on the popularity of the play and the anticipation over the film by producing a novel adaptation, also titled *Damaged Goods*, in 1913—between the debut of the play and the debut of the film.

6. See Tavera's "Her Body, *Herland*." In *Herland*, Gilman advocates sex education occurring outdoors in nature.
7. Alcott, *Eight Cousins*, 224. In fact, Gilman's short story "Joan's Defender" (1916) is nearly identical in plot to *Eight Cousins*.
8. Carla Bittel, "Woman, Know Thyself: Producing and Using Phrenological Knowledge in 19th-Century America," *Centaurus* 55, no. 2 (May 2013): 104–30.
9. Meyer, *Helen Brent, M.D.*, 61–2. Hereafter cited in the body of the text.
10. Gilman, *The Crux*, 139. Hereafter cited in the body of the text.
11. Altschuler, *The Medical Imagination*, 58.
12. Pearl James, *The New Death: American Modernism and World War I* (University of Virginia Press, 2013), 13.
13. Mary Spongberg, *Feminizing Venereal Disease: The Body of the Prostitute in Nineteenth-Century Medical Discourse* (New York University Press, 1997), 6.
14. Emily Martin, *Flexible Bodies: Tracking Immunity in American Culture—From the Days of Polio to the Age of AIDS* (Boston: Beacon Press, 1994), 136; see also Matt Franks, "Breeding Aliens, Breeding AIDS: Male Pregnancy, Disability, and Viral Materialism in 'Bloodchild,'" in *The Matter of Disability: Materiality, Biopolitics, Crip Affect*, edited by David T. Mitchell, Susan Antebi, and Sharon L. Snyder (Ann Arbor: University of Michigan Press, 2019), 182–203.
15. Martin, *Flexible Bodies*, 12, 131–2, 134, 139.
16. Priscilla Wald, *Contagious: Cultures, Carriers, and the Outbreak Narrative* (Durham, NC and London: Duke University Press, 2008), 14.
17. Jeffrey P. Moran, *Teaching Sex: The Shaping of Adolescence in the Twentieth Century* (Cambridge, MA: Harvard University Press, 2000), 52.
18. For a more detailed historical account of the "Chicago experiment" of 1913, see Moran's *Teaching Sex*, 50–4.
19. Moran, *Teaching Sex*, 69. See also D'Emilio and Freedman, *Intimate Matters*, 211; and Allan M. Brandt, *No Magic Bullet: A Social History of Venereal Disease in the United States since 1880* (New York: Oxford University Press, 1987), 52–121.
20. Moran, *Teaching Sex*, 70.
21. Martin, *Flexible Bodies*, 25–6.
22. Ibid. 26.
23. Ibid. 54.
24. Ibid. 109.
25. Quoted in Martin, *Flexible Bodies*, 56.
26. Martin, *Flexible Bodies*, 56.
27. Spongberg, *Feminizing Venereal Disease*, 6. By the 1830s, most medical authorities agreed that "it was quite possible for all women to carry some taint of venereal

disease," and though this prevailing sentiment was challenged by a perceived "gulf between the upright woman and the fallen woman," this foundational rhetoric made it possible to transfer the origins of venereal disease from females bodies, generally, to female prostitutes, specifically. In other words, prostitutes could not have been considered harbingers of venereal disease if the female sex had not first been considered "diseased" by her very nature. See also "The Attack on Prostitution" section from D'Emilio and Freedman, *Intimate Matters*, 208–15.
28. Stone, *Black Well-Being*, 144–5, 153.
29. Pernick, *The Black Stork*, 144.
30. Secretary of War Newton Baker collaborated with ASHA during World War I to create the CTCA just eleven days after the declaration of war (Brandt 59). Civilians and military officers alike feared US troops would return from abroad with venereal diseases not only because soldiers would be exposed to "foreign" environments; civilians feared military camps lacked structure and the moral guidance soldiers received at home. By the end of World War I, the United States government had not only established a government-sanctioned public sex education program but also founded the US Public Health Department, with its own special division in charge of containing venereal diseases and promoting sex education.
31. Schaefer, *"Bold! Daring! Shocking! True!"*, 21–2.
32. Although I was unable to acquire permissions for the movie posters or film stills of *The Black Stork* (1917) as this book went to press, Martin S. Pernick provides useful and revealing stills from *The Black Stork* in chapter 8 of his study of the film (see pages 143–58). I highly encourage the reader to compare the images from the heralds for *Damaged Goods* (1914) in this book alongside the images containing stills of *The Black Stork* in Pernick's book as you read this R_x.
33. Ibid. 22.
34. Ibid. 23.
35. Ibid. See also Annette Kuhn, *Cinema, Censorship, and Sexuality, 1909–1925* (New York: Routledge, 1988).
36. Schaefer, *"Bold! Daring! Shocking! True!"*, 23, 24.
37. Pernick, *The Black Stork*, 146.
38. Charlotte Perkins Gilman, "Brieux's Play, 'Damaged Goods,'" in *The Forerunner* 4, no. 4 (1913), 112, <https://babel.hathitrust.org/cgi/pt?id=mdp.39015014168648&view=1up&seq=120> (accessed December 12, 2021).
39. Ibid. 112.
40. Meyer, Letter to the Editor, 548.
41. Charlotte Perkins Gilman, "The Vintage," *The Yellow Wall-Paper, Herland, and Selected Writings*, ed. Denise D. Knight (New York: Penguin Books, 2009), 297. Hereafter cited parenthetically in the body of the text.
42. Spongberg, *Feminizing Venereal Disease*, 166. See also Brandt, *No Magic Bullet*, 26–30. Prince Morrow argued that mothers suffered most from venereal disease infection and that "[t]hese crimes against the family will continue until women know, as they have a perfect right to know, the facts which so vitally concern their own health and the health and lives of their children" (qtd. in Brandt, 29). His rationale for sex education appears

feminist, and he would in fact consider it feminist, as would Gilman; yet it is embroiled in a heterosexist worldview that simultaneously deifies motherhood.
43. Moran, *Teaching Sex*, 31. The organization was founded in 1905 by Prince Morrow and the New York Academy of Medicine. It was the first of many sex hygiene organizations. The popularity of and demand for sex hygiene resulted in hundreds of regional and state organizations and by 1910 Morrow was encouraged to found a national organization, the American Federation for Sex Hygiene. Upon Morrow's death in 1913, this organization would gain new leadership and a new name, the American Social Hygiene Association (ASHA), which would establish a national curriculum for institutionalized public sex education. For a more comprehensive history of sex education in the United States, see Moran's *Teaching Sex*.
44. Foucault, *The History of Sexuality, Volume I*, 27, 92, 99.
45. D'Emilio and Freedman, *Intimate Matters*, 204–5. According to D'Emilio and Freedman, Prince Morrow "placed the blame not on the female prostitute, but on 'masculine unchastity'" (204). Although they credit Morrow with founding the social hygiene movement itself, D'Emilio and Freedman acknowledge that Morrow's followers and later social hygiene movement supporters did not wholly agree with Morrow's conclusions in *Social Diseases and Marriage*. Thus, many Progressive-era theorists and social reformers—including Charlotte Perkins Gilman—identified prostitution as synonymous with venereal disease, even though Morrow did not hold such a position.
46. Prince Morrow, *Social Diseases and Marriage* (New York and Philadelphia: Lea Brothers and Co., 1904), 332.
47. According to Mary Ziegler, thirty-three states passed eugenic sterilization laws in the period from 1909 to 1930 (212). She notes that Gilman primarily supported birth control for preventing reproduction among "defectives" such as prostitutes, but she also endorsed involuntary sterilization for "defectives" as an alternative (228). Judith Allen also discusses Gilman's specific attitudes toward prostitution, an institution that Gilman considered among "the three greatest evils" of society (qtd. in Allen, 175). Like Ziegler, Allen finds Gilman's rationale was based in feminist theory to which she significantly contributed, though Allen admits Gilman's rationale for opposing prostitution would "disturb or offend current feminist sensibilities" (174). Allen credits Gilman with providing "a sound biological basis for feminism through a reworking of contemporary evolutionary theory" (174), prefiguring such feminist theorists as Simone de Beauvoir (193).
48. Jan MacKell, *Brothels, Bordellos, and Bad Girls: Prostitution in Colorado, 1860–1930* (Albuquerque: University of New Mexico Press, 2004). MacKell dispels a prominent Wild West myth of settlement in her book, proving that most Colorado towns and cities were settled by prostitutes, not miners or cowboys. Although miners did travel west in search of wealth or land, their settlements appeared more like camps than towns. In the 1880s, prostitutes followed the miners, many of whom welcomed their companionship and their business, since profitable parlor houses, bordellos, cribs, and brothels generated more business and allowed for new business ventures. Certainly, there was some opposition, and as more women moved west during the early 1910s, prostitution as a profession was challenged based

upon moral grounds. In many cities, prostitution was outright prohibited by law, but most civic leaders privately endorsed it: "[C]ity officials recognized the value of assessing fines versus closing the bordellos down. Like most of Colorado's towns, the city simply enacted a monthly fine and enjoyed the profits" (123). Judith Allen also finds Gilman's *The Crux* "recast[s] prevailing stereotypes" of the "wild west" (190); Gilman even confirms MacKell's claim that prostitution was an integral factor for settling the western frontier, since for Gilman, "prostitution in the West was a coordinate of a strong marriage market for women" (177). In other words, the fact that prostitution was a financially successful business venture proved not only the opportunity for a successful marriage market "out west," but the *necessity* of it since, as the logic goes, "clean" women could "set the eugenic wrongs to right [and] put the prostitute out of business," even as they failed to realize how much western towns relied upon prostitution as a business venture for the town's success (178).
49. Wald, *Contagious*, 22.
50. Ibid. 21.
51. For the term "baby utopia," see Charlotte Perkins Gilman, *Moving the Mountain* (Blacksburg, VA: Wilder Publications, Inc., 2011); see also Val Gough, "'In the Twinkling of an Eye': Gilman's Utopian Imagination," in *A Very Different Story: Studies on the Fiction of Charlotte Perkins Gilman* (Liverpool: Liverpool University Press, 1998), 131. In her preface to *Moving the Mountain*, Gilman called the novel her "short distance Utopia" or "baby Utopia" (5). Scholars have come to consider this "baby utopia" as Gilman's "blueprint" utopia. In other words, scholars consider *Moving the Mountain* a space for utopian play in which Gilman experiments with pragmatic social reform measures that she intended her readers to consider seriously (Gough 131).
52. Barker-Benfield, "Sexual Surgery in Late-Nineteenth-Century America," 283.
53. Ben Barker-Benfield, "The Spermatic Economy: A Nineteenth Century View of Sexuality," *Feminist Studies* 1, no. 1 (1972), 54. For more on long nineteenth-century public opinion toward prostitutes and prostitution, see Horowitz, *Rereading Sex*, 118–22, 151, 204.
54. Charlotte Perkins Gilman, "Birth Control," *The Forerunner* 6, no. 7 (1915), 180, accessed June 4, 2015, <https://babel.hathitrust.org/cgi/pt?id=coo.31924106110657&view=1up&seq=191&skin=2021> (accessed December 12, 2021).
55. Ibid.
56. Gilman, *Moving the Mountain*, 46.
57. Janet Beer and Anne Heilmann, "'If I Were a Man': Charlotte Perkins Gilman, Sarah Grand, and the Sex Education of Girls," in *Special Relationships: Anglo-American Antagonisms and Affinities 1854–1936*, edited by Janet Beer and Bridget Bennett (Manchester and New York: Manchester University Press, 2002), 193. Beer and Heilmann are two of the only other scholars beside myself who have focused on Gilman's relationship to early sex education theory and practice. Beer and Heilmann claim that there were two primary approaches to sex education at the fin de siècle: maternalist and professionalist. Maternalists focused on domestic and public health methods of sex education, emphasizing "a woman's right to know" to protect herself and her future children from disease.

Maternalists adopted an affective position, as they feared unchaste men could impress the next generation with their immoral behavior and physical illness. Professionalists promoted public sex education taught by men for an audience primarily of boys and young men. They believed that young women must be trained for motherhood, while young men must learn to channel their sexual energies for procreative purposes.

58. Both Mary Ziegler and Dana Seitler independently define eugenic feminism as the application of eugenic theory to the politics of early feminism, which gave feminists such as Charlotte Perkins Gilman, Margaret Sanger, and Victoria Woodhull a voice in scientific and medical discourse. Eugenic feminism might seem like a contradiction in terms, but both Zeigler and Seitler highlight how it provided women activists with an opportunity for greater personal autonomy because women as biological mothers would literally be responsible for the future of race health. See Ziegler's "Eugenic Feminism" and Dana Seitler's *Atavistic Tendencies: The Culture of Science in American Modernity* (Minneapolis: University of Minnesota Press, 2008), 181–5.

59. Linda Gordon, *The Moral Property of Women: A History of Birth Control Politics in America* (Chicago: University of Illinois Press, 2002), 57, 59, 60; see also Janet Farrell Brodie, *Contraception and Abortion in Nineteenth-Century America* (Ithaca, NY: Cornell University Press, 1994), 262. The voluntary motherhood movement is considered a precursor to the birth control movement. It was most active in the United States from the 1870s through the 1890s.

60. I use the word "undesirable" here rather than "unwanted," for Gilman certainly wants children. She wrote extensively on the significance of motherhood, and in fact, deifies motherhood in *Herland*, a point which many scholars of utopian studies have commented upon.

61. Annie Nathan Meyer, *It's Been Fun: An Autobiography* (New York: Schuman, 1966), 218.

62. In a forthcoming article with *Legacy: A Journal of American Women Writers*, I examine Meyer's unpublished feminist dystopian sketch within the context of a larger trend among utopian/dystopian women writers that deploys global in/fertility as the after-effect of reproductive health dysfunction. On the one hand, Mary E. Bradley Lane's *Mizora* (1888–9) and Charlotte Perkins Gilman's *Herland* (1915) describe fertility in an all-female utopia as the result of parthenogenesis, which deviates from traditional heterosexual intercourse to give women autonomy over their own bodies. Conversely, Margaret Atwood's *The Handmaid's Tale* (1985) and P. D. James's *The Children of Men* (1991) imagine global infertility as alternatively the result of birth control or male sterility. I explore how Meyer uses the trope of global infertility as a critique of institutional medicine and its regulation of the pregnant female body. In her autobiography, Meyer describes an unpublished novel of hers "about a woman who craved maternity, but who did not want either marriage or just sleeping with a man. She had her child by artificial insemination, a theme which shocked two publishing houses to the marrow, but which today is written of quite casually in the daily newspapers." Because of its shocking subject, Meyer claims she "didn't continue to offer it to other houses" (*Fun* 3). It is possible that this novel is the same work of

dystopian fiction she sketches in her 1922 diary entry, although there is a slight date discrepancy (which may be attributed to Meyer's memory) as well as a difference in the reproductive health subject, "artificial insemination" rather than "birth control." Nevertheless, as her first novel, and one that specifically deals with syphilis rather than reproductive technologies, Meyer's *Helen Brent, M.D.* appears unique in terms of historical context and Meyer's canon. Meyer's 1922 diary entry detailing the plot and organization of her feminist utopian novel can be found here: Annie Nathan Meyer, Oct. 14, 1922. Journal Entry. Series MS-7: Annie Nathan Meyer Papers, Box 12, Folder 6, The Jacob Rader Marcus Center of the American Jewish Archives.
63. Meyer, *It's Been Fun*, 3.
64. Myrna Gallant Goldenberg, "Annie Nathan Meyer: Barnard Godmother and Gotham Gadfly" (dissertation, University of Maryland–College Park, 1987), 147, n. 57.
65. Lynn D. Gordon, "Annie Nathan Meyer and Barnard College: Mission and Identity in Women's Higher Education, 1889–1950," *History of Education Quarterly* 26, no. 4 (1986), 508.
66. McGregor, *From Midwives to Medicine*, 69, 74, 126. McGregor offers a comprehensive history of gynecology and its development as a serious, respected, professional field of science.
67. It's worth noting that T. Gaillard Thomas became a famous gynecologist in his own right, as Thomas was the first doctor to perform and publish an account of vaginal ovariotomy (in 1870).
68. Lillian R. Furst, *Between Doctors and Patients: The Changing Balance of Power* (Charlottesville and London: University Press of Virginia, 1998), 148, 128. This class division may have been compounded when hospitals became closely associated with colleges and universities as a means of providing hands-on experience prior to or after graduation. In other words, our modern concept of "residency" after nursing school or medical school graduation developed during the late nineteenth century, but since the practice was not yet regulated, patients were exploited by hospitals for medical residency. Furst identifies J. Marion Sims's Woman's Hospital in New York as one of many hospitals that applied a social class hierarchical structure toward patients.
69. Morantz-Sanchez, *Sympathy and Science*, 110.
70. D'Emilio and Freedman, *Intimate Matters*, 141.
71. Ibid. 156.
72. Ibid. 155.
73. McGregor, *From Midwives to Medicine*, 202.
74. The social purity movement was a turn-of-the-century health reform movement that sought to eradicate venereal disease and prostitution. Although we do not know whether Meyer was an active participant in the social purity movement, we do know that she was an active health reformer alongside her husband, Alfred Meyer, and together they may have defended social purity, or at least, venereal disease eradication. It is also worth noting that Meyer had a tenuous relationship with the New York City feminist movement specifically because she was not a suffragist. She was, in fact, an active member of the anti-suffrage movement, a point she continues to

defend in her memoir, *It's Been Fun* (1966). Anti-suffrage, however, does not translate to "anti-feminist," since Meyer had "precise reasons" for her anti-suffrage sympathies: "Antis had always stood for conscientious use of the ballot, once it was ours," yet it should not be "ours" until women achieve a fair education, Meyer explains (*Fun* 205). Meyer feared irresponsible and ignorant voting, a position many Antis held, according to Manuela Thurner. Antis and suffragists were not necessarily oppositional to one another; rather, they were working toward the same goals—women's rights—but in different ways (Thurner 37). Meyer, in fact, was stridently feminist, but her activist work lay primarily in achieving higher education and professional careers for women.

75. Brandt, *No Magic Bullet*, 40, 161. Scientists would not find a cure for syphilis until penicillin was discovered in 1929, and then implemented as a treatment in 1943.
76. Harriet A. Washington, *Medical Apartheid: The Dark History of Medical Experimentation on Black Americans from Colonial Times to the Present* (New York: Anchor Books, 2006), 159.
77. As Londa Schiebinger reveals, flowers played a significant role in early gynecological study. Even before gynecology was established as a professional field of medicine, scientists such as Carl Linnaeus compared female anatomy with flower biology as a means of explaining human sexuality, albeit from a decidedly heterosexual position (4). One of the first textbooks to include a detailed diagram of female anatomy and physiology depicts the female body as opening like a flower (Horowitz, *Rereading Sex*, 21). Therefore, I do not find it coincidental that Alcott names her protagonist "Rose" or that Meyer names one of her minor characters "Rose." Alcott does so to reaffirm comparative anatomy for sex education, especially since she finds female reproductive health shaped by environmental forces rather than biological ones. Meyer, on the other hand, finds this traditional sex education approach faulty. This is perhaps why "Rose" dies but "Lotus" lives. The traditional comparative anatomy approach censors sexual knowledge, especially for a female audience, whereas Meyer's liberal approach, which she promotes in Dr. Brent's education of Lotus, allows for sexual knowledge dissemination and survival.
78. D'Emilio and Freedman, *Intimate Matters*, 156, 150–6.
79. Alaimo, *Bodily Natures*, 146. Her emphasis.
80. Brandt, *No Magic Bullet*, 192.
81. Ibid. 199.
82. Washington, *Medical Apartheid*, 192. Her emphasis.
83. Pernick, *The Black Stork*, viii. My emphasis.
84. See Alys Eve Weinbaum, "Writing Feminist Genealogy: Charlotte Perkins Gilman and the Reproductive Rationalism of Racial Nationalism," in *Wayward Reproductions: Genealogies of Race and Nation in Transatlantic Modern Thought* (Durham, NC: Duke University Press, 2004), 61–105; see also Tavera, "Her Body, *Herland*," 13. Scholarship on Gilman and race is highly critical of Gilman (and understandably so) because her birth control politics promote the sterilization of people of color and people with disabilities. For instance, Lynne Evans finds that the political structure of Gilman's *Herland* mimics the patriarchy of nineteenth-century society even in its formulation of a matriarchy. Gilman deploys power based upon a hierarchy of race

and (dis)ability, using eugenic theory as a rationale for her hierarchy. Meanwhile, Dana Seitler traces the politics of eugenic feminism in Gilman's "The Yellow Wallpaper," *The Crux*, and *Herland*, finding a regeneration narrative that works against a cultural fear of atavism, or the biological retrogression of humanity toward our primitive, animalistic, or savage ancestry.

85. Samuels, *Fantasies of Identification*, 11, 16; see also Schuller, *The Biopolitics of Feeling*, 17.
86. Dana Seitler, Introduction to *The Crux* by Charlotte Perkins Gilman (Durham, NC and London: Duke University Press, 2003), 16.
87. Ibid. 16.
88. Disability scholar Paul Longmore historicizes the concept of the poster child as a product of American charity fundraising, beginning in the 1930s and gaining in recognizability with the popularity of televised campaigns such as the Easter Seals Telethon. The concept of the poster child works as a theoretical concept that describes how specific diagnoses, disabilities, and conditions become recognizable to the public through stereotypical representations of disability. For more on the poster child, see Paul Longmore, "'Heaven's Special Children': The Making of Poster Children," in *The Disability Studies Reader*, 4th edition, ed. Lennard J. Davis (New York: Routledge, 2013), 34–41.
89. Seibers, "Returning the Social to the Social Model," 44. Seibers has been engaging at the margins of new materialism and material feminisms for over a decade, even though he does not explicitly articulate his theory of complex embodiment within the parameters of these fields. Seibers previously published an essay in *Material Feminisms*, edited by Stacy Alaimo and Susan Hekman (Bloomington: Indiana University Press, 2009), titled "Disability Experience on Trial," which describes how the social model of disability takes a (new) materialist turn when physical spaces like the courtroom or the bedroom create the conditions of disability for individuals who use wheelchairs.
90. Seibers, "Returning the Social to the Social Model," 44.
91. Ibid. 39, 42, 44.
92. Ibid. 44. My emphasis.
93. Joshua Kupetz, "Disability Ecology and the Rematerialization of Literary Disability Studies," in *The Matter of Disability: Materiality, Biopolitics, Crip Affect*, edited by David T. Mitchell, Susan Antebi, and Sharon L. Snyder (Ann Arbor: University of Michigan Press, 2019), 61.

CONCLUSION—MEDICAL THEATER: THE BIRTH OF ANTI-LYNCHING PLAYS AND REPRODUCTIVE JUSTICE

Black Souls is not a work of medical fiction. The play, however, participates in the tradition of medical theater, as women playwrights of anti-lynching plays drew upon the medico-legal discourse of the late nineteenth and early twentieth centuries to rescript the black theatrical body from its racist, sexist, and ableist roots in the theater of lynching, the surgical theater, and anatomical and postmortem exhibitions, among others. Historian Harriet A. Washington traces a tradition of putting Black bodies on public display in the medical theater, beginning with Dr. J. Marion Sims, who infamously performed dozens of surgeries between 1845 and 1849 on no less than seventeen Black slave women, including Anarcha, Lucy, and Betsy, in pursuit of a fix for the postpartum condition of vesicovaginal fistula. Initially these surgeries were performed before a live audience of white male doctors, who assisted Sims by holding down the slave women as he made incisions without the use of anesthesia.[1] Although the practice of live surgical theater in Sims's clinic eventually ended, the black theatrical body emerged in a number of public exhibitions throughout the long nineteenth century. Beginning in the 1780s and continuing well into the antebellum period, Black bodies like that of Emily Brown were regularly "burked," or stolen, from graveyards to become cadavers for anatomical dissection before an audience of medical school students.[2] Africans suffering from albinism appear in P. T. Barnum's circus during the 1870s and 1880s, advertised as "white negroes," "white Ethiopians," and "leopard boys."[3] And from the 1890s to the 1930s, journalists advertised specific times and locations for lynchings in advance of the mob violence itself so that crowds could gather to watch. They would even take photographs and sell them as souvenirs.[4]

Ann M. Fox identifies "two powerful theatrical misappropriations of the African American body" that women playwrights of anti-lynching plays not only encountered but also used their plays to counter: "those embodied onstage in minstrel shows and supposedly serious plays by ostensibly sympathetic white playwrights, and those staged in medical theater, including the pseudoscientific knowledge that deemed the African American body to be feeble, inferior, and at the disposal of medical culture."[5] To this, Koritha Mitchell adds a third theatrical performance against which women playwrights must contend: the theater of lynching. In fact, Mitchell considers the theater of lynching the primary impetus inciting Black women writers such as Angelina Weld Grimké, Mary Powell Burrill, and Georgia Douglas Johnson to produce anti-lynching plays that work to re-script the theater of lynching through embodied speech acts such as gesture, singing, or dialogue. Soyica Diggs Colbert agrees with Fox and Mitchell, arguing that the black theatrical body, a term which she coins, works as a form of reparation that remakes history from the perspective of African American playwrights. Colbert further identifies *Rachel* as a "stunning example" of how the black theatrical body remakes the history of Black female reproductivity, as Rachel "attempt[s] to take control of the racial trauma and violence endemic to her world through the curtailment of her own reproduction."[6] Grimké knows that a Black woman's personal refusal to participate in the biopolitics of American reproduction will not wholly upturn the hegemonic system itself. Yet it will work as a form of self- and community preservation in the meantime. The word "meantime" is key to Mitchell's study of anti-lynching drama: "How did blacks help each other cope while lynching remained a reality? Yes, they hoped there was a 'brighter coming day,' but what were they planning to do in the meantime?" Mitchell asks.[7]

I agree with Mitchell and Colbert that the most exigent form of the black theatrical body compelled women playwrights to write against the theater of lynching as a form of individual and community survival. Yet I also want to highlight the evolution of medical theater alongside Fox, of which the theater of lynching is one iteration. Women playwrights like Angelina Weld Grimké and Annie Nathan Meyer recognize how medical theater plays a role in the emergence of the theater of lynching specifically because they were themselves entangled in medical discourse. It is no coincidence that Grimké's Mara Marston is the daughter of a retired physician, Dr. Richard Marston. Grimké knows how medico-legal discourses are deployed not only to uphold black stereotypes of the black rapist beast, of black female hypersexuality, and of black contagion and anti-amalgamation, but also to rationalize violence against Black bodies. *Rachel* (1916) and *Mara* (c. 1920) expose these stereotypes as false and implicate white masculinity as responsible for circulating false culture narratives of embodied

Blackness. They eschew replicating the physical violence of the theater of lynching in favor of performing reproductive loss such as infanticide, abortion, and celibacy through the practice of (melo)dramatic storytelling and dialogue that highlights the traumatic after-effects of lynching on Black family and community members, especially Black mothers.[8]

Throughout *(P)rescription Narratives*, I have argued that women writers of medical fiction imagine the act of storytelling as therapeutic, as a kind of narrative medicine in which empathy functions as an effective and affective antidote to the shame medico-legal discourse engineers under an American culture of censorship. I want to close this book with a discussion of Grimké's and Meyer's anti-lynching plays because the cultural work of drama in the aftermath of Comstockian censorship highlights the hope of anti-lynching woman playwrights that dramatic performance will produce the affect that medical novels such as *Helen Brent, M.D.* and Frances Ellen Watkins Harper's *Iola Leroy* might not have effected, effectively. In the wake of Margaret Sanger's birth control campaign and the death of Anthony Comstock, the shame of reproductive health disparities adopt a different tenor. While Sanger and her birth control supporters shame Black women and women with disabilities into using contraception as a way to protect and promote "race health," Black women writers like Grimké expose how shame engineered under censorship law and eugenic birth control politics creates the conditions of mental illness among Black women through the trauma of reproductive loss. Grimké and Meyer further recognize that attempts to heal from these traumatic experiences of reproductive loss are limited. Rachel attempts suicide on multiple occasions, and neither a medical practitioner nor a member of the family can heal her. Likewise, Dr. Marston cannot heal Mara in either version of the play, the anti-lynching plot or the romance plot. He suggests that death might be the kindest way to alleviate the suffering Mara experiences. Like Grimké, Meyer recognizes that even upstanding members of the Black community like her protagonist Andrew Morgan cannot stop the theater of lynching once it is in motion. She ultimately places the burden of hope and of reparation on members of her audience who have the will to change cultural narratives of Black reproductivity.

Annie Nathan Meyer serves as a useful kind of lynchpin in the transition from the (bio)politics of women writing medical fiction to the (bio)politics of women writing anti-lynching plays in the pursuit of reproductive rights for women. Yet, as founder of the genre of the anti-lynching play, Grimké initiates this generic transition as well as conversations about Black reproductivity. I opened this book with the politics of reproductive rights in *Helen Brent, M.D.* Therefore, it only seems fitting to close it with the politics of reproductive justice in *Black Souls* as a way of illustrating the evolution of Annie Nathan Meyer as a representative writer, since she engages the medical imagination in two different genres of writing. Moving from medical fiction to anti-lynching plays, and from reproductive rights to reproductive justice, further bookends the evolution of fin de siècle conversations about reproductive health from the beginning of censorship law in 1873 to the onset of its modern legacy during the birth control movement of the 1920s. Margaret Sanger's *The Birth Control Review* privileges the voices of white women writers like Charlotte Perkins Gilman, whose utopian novels *Moving the Mountain* (1911) and *Herland* (1915) represent precisely the conservative feminist vision of society that Sanger hopes birth control practices might realize, especially in its partnership with the eugenics movement.[9] Grimké and Meyer imagine birth control as another form of biopolitics not unlike lynching, since both birth control and lynching forcibly regulate the bodies of Black women. Subsequently, the oppositional practices of woman-authored anti-lynching dramas perform a similar kind of (p)rescription as woman-authored medical fiction in their emphasis on what Mitchell calls "embodied practices of black belonging."[10]

Since the recovery of Grimké's *Rachel* in the 1990s, scholarship on the play increasingly discusses it as a work of birth control literature, or what Beth Widmaier Capo calls "textual contraception." Capo herself briefly references *Rachel* as a work of textual contraception, though like many scholars, Capo predominately focuses on Grimké's short stories published in *The Birth Control Review*, "The Closing Door" (1919) and "Goldie" (1920).[11] Although I discuss *Rachel* as unequivocally a work of birth control fiction, I further read both of Grimké's plays, *Rachel* and *Mara*, as partial works of medical fiction that promote a reproductive justice platform in support of the right of Black women to have a child and to raise that child in a healthy sociocultural environment. Importantly, I do not argue that the reproductive justice movement of the 1990s necessarily finds its origins in the anti-lynching movement or the anti-lynching plays of women playwrights. I instead invoke the principles of the reproductive justice movement, which I argue not only appear in the anti-lynching plays of women playwrights such as Grimké and Meyer, but also are exigent in the biopolitical response of women playwrights like Grimké, who self-consciously engages in birth control discourse by publishing in *The Birth Control Review*. Activists of the reproductive justice movement of the 1990s define "reproductive justice" as "activism for reproductive rights within the larger social justice movement."[12] Although it was concerned with access to contraception, abortion, reproductive technologies, and basic gynecological knowledge and screening services like the preceding crusade, an important platform of the reproductive justice movement of the 1990s was the anti-sterilization of women of color and the right of women of color to have children.

This latter platform is key to understanding how anti-lynching playwrights approach the subject of reproductive health and its affect differently than prose works of medical fiction such as Watkins Harper's *Iola Leroy* (1892), or even other works of textual contraception such as Nella Larson's *Quicksand* (1928) or Langston Hughes's "Cora Unashamed" (1933). The anti-lynching plays of women writers provoke an affective response to the privileging of white feelings at the expense of violence against Black bodies and they do this specifically by appealing to the concerns of mothers. As the birth control campaign made censorship under Comstock law impotent,[13] the practice of lynching replaced Comstock law as a form of suppression of Black bodies and Black voices. Grimké and Meyer risk the threat of mob violence at worst, or social ostracism at best, to force audiences to acknowledge the specific health concerns of Black women, while they simultaneously criticize society for privileging white feelings at the expense of Black lives. Scholars agree that the primary audience of woman-authored anti-lynching plays was women, whether white women or Black women, or both. As Joyce Meier explains, anti-lynching playwrights, including Grimké, wrote their plays for Black women in an effort to express their solidarity in suffering, while they wrote to white mothers who were "oblivious" to the suffering of Black women and who, because of their status as mothers, might "reach across the chasm of race and class" to alleviate the reproductive trauma of Black women.[14] Anti-lynching playwrights offer a productive way of closing this book, as Black women carry the after-effects of Comstockian censorship into the twentieth century—and into future research of Black disability studies—when systemic racism threatens to lynch their living children and prevent access to healthcare resources that might stop the cycle of multiple childbirths.

Like woman-authored medical fiction, anti-lynching dramas are more than a form of protest art. Koritha Mitchell admits that anti-lynching dramatists do reject a specific cultural narrative: the black rapist myth. However, she also emphasizes that Black-authored lynching dramas perform more than just an appeal to white audiences for empathy, especially when they take the form of a one-act play that appears in print publication venues like *The Crisis* or *Opportunity*. Because playwrights of one-act plays such as Mary Powell Burrill's *Aftermath* (1919) and Georgia Douglas Johnson's *Safe* (c. 1929) were meant to be read aloud, they also perform the work of community-building as they help Black audiences cope with the traumatic after-effects of lynching. Johnson's *Safe* offers a clear vision of how the (bio)politics of lynching and the (bio)politics of birth control align in their shared eugenic practice of limiting the reproduction of Black bodies. Liza Pettigrew strangles her newborn son to death as the lynching of Sam Hosea occurs right outside her bedroom window, and it is Dr. Jenkins who conveys the message to Liza's husband John, her mother Mandy, and the audience, who hear the cries of the baby and the cries of Sam from offstage. Dr. Jenkins tells us, "she kept muttering over and over again: 'Now he's safe—safe from the lynchers! Safe!'"[15] Johnson not only imagines lynching as a metaphor for birth control, but also imagines birth control as an affective response to lynching. Johnson derives her metaphor of lynching as a form of birth control from Angelina Weld Grimké, whose play *Rachel* was the first anti-lynching drama by an African American playwright, and as such, established the generic conventions.[16] Rachel's neighbor Mrs. Lane is the first to articulate the theme of the play—and of Black women's birth control stance—when she rejects the idea of birthing more than one child, insisting that, "If I had another—I'd kill it. It's kinder."[17]

Mitchell defines this particular convention of anti-lynching drama using the term, "de-generation," by which she means the removal and prevention of future generations of the Black race.[18] All anti-lynching dramas involve the removal of a character—usually a Black male character—from the family unit through the act of lynching, which forcibly prevents that character from continuing his generational lineage as a biological parent. However, in many anti-lynching dramas written by women, removal and prevention occurs twice over as a female character embodies reproductive intervention and control through the performance of celibacy, abortion, or infanticide *because of the lynching* of a Black family member. Grimké establishes this convention in *Rachel*, as her mother Mrs. Loving and her neighbor Mrs. Lane raise Rachel's awareness of the connection between the lynching of Black men like Rachel's father and brother and the reproductive labor of Black women, who produce victims for the lynch mob. Although she refuses to recreate the violence of the lynch mob on stage, Grimké is nevertheless clear about the violence of "de-generation" in her depiction of birth control. Rachel's affective response to Mrs. Loving's story of the deaths of her son and husband at the hands of the lynch mob, and to Mrs. Lane's warning against having children, is to physically and metaphorically destroy her unborn children by tearing apart the roses that John Strong gave her during his marriage proposal. Grimké meets the violence of the mob with the violence of birth control as Rachel "snatches the rosebuds from the vase, grasps them roughly, tears each head from the stem, and grinds it under her feet" (63). The audience knows Rachel is also destroying her future children because, earlier in the scene, Jimmy comments, "Rosebuds are just like little 'chilyun,' aren't they, Ma Rachel? If you are good to them, they'll grow up into lovely roses, won't they?" (60). Rachel agrees with Jimmy, and then carries the metaphor into her verbal rejection of John when he comes to visit during the third act. "Rachel,—why—why—did you—kill the roses—then?" John asks, thinking that he has offended her in some way. Echoing Mrs. Lane, Rachel responds, "Don't you believe—it—a—a—kindness—sometimes—to kill?" Horrified, John realizes what the audience has known all along: That they are no longer talking about roses, but about children, prompting him to ask, "Do you mean—just—the roses?" (88).

Grimké adopts a more graphic representation of "de-generation" in her short story "The Closing Door," one that successors such as Georgia Douglas Johnson would recreate in their anti-lynching dramas. In fact, "The Closing Door" ends similarly to Johnson's *Safe*, with the act of infanticide: "Agnes

Milton had taken a pillow off of by [sic] bed and smothered her child," a newborn boy, the narrator Lucy tells us matter-of-factly.[19] Just like Rachel and Liza, Agnes directly associates the lynching of her brother Bob with the necessary death of her newborn son as a way of keeping Black boys "safe" from harm. Grimké publicly responded to charges of promoting "race suicide" and infanticide in *Rachel* and "The Closing Door," respectively. She opens her published defense of *Rachel* by attacking these charges head-on: "Since it has been understood that 'Rachel' preaches race suicide, I would emphasize that that is not my intention. To the contrary, the appeal is not primarily to colored people, but to the whites," Grimké explains, as a white audience might empathize with Grimké on the subject of motherhood.[20] Echoing Layne Parish Craig, who surmises that Grimké promotes the same birth control politics in "The Closing Door" as she does in *Rachel*,[21] I agree alongside many scholars of anti-lynching drama that neither Johnson nor Grimké literally promotes infanticide; rather, they imagine both lynching and infanticide as metaphors for retroactive birth control, or "de-generation." Grimké offers a "complicated and nuanced position" on the subject of "black woman's birth control," Lorna Raven Wheeler explains in her queer reading of "The Closing Door."

Wheeler opens her essay with a question that many contemporary scholars, including Gloria T. Hull, Daylanne K. English, and Layne Parish Craig, have asked of Grimké: "What is a 'nice girl' like Angelina Weld Grimké doing working with the social activists of the birth control movement who, some would argue, lean toward eugenics?"[22] If the violence of infanticide was not problematic enough for early twentieth-century reviewers, Grimké appears to polarize her present-day and future audiences even further by associating herself with a known eugenicist: Margaret Sanger, editor of *The Birth Control Review*. Whereas Hull, English, and Craig, among others, critique Grimké for her apparent alliance with Sanger, Wheeler suggests that Grimké uses the publication of "The Closing Door" in *The Birth Control Review* to promote a more expansive definition of birth control that includes abortion and celibate lesbianism while "simultaneously critiqu[ing] the very eugenics that Margaret Sanger and company advocate, claiming that even unborn black babes are unsafe in America."[23] I agree with Wheeler, but I would like to take the claim one step further: Grimké's position on birth control is expansive and nuanced specifically because her politics promote an early form of reproductive justice that is not just about the right to birth control, but also about the right to have a wanted child and to raise that child in a healthy sociocultural environment. Rachel wants children. She wants to be a mother so much that she deifies it, calling motherhood "the most holy thing in life" (28). As Michelle Hester reminds us, Rachel is named for the biblical character from the Old Testament, Jacob's barren wife, who exclaims, "Give me children, or I'll die."[24] Her declaration effectively prophesies the conception and birth of her sons Joseph and Benjamin, as well as her own death in childbirth with her second son, Benjamin. Grimké's Rachel fulfills the prophecy of the biblical Rachel: In choosing not to have biological children, and taking an oath "that no child of mine shall ever lie upon my breast" (63), Rachel dies a kind of spiritual death that Mrs. Loving describes as a living death. Since her oath, which Mrs. Loving does not know about, Rachel "lay in bed hardly moving, scarcely speaking," Mrs. Loving tells Tom. "Only her eyes seemed alive. I never saw such a wide tragic look in my life. It was as though her soul had been mortally wounded" (78).

In what follows, I argue that Grimké imagines the lack of reproductive choices among Black women as responsible for creating the conditions of mental illness, and specifically depression and suicide. *Rachel* is a work of partial medical fiction not because there is the presence of a medical professional such as a doctor or nurse, or even because Grimké makes specific references to medical theories or prominent medical researchers. *Rachel* is a work of partial medical fiction because Grimké attends to the social impact of specific health conditions of members of marginalized communities, just as Charlotte Perkins Gilman does in "The Yellow Wallpaper" when she imagines postpartum psychosis as a product of a complex network of systems that affect gender and disability, including but not limited to sexist medicine, legal censorship, and gendered private and public spaces. Instead of suffering postpartum depression or postpartum psychosis, Rachel suffers from depression and the after-effects of attempted suicide. Her experience of mental illness emerges from a complex network of systems that affect gender, disability, and race, including Jim Crow laws, racist and ableist birth control policies, and the trauma of lynching theater. Grimké did not simply begin a new genre of drama. She also began a new conversation about reproductive health and medicine as a result of her intersectional position on the generic convention of "de-generation."

Rachel appears to be performing a public service to her unborn children, herself, and the Black community by choosing abstinence as a form of birth control and refusing to produce subjects for lynching who will perpetuate the economy of oppression under Jim Crow. Yet Rachel's refusal to have children also seemingly plays into eugenic arguments à la Sanger and her birth control supporters, who are in favor of the forced contraception of Black women as a way to protect and promote "race health." Under the conditions of Jim Crow law and racist birth control policy, Rachel's options are presented as a Hobson's choice. Rachel is given the illusion of choice when, in fact, neither option is desirable: She must produce children, thereby legitimizing the risk of lynching as a form of "birth control" among women of color, or she must endorse abstinence as a form of contraception that achieves the exact same ends of fewer women of color producing "undesirable" Black children. Rachel's grief and subsequent mental illness resulting from this illusion of choice lead her to attempt suicide, or at the very least, express suicidal ideation. The first time Rachel expresses suicidal ideation in the play is during the scene in which she tells Jimmy the bedtime story of the Land of Laughter. Jimmy, who is still not ready for sleep, follows up the bedtime story with a request for Ma Rachel to sing to him. She protests, but finally agrees, only because it is "perhaps for the last time." When Jimmy asks, "[W]hy the last time?" Rachel, "[s]haking her head sadly, goes to the piano," and then whispers again and again, "The last time" (74).

Joyce Meier reads *Rachel* as the thematic antecedent of works of literary fiction by Black women writers such as Johnson's *Safe*, Larson's *Quicksand*, and Toni Morrison's *Beloved* that consider the refusal of motherhood the only viable option for protecting Black children from the realities of racism, sexism, and classism. Meier characterizes this theme as "black motherlessness," yet it is important to emphasize that these motherless Black female characters who "choose to give up the child they are having or already have" through celibate lesbianism, abortion, or infanticide are giving up a wanted child.[25] This unfulfilled desire has serious repercussions for the mental health of the would-be mother; as Meier observes in an endnote, "there is some evidence in the play that Rachel's pained awareness of her powerlessness as a black mother will eventually lead to suicide."[26] I would like to pull this observation out of Meier's endnote and foreground the effect of Hobson's choice. Contrary to Meier's prediction that Rachel will attempt suicide post-play, I believe there is evidence Rachel has already attempted suicide between the events of acts two and three, after realizing that she cannot marry John Strong and become a biological mother. In the third act, Mrs. Loving describes finding Rachel "a week ago today" in her bedroom, "unconscious, lying on her face" (83). "Three men broke down the door," Mrs. Loving explains to John, and when they entered the room, Mrs. Loving found the torn roses on the floor and an empty vase, representing the unborn children, as we might recall, and Rachel's empty womb, respectively. "For a few minutes I thought she was dead" (83), Mrs. Loving confesses, but she has the clarity of mind to call the doctor, who arrives to physically resuscitate Rachel and help her regain consciousness but who cannot heal her mental illness. Mrs. Loving acknowledges that Rachel "is very much depressed," but the fact that Rachel locks her door, that she is found unconscious and nearly dead, and that the stage directions tell readers Rachel is found unconscious on the same day she makes her oath, collectively suggests that the events relay an attempted suicide.

If the narrative, events, and stage directions are not sufficient to convince readers that Rachel suffers mental illness because of an unfulfilled desire for children and motherhood, the ironic tone of voice in her monologues might further convince readers that *Rachel* articulates a reproductive justice approach that calls for a Black woman's right to have children rather than the right to contraception. Meier rightly raises the question of tone in Rachel's ironic laughter, which borderlines on a kind of Black madness that highlights the "irreconcilable contradictions" between (white) Victorian ideals and the realities of Black life.[27] There is also an irreconcilable contradiction between the objectives of the birth control movement and the desires of Black women. Therí Alyce Pickens, in fact, identifies Grimké's Rachel as a Black mad character who simultaneously disrupts white racism to expose its material effects yet cannot manifest increased agency for herself.[28] How Rachel performs this Black madness is what interests me because her performance raises an awareness of how socioeconomic and material conditions affect mental illness, which initiates a trend in anti-lynching plays of engaging the medical imagination for reproductive justice (bio)politics. In one of her final monologues from act three, Rachel laments the illusion of choice for Black women like her. "God is laughing," Rachel justifies of her own ironic laughter:

> We're his puppets.—He pulls the wires.—and we're so funny to Him.— I'm laughing too—because I can hear—my little children—weeping. They come to me generally while I'm asleep, but I can hear them now.— They've begged me—do you understand?—begged me—not to bring them here; and I've promised them—not to—I've promised. (91)

Rachel highlights the socially constructed nature of her own lack of agency as a Black woman who desires children but cannot give birth to them in good conscience under the conditions of Jim Crow. She calls herself and other Black women "puppets" with "wires," indicating that her actions give audiences (of white women) the illusion of choice when they are far enough away from the subject to miss seeing the wires. Up close, the wires tell a story of dependency upon systems that control the actions of the puppets regardless of the will of the puppet, or Black woman.

Black madness elides a linear progressive narrative of overcoming adversity, opting instead for "delineat[ing] the costs of hope and the aftermath of degradation."[29] And this is where the medical imagination of anti-lynching plays diverges sharply from its literary predecessors, prose works of medical fiction. Grimké's hope lies in the affective nature of the onstage drama and its ability to move an audience to change their perspective, their values, and ultimately their behavior toward the subjects of Black women's health specifically, and race relations in America more broadly. As scholars have repeatedly emphasized, Grimké publicly claimed in a published essay for *The Competitor* that she wrote *Rachel* for a white audience; and we have no reason to doubt her claims of authorial intent, especially since she wrote *Rachel* with the express intention of its being performed on stage. Unlike the one-act anti-lynching plays that *Rachel* inspired, which were not meant to be performed on stage but rather read in print publication form,[30] Grimké explicitly wrote *Rachel* as a submission for the National Association for the Advancement of Colored

People's (NAACP) drama contest, which was held in March 1915 and advertised in *Crisis*. *Rachel* won the contest, and Grimké's prize for winning was the full-stage production of *Rachel*, which premiered on Friday, March 3, 1915 at the Myrtilla Miner Normal School in Washington, DC.[31]

Grimké's unpublished play *Mara* offers further insight into her nuanced politics of reproductive justice, not only because she once again couches birth control politics in an anti-lynching play, but also because she broaches a broader reproductive justice agenda on the traumatic after-effects of rape and amalgamation. *Mara* also exhibits the failure of the medical imagination to heal from the trauma of reproductive loss. What little scholarship exists on *Mara* largely attends to the generic conventions of the play or the politics of recovery, since *Mara* has never been published or performed and remains in manuscript form in the archives of the Moorland-Springarn Research Center at Howard University. Like *Rachel*, *Mara* is a melodramatic play whose titular protagonist and her family not only suffer the after-effects of lynching but also are themselves lynched in the final act of the play. At least, that's one version. Christine R. Gray emphasizes that Grimké produced multiple drafts and variant texts under the working title of *Mara*. She further identifies (as do I) two main plots emerging from these variant texts, which Gray differentiates by calling one "the anti-lynching plot" and the other "the romance plot."[32] In my own study of the variant texts from the Grimké archives, I find evidence of the medical imagination, and specifically, of Dr. Marston performing acts of healing on his daughter Mara, whose body ultimately cannot be healed. Like *Rachel*, *Mara* concludes with the female protagonist performing Black madness in such a way as to disrupt notions of whiteness and the practices of white racism. She accomplishes this disruption through Mara's performance of reproductive loss, which highlights how the lack of reproductive justice adversely affects a Black woman's mental health. Or perhaps Grimké was a Black mad writer with a Black mad process bent on disrupting hegemonic notions of "canon" by allowing her plays to bleed across plot lines. After all, Gray argues that "the dated material found in the *Mara* files" exhibits evidence that "*Mara* was one of Angelina Grimké's early drafts as she created her entry for the contest, the one for which *Rachel* was selected."[33]

Mara tells the story of a young Black woman named Mara Marston who, in the anti-lynching plot, is abducted and raped on her eighteenth birthday by the son of a wealthy white plantation owner, Lester Carew. Upon her return home to "The Cedars," Mara's father Dr. Richard Marston, who is a retired physician, avenges his daughter by killing Lester Carew, while Mara exhibits madness as a result of sexual trauma. The play literally ends in silence, the stage directions tell us, after a lynch mob murders the entire Marston family as punishment for killing Lester. In fact, Grimké writes in the opening sentence of Act IV, Scene 2, "No word is spoken throughout this scene."[34] The only sounds the audience should hear, or imagine as readers, is "[t]he shrieks of Mrs. Marston" as she and her family, Dr. Marston and Mara, are being lynched. As in most anti-lynching plays, the lynching itself occurs off stage, yet "[t]here is a long terrible silence" before the "curtain falls" and the play officially ends. In contrast, the romance plot tells the story of retired physician Dr. Richard Marston and his wife Ellen Marston, who keep their daughter Mara isolated from the world because of the threat of racism, which has already caused the married couple to lose six children prior to Mara's birth. On her eighteenth birthday, Mara meets and falls in love with Lester Carew, the son of a wealthy white plantation owner, whose lust for Mara results in her willing engagement in a sexual affair with him. When Lester's lust for Mara does not last, the spurned Mara spirals into madness and dies of grief like her literary heroine, Elaine from Alfred, Lord Tennyson's "Lancelot and Elaine"—or as I imagine, perhaps more like the suicidal Ophelia of William Shakespeare's *Hamlet*. In what I presume to be the ending of "the romance plot," Grimké writes in the stage directions, "There are one or two convulsive movements, then she relaxes; a beautiful smile comes onto her face" before she becomes "strangely still." Dr. Marston performs his medical duty, as "he feels for her pulse, her heart, examines her eyes, and then as though stunned stands looking down."

Gray calls out scholars for practicing a kind of selective censorship that privileges the anti-lynching play and suppresses the romance play, thereby eliding the textual possibilities that cross-pollinate Grimké's body of work. Admittedly, the "romance plot" ends with the specter of lynching hanging over the play, as Dr. Marston declares his intent to kill Lester Carew in retribution for Mara's death. Both Mrs. Marston and Dr. Marston know that even if he is successful, Dr. Marston will not return. Mrs. Marston asks of Dr. Marston, "Do you know there has already—been—a—a lynching in the town?" Dr. Marston affirms yes, that he does know, but insists on going anyway regardless of the certain death Mrs. Marston foreshadows.[35] I agree with Gray that we must attend to the dominant plots of both plays and as much of the variant texts. Thus, in attending to the differences—and similarities—between the manuscripts of the anti-lynching plot and the romance plot, I want to highlight two primary issues for reading within a crip affect framework and from the vantage point of reproductive justice. First, both the anti-lynching plot and the romance plot address thematic subjects that fall under the politics of reproductive justice, since Mara's death in both versions reaffirms the "de-generation" of Black families as a key convention in anti-lynching plays and in Grimké's plays overall. Second, Dr. Marston unsuccessfully attempts to heal the suffering of Mara, which suggests Grimké is skeptical of the efficacy of the kind of Black communal nursing that Watkins Harper promotes in *Iola Leroy*. In the anti-lynching plot, the theater of lynching once again enforces "de-generation" through the act of rape and lynching, while in the romance plot, the black theatrical body of

Mara performs "de-generation" through death and her death explicitly results from sexual exploitation. According to the medico-legal discourse of the nineteenth century, and specifically the politics of anti-amalgamation, Mara cannot logically be the object of Lester Carew's desire. Neither can Mara's grandmother, "a beautiful quadroon slave forced to be the concubine of [her] master, Roger Carew," even though the rape of Mara's grandmother results in the birth of Dr. Richard Marston, Mara's father.[36]

Annie Nathan Meyer succinctly summarizes the message of *Mara* using the rhetoric of eugenics and atavism in the final act of her own play *Black Souls*: "How dare you think you can take us black women into your arms without your lusts getting into the blood of your children? If you want your women to stay clean, you've got to stay clean yourselves," Phyllis Morgan accuses Governor Verne.[37] Phyllis appeals to a white audience's belief in eugenics and atavism by invoking lust as an inheritable trait that contributes to the de-evolution of white offspring. Importantly, Phyllis is referring to the affair between Luella Verne, a white woman and the state governor's daughter, and David Lewis, who is Phyllis's brother and a Black professor at Magnolia College. David is lynched during the play because a mob assumes that a Black man cannot be the object of a white woman's desire. Yet Phyllis is also defending herself against the sexual advances of Governor Verne, who once raped her prior to the events of the play. Phyllis's husband reiterates the hypocrisy of amalgamation practices and the theatrics of lynching that defend the rape of Black women yet criminalize the desires or the alleged rape of white women: "You think nothing of forcing a colored woman," Andrew Morgan accuses Governor Verne, "but there's one ideal in your pig-headed egoism you cling to—that your white women must be guarded against the black man."[38] It is precisely this hypocrisy that motivates the behavior of Lester Carew and his father Roger Carew in Grimké's *Mara*, as both men assume and perpetuate the myth of black hypersexuality and of the always-available Black female body. In fact, one draft of the romance plot version of *Mara* was titled *Lust*, a word that not only invokes Phyllis's accusation of white male "lusts getting into the blood of [their] children," but also characterizes "Lester," whose name is only one vowel away from "lust."

The romance plot of Mara may be about "the awakening of Mara's sexuality," as Gray argues, but the multiple rewrites—dozens of them—of the conversation between Mara and Carew suggest that Grimké may not have been wholly committed to Mara's complicity or her consent to sexual intercourse. Many of the versions begin with or contain similar lines, indicating that they are rewrites of the same scene. Often, these versions open with Mara's surprised exclamation of "Y—o—u!" when Carew rides up to the gate on horseback for a second chance meeting with her. He often asks, "Didn't you say you wished me to come back?" in response to her surprise, and then he declares some version of desire for her, as in "you made me" come or "you draw me" in. Mara's responses change widely. In one version, Carew kisses her, and she declares, "Why!—Why!—That's the most beautiful thing that has ever happened to me. Why I didn't know!"[39] In another version, she hesitates to let him even kiss her hand, declaring, "my soul tells me many things that my mind does not understand—until—afterwards." As Gray points out, there are versions in which Mara declares a feeling of love or infatuation, as when she confesses, "I have thought of you . . . When I have not been thinking of you, you have been just behind every thought."[40] Yet other versions of this conversation are decidedly sinister, as Carew pressures Mara even while she expresses interest toward him. In one version of the conversation, he makes Mara feel guilty for inviting him back: "Do you realize I have ridden twenty miles—to see you?" When she asks him to leave, he charges, "Where is the worry, Mara, in sitting here beside me and talking a few minutes?" Again, she asks him to leave, so he insists that she will be "sorry" when he is gone: "Won't you do just this—to please me? If you don't after I'm gone for always you'll remember me and be sorry."[41] Grimké appears to be exploring issues of sexual consent during a period when women, regardless of their race, could neither report rape nor hold the rapist accountable.

Grimké and Meyer expose the dangers of circulating myths of black female hypersexuality during and after slavery, as well as during and after Comstockian censorship, for its circulation results in rape and sexual exploitation, mental illness and death, and above all, "de-generation" and the regulation of Black reproductivity and the Black female body. Although Dr. Marston attempts to heal Mara of her suffering in both versions of the plot, he cannot. Nor does he want to heal her. Dr. Marston ultimately admits to his wife that perhaps it is best for death to release Mara from her pain rather than live with the traumatic after-effects. In a scene from Act IV, which might follow either Mara's return from the storm during which she was raped or her mental illness following Lester's rejection, Dr. Marston asks his wife to "bring me my medicine chest," and then concocts "a sleeping draught to quiet her." Mrs. Marston asks if Mara will get better after he has treated her, but Dr. Marston gives her no hope:

> Mrs. Marston: Richard—her mind will be—better?
> Dr. Marston: I doubt it.
> Mrs. Marston: You mean—it is—hopeless?
> Dr. Marston: Yes. You must remember Mara is different from most girls. The balance of her mind and body and soul—is very delicate. The balance, once disturbed—[Breaks off]
> Mrs. Marston: Richard—she—she—will—live?
> Dr. Marston: I hope not.—I think not.
> Mrs. Marston: Richard!
> Dr. Marston: It is the kindest thing—to wish—her now.[42]

Just like the "romantic" conversation between Mara and Carew, which is arguably a kind of revision of the *Romeo and Juliet* balcony scene, Grimké rewrote this scene between Mrs. Marston and Dr. Marston multiple times. One thing is clear: Each rewrite of this scene recalls Rachel's appeal to John Strong that perhaps it is "a—kindness—sometimes—to kill" (88). Dr. Marston recognizes the limits of medicine in his acknowledgment that if he cannot heal Mara, he hopes she will die. In another version of this scene, Mrs. Marston insists that Dr. Marston "send to town for a specialist," but Dr. Marston claims, "there is nothing a specialist could do" that he has not already done as a once-practicing physician. Once again, when Mrs. Marston asks if Mara will recover, Dr. Marston ultimately says no, and then adds that he is "glad to say—no!" He turns the guilt, or perhaps the opportunity for compassion, toward Mrs. Marston as her mother, "Do you mean that you—her mother—can wish her to live—so?"[43] Whether Dr. Marston is referring to the sexual trauma, the shame of premarital sexual intercourse, or the experience of mental illness, Grimké nevertheless highlights the limitations of medicine and of the reproductive rights of Black women in all possible scenarios.

Although medical ideologies and the representation of medical practice play a minor role in *Mara*, I find the fact of Dr. Richard Marston's profession as a physician significant to the play itself because it draws our attention as readers toward the representation of health in Grimké's body of drama, and specifically, the deterioration of Mara's and Rachel's mental health in the wake of reproductive loss. Meyer does not foreground the after-effects of lynching on the health of Black women in quite the same way, though as a work of anti-lynching drama that inherits the generic conventions of Grimké's *Rachel*, Meyer's *Black Souls* is unequivocally about reproductive justice for Black women. What Meyer does explicitly accomplish in *Black Souls* that Grimké does not in either *Rachel* or *Mara* is to call out white women for ignoring the values of Black women in conversations about reproductive health. As Carla Kaplan explains, the character of "Luella embodies Angelina Weld Grimké's (and other black women's) view of white women as 'about the worst enemies with which the colored race has to contend.'"[44] Meyer is unapologetic in linking Luella with women like Ruby Bates, who was responsible for the convictions of the Scottsboro boys, and holding them accountable for their role in perpetuating racial violence. Kaplan makes a convincing argument for Meyer's own allyship of Black men and women in the cause of racial justice, who as a Black lives ally "looked at her own whiteness critically and was skeptical about white feelings," Kaplan explains.[45] Luella may have loved David, but she is still "guilty of his death" because she was not self-critically aware of the repercussions her actions would have for him.[46] Meyer appears to be calling out white feminism for actively harming Black men and women rather than simply ignoring them. She recognizes "the trouble with white women," even if she cannot dismantle the system.[47] As a link between the woman-authored medical fiction of the Comstock Law era and the woman-authored anti-lynching dramas of the Jim Crow era, Annie Nathan Meyer reminds us of how cultural narratives of race, gender, and disability adapt from one period to the next. If we are not done with them, and they are not done with us, then I must echo Meyer and Grimké in their hope for the power of narrative to affect change, for it is now our responsibility to confront the cultural narratives that we inherit from one generation to the next, to critically consider their affective operation, and to work to reshape those affective narratives for greater inclusivity and empathy.

NOTES

1. Washington, *Medical Apartheid*, 65. An important distinction should be made: Washington does not claim that Dr. J. Marion Sims begins the practice of experimentation on Black slaves, but that he may be the earliest known surgeon to perform experiments on Black slaves before a live audience. Washington acknowledges a number of earlier surgeons who performed surgical experiments on the bodies of Black slaves, including Dr. François Marie Prévost of Louisiana, Dr. Ephraim McDowel of Kentucky, and Dr. P. C. Spencer of Virginia (70).
2. Ibid. 130–1.
3. Ibid. 94–5.
4. Koritha Mitchell, *Living with Lynching: African American Lynching Plays, Performance, and Citizenship, 1890–1930* (Urbana: University of Illinois Press, 2011), 6.
5. Ann M. Fox, "A Different Integration: Race and Disability in Early-Twentieth-Century African American Drama by Women," *Legacy* 30, no. 1 (2013), 156.
6. Soyica Diggs Colbert, *The African American Theatrical Body: Reception, Performance, and the Stage* (Cambridge: Cambridge University Press, 2011), 53.
7. Mitchell, *Living with Lynching*, 31.
8. Ibid. 37.
9. Tavera discusses Charlotte Perkins Gilman's *Herland* as a work of partial medical fiction in its discursive engagement with Margaret Sanger's birth control movement, the eugenics movement, and early sex education theory. This latter discourse, early sex education theory, was made exigent by the syphilis epidemic, the Anti-Venereal Disease Campaign of the 1910s (which emerged in response to the syphilis epidemic), and the birth control movement, and was influenced by the eugenics movement as crystallized in the work of Maurice Bigelow. Layne Parish Craig similarly reads Gilman's *Herland* as a work of birth control fiction that ultimately provided a model for Sanger, whose politics became increasingly conservative so that she could gain a public following.
10. Mitchell, *Living with Lynching*, 14. I use the term "anti-lynching" drama or play rather than "lynching" drama or play because I seek to emphasize the oppositional function of the genre. I understand the cultural work of anti-lynching drama to be akin to the cultural work of antiracist prose literature such as Ibram X. Kendi's *How to be an Antiracist*.
11. Beth Widmaeier Capo, *Textual Contraception: Birth Control and Modern American Fiction* (Columbus: The Ohio State University Press, 2007), 93–6.

12. Joan C. Chrisler, "A Reproductive Justice Approach to Women's Health," *Analyses of Social Issues and Public Policy* 14, no. 1 (2014), 206. For a comprehensive history of the reproductive justice movement of the 1990s, I recommend Michelle Murphy's *Seizing the Means of Reproduction: Entanglements of Feminism, Health, and Technoscience* (Durham, NC: Duke University Press, 2012), Wendy Kline's *Bodies of Knowledge: Sexuality, Reproduction, and Women's Health in the Second Wave* (Chicago: University of Chicago Press, 2010), and Jennifer Nelson's *Women of Color and the Reproductive Rights Movement* (New York: New York University Press, 2003). Importantly, Kline makes connections between J. Marion Sims's experiments on Anarcha, Lucy, and Betsy during the 1850s and the experiments on women of color during the Depo-Provera trials, which indicates a historical legacy of evidence of the need for reproductive justice. Given that early women's rights activists worked to raise awareness of the rape of Black female slaves during and after slavery, arguably the principles of reproductive justice find their origins as early as the 1830s with activists like Mary Gove Nichols and Paulina Wright Davis. This is why I hesitate to identify a definitive origin for the principles of reproductive justice, as there are many possible origins, including but not limited to the anti-lynching plays of women playwrights.
13. Werbel, *Lust on Trial*, 293, 297–9. Werbel acknowledges that there were many factors leading to the demise of Comstock law, and that Sanger's birth control movement was only one factor, albeit an important one. Comstock was losing power after the Knoedler trial of 1883, which divided the loyalties of Comstock's supporters because many of them had financially invested in works of "high art" that contained paintings of nudes and that Comstock's prosecution ruled "obscene." The risk of financial loss resulted in conversations about "high" versus "low" art, and specifically whether paintings of nudes are equivalent to "cheap" pornographic photography, as well as whether consumption of art depicting nude bodies is akin to other forms of "obscene" behavior such as prostitution. In other words, the Knoedler case led to questions of hierarchizing obscenities. Sanger's birth control campaign capitalized on this hierarchy in its emphasis on concerns of physical health over aesthetic forms of obscenity in the wake of the syphilis epidemic and her own personal loss of her mother due to repeated childbearing.
14. Joyce Meier, "The Refusal of Motherhood in African American Women's Theater," *MELUS* 25, no. 3/4 (2000), 135.
15. Georgia Douglas Johnson, "Safe," in *Strange Fruit: Plays on Lynching by American Women*, edited by Kathy A. Perkins and Judith L. Stephens (Bloomington: Indiana University Press, 1998), 115.
16. Mitchell, *Living with Lynching*, 60, 10; see also Kathy A. Perkins and Judith L. Stephens, who, in the Introduction to *Strange Fruit*, identify Angelina Weld Grimké's *Rachel* as "the earliest known example of a full-length drama written in the anti-lynching tradition" (24). Indeed, Mitchell claims Grimké started the tradition—and perhaps wrote the first full-length, non-musical African American drama as well—thereby establishing the genre conventions for other playwrights to follow.
17. *Rachel*, 58. Hereafter cited in the body of the text.
18. Mitchell, *Living with Lynching*, 60, 70–6.

19. Angelina Weld Grimké, "The Closing Door," *The Birth Control Review* 3, no. 10 (1919), 12, <https://babel.hathitrust.org/cgi/pt?id=hvd.hnp3k3&view=1up&seq=428&skin=2021> (accessed December 12, 2021).
20. Angelina Weld Grimké, "'Rachel' The Play of the Month: The Reason and Synopsis by the Author," *The Competitor* 1, no. 1 (1920), 51, <https://babel.hathitrust.org/cgi/pt?id=pst.000066962656&view=1up&seq=61&size=150> (accessed December 12, 2021).
21. Layne Parish Craig, *When Sex Changed: Birth Control Politics and the Literature between the World Wars* (New Brunswick, NJ: Rutgers University Press, 2013), 78.
22. Lorna Raven Wheeler, "The Queer Collaboration: Angelina Weld Grimké and the Birth Control Movement," in *Critical Insights: LGBTQ Literature*, edited by Robert C. Evans (Amenia, NY: Grey House Publishing, 2015), 179.
23. Ibid. 189.
24. Michelle Hester, "An Examination of the Relationship Between Race and Gender in an Early Twentieth-Century Drama: A Study of Angelina Weld Grimké's *Rachel*," *The Journal of Negro History* 79, no. 2 (1994), 251; see also Book of Genesis 30:1, in the Revised Standard Version of the Bible, where the author narrates, "When Rachel saw that she bore Jacob no children, she envied her sister; and she said to Jacob, 'Give me children, or I shall die!'"
25. Meier, "The Refusal of Motherhood in African American Women's Theater," 118.
26. Ibid. 137, n. 7.
27. Ibid. 124.
28. Pickens, *Black Madness::Mad Blackness*, 14.
29. Ibid. 17.
30. Mitchell, *Living with Lynching*, 36, 39–40.
31. Mitchell, *Living with Lynching*, 10–11, 57, 60; see also Christine R. Gray, "*Mara*, Angelina Weld Grimké's Other Play and the Problems of Recovering Texts," in *Black Women Playwrights: Visions on the American Stage*, edited by Carol P. Marsh-Lockett (New Brunswick, NJ: Routledge, 1999), 74.
32. Gray, "*Mara*, Angelina Weld Grimké's Other Play," 74.
33. Ibid. 74.
34. Angelina Weld Grimké, *Mara*, c. 1914, Angelina Weld Grimké Collection, Box 38–14, Folder 234, Moorland-Spingarn Research Center at Howard University.
35. Ibid. Box 38–14, Folder 236.
36. Ibid. Box 38–14, Folder 231.
37. Annie Nathan Meyer, "Black Souls," in *Strange Fruit: Plays on Lynching by American Women* (Bloomington: Indiana University Press, 1998), 172.
38. Ibid. 170.
39. Grimké, *Mara*, c. 1914, Angelina Weld Grimké Collection, Box 38–14, Folder 234.
40. Gray, "*Mara*, Angelina Weld Grimké's Other Play," 77.
41. Grimké, *Mara*, c. 1914, Angelina Weld Grimké Collection, Box 38–14, Folder 234.
42. Ibid. Box 38–14, Folder 236.
43. Ibid. Box 38–14, Folder 236.
44. Carla Kaplan, *Miss Anne in Harlem: The White Women of the Black Renaissance* (New York: Harper Collins, 2013), 181.

45. Carla Kaplan, "Before There Was Karen, There Was Miss Anne," Biographers International Organization, <https://biographersinternational.org/before-there-was-karen-there-was-miss-anne/> (accessed December 12, 2021). Although this article falls within the context of public humanities, I find it useful for describing exactly how the racial politics of the late nineteenth century affect the racial politics of the twenty-first century. Kaplan clearly explains the importance of Black advocacy among white women, as well as how to be an effective ally: "These women drew attention away from themselves. They left few records and made telling their stories challenging. That was by design. They believed that unlearning white privilege—not living as Miss Anne, or Karen, Barbecue Becky, or Permit Patty—means more than voicing solidarity and support. Their lesson is that racial justice cannot—must not—be based on further privileging of white feelings, again. The point remains salient today."
46. Meyer, "Black Souls," 172.
47. Schuller, *The Trouble with White Women*, 4. It bears repeating: "The trouble with white feminist politics is not what it fails to address and whom it leaves out. The trouble with white feminism is what it does and whom it suppresses."

BIBLIOGRAPHY

Archival Collections

The Jacob Marcus Rader Center of the American Jewish Archives, Hebrew Union College, Cincinnati, Ohio: MS-7: Annie Nathan Meyer Papers

Moorland-Spingarn Research Center, Howard University, Washington, DC: Angelina Weld Grimké Collection

Primary Sources

Alcott, Louisa May. *Eight Cousins*. New York: Puffin Books, 1995.

Broun, Heywood and Margaret Leech. *Anthony Comstock: Roundsman of the Lord*. New York: The Literary Guild of America, 1927.

Clarke, Edward H. *Sex in Education, or a Fair Chance for Girls*. Boston: J. R. Osgood and Company, 1875.

Comstock, Anthony. *Morals Versus Art*. New York: Ogilvie & Co., 1887.

Comstock, Anthony. *Traps for the Young*. New York: Funk & Wagnalls Co. 1883.

Davis, Rebecca Harding. *Kitty's Choice: A Story of Berrytown*. Philadephia: J. B. Lippincott and Company, 1874.

Davis, Rebecca Harding. "The Wife's Story." *The Atlantic Monthly* 14 (1864).

Gibbs, Philip. *The New Man: A Portrait of the Latest Type*. London: Sir Isaac Pitman & Sons, Ltd., 1913. <https://babel.hathitrust.org/cgi/pt?id=hvd.3 2044014280564&view=1up&seq=9>.

Gilman, Charlotte Perkins. "Birth Control." *The Forerunner* 6, no. 7 (1915): 177–80. <https://babel.hathitrust.org/cgi/pt?id=coo.31924106110657&view=1up&seq=191&skin=2021>.

Gilman, Charlotte Perkins. "Brieux's Play, 'Damaged Goods.'" *The Forerunner* 4, no. 4 (1913): 112. <https://babel.hathitrust.org/cgi/pt?id=mdp.39015014168648&view=1up&seq=120>.

Gilman, Charlotte Perkins. *The Crux*. Durham, NC and London: Duke University Press, 2003.

Gilman, Charlotte Perkins. *Mag-Marjorie and Won Over*. Forest Hills, NY: Ironweed Press, Inc., 1999.

Gilman, Charlotte Perkins. *Moving the Mountain*. Blacksburg, VA: Wilder Publications, Inc., 2011.

Gilman, Charlotte Perkins. "The Vintage." In *The Yellow Wall-Paper, Herland, and Selected Writings*, edited by Denise D. Knight, 319–27. New York: Penguin Books, 2009.

Gilman, Charlotte Perkins. "Why I Wrote The Yellow Wallpaper." In *The Yellow Wallpaper and Other Stories*, edited by Robert Schulman, 331–2. Oxford: Oxford University Press, 2009.

Gilman, Charlotte Perkins. "With Her in Ourland." *The Forerunner* 7 (1916).

Grand, Sarah. "The New Aspect of the Woman Question." *The North American Review* 158 (1894): 270–6. <https://archive.org/details/jstor-25103291/page/n1/mode/2up?q=new+woman>.

Grimké, Angelina Weld. "The Closing Door." *The Birth Control Review* 3, no. 10 (1919): 8–12. <https://babel.hathitrust.org/cgi/pt?id=hvd.hnp3k3&view=1up&seq=424&skin=2021>.

Grimké, Angelina Weld. "'Rachel' The Play of the Month: The Reason and Synopsis by the Author." *The Competitor* 1, no. 1 (1920): 51–2. <https://babel.hathitrust.org/cgi/pt?id=pst.000066962656&view=1up&seq=61&size=150>.

Grimké, Angelina Weld. *Rachel: A Play in Three Acts*. Boston: The Cornhill Company, 1920.

Harper, Frances Ellen Watkins. *Iola Leroy, or Shadows Uplifted*, edited by Koritha Mitchell. Ontario: Broadview Press, 2018.

Johnson, Georgia Douglas. "Safe." In *Strange Fruit: Plays on Lynching by American Women*, edited by Kathy A. Perkins and Judith L. Stephens, 110–15. Bloomington: Indiana University Press, 1998.

Kenton, Edna. "The Pap We Have Been Fed On VIII: 'Lady Doctresses' of Nineteenth Century Fiction." *The Bookman* 44 (1916): 280–7. <https://www.unz.com/print/Bookman-1916nov-00280/>.

Meyer, Annie Nathan. "Black Souls." In *Strange Fruit: Plays on Lynching by American Women*, edited by Kathy A. Perkins and Judith L. Stephens, 133–73. Bloomington: Indiana University Press, 1998.

Meyer, Annie Nathan. *Helen Brent, M.D.* Hastings, NE: Hastings College Press, 2020.
Meyer, Annie Nathan. *It's Been Fun: An Autobiography.* New York: Schuman, 1966.
Meyer, Annie Nathan. Letter to the Editor, *The Bookman* 45 (1917): 548. <http://babel.hathitrust.org/cgi/pt?id=mdp.39015030008950;view=1up;seq=573>.
Mitchell, S. Weir. *Fat and Blood.* Philadelphia: J. B. Lippincott Company, 1891.
Mitchell, S. Weir. *Wear and Tear, or Hints for the Overworked.* Philadelphia: J. B. Lippincott Company, 1887.
Morrow, Prince. *Social Diseases and Marriage.* New York and Philadelphia: Lea Brothers and Co., 1904.
Phelps, Elizabeth Stuart. *Doctor Zay.* Lexington, KY: CreateSpace Independent Publishing Platform, 2013.
"Recent Fiction: *Helen Brent, M.D..*" *The Critic* 543.16 (1892): 30–1. <http://babel.hathitrust.org/cgi/pt?id=mdp.39015047773554;view=1up;seq=34>.
Review of *A Country Doctor* by Sarah Orne Jewett. *The Dial* (1884): 66. <https://babel.hathitrust.org/cgi/pt?id=hvd.32044089408348&view=1up&seq=80&q1=A%20Country%20Doctor>.
Review of *Doctor Zay* by Elizabeth Stuart Phelps. *The Atlantic Monthly* 50 (1882): 432. <https://babel.hathitrust.org/cgi/pt?id=uiug.30112110809743;view=1up;seq=466m>.
Review of *Kitty's Choice: A Story of Berrytown* by Rebecca Harding Davis. *Godey's Lady's Book and Magazine* 88 (1874): 184. <https://babel.hathitrust.org/cgi/pt?id=pst.000020202385&view=1up&seq=176&q1=Berrytown>.
Review of *The Portrait of a Lady* and *Doctor Breen's Practice. The Atlantic Monthly* 49 (1882): 126–30. <https://babel.hathitrust.org/cgi/pt?id=coo.31924080787504;view=1up;seq=132>.
United States v. Bennett 24 Fed. Cas. 1093, No. 14,571 (SDNY 1879). <https://law.resource.org/pub/us/case/reporter/F.Cas/0024.f.cas/0024.f.cas.1093.pdf>.
United States v. One Book Entitled "Ulysses" 72 F.2d 705 (2d Cir. 1934). <https://law.justia.com/cases/federal/appellate-courts/F2/72/705/1549734/>.
Wright, Sir Almroth. *The Unexpurgated Case Against Woman Suffrage.* New York: Paul B. Hoeber, 1913.

SECONDARY SOURCES

Adams, Katherine. "Feminist Alcott?" In *Critical Insights: Louisa May Alcott*, edited by Gregory Eiselein and Anne K. Phillips, 52–65. Amenia, NY: Grey House Publishing, Inc., 2016.
Ahmed, Sara. "Affective Economies." *Social Text* 22, no. 2 (2004): 117–39.

Alaimo, Stacy. *Bodily Natures: Science, Environment, and the Material Self.* Bloomington and Indianapolis: Indiana University Press, 2010.

Allen, Judith. "Reconfiguring Vice: Charlotte Perkins Gilman, Prostitution, and Frontier Sexual Contacts." In *Charlotte Perkins Gilman: Optimist Reformer*, edited by Jill Rudd and Val Gough, 173–99. Iowa City: University of Iowa Press, 1999.

Altschuler, Sari. *The Medical Imagination: Literature and Health in the Early United States.* Philadelphia: University of Pennsylvania Press, 2018.

Appiah, Kwame Anthony. "The Case for Capitalizing the B in Black." *The Atlantic*, June 18, 2020. <https://www.theatlantic.com/ideas/archive/2020/06/time-to-capitalize-blackand-white/613159/>.

Barad, Karen. *Meeting the Universe Halfway: Quantum Physics and the Entanglement of Matter and Meaning.* Durham, NC and London: Duke University Press, 2007.

Barad, Karen. "Posthumanist Performativity." In *Material Feminisms*, edited by Stacy Alaimo and Susan Hekman, 120–54. Bloomington and Indianapolis: Indiana University Press, 2008.

Barker-Benfield, Ben. "Sexual Surgery in Late Nineteenth-Century America." *International Journal of Health Services* 5, no. 2 (1975): 279–98.

Barker-Benfield, Ben. "The Spermatic Economy: A Nineteenth Century View of Sexuality," *Feminist Studies* 1, no. 1 (1972): 45–75.

Beer, Janet and Anne Heilmann. "'If I Were a Man': Charlotte Perkins Gilman, Sarah Grand, and the Sex Education of Girls." In *Special Relationships: Anglo-American Antagonisms and Affinities 1854–1936*, edited by Janet Beer and Bridget Bennett, 178–201. Manchester and New York: Manchester University Press, 2002.

Birmingham, Kevin. *The Most Dangerous Book: The Battle for James Joyce's Ulysses.* New York: Penguin Books, 2015.

Bittel, Carla. "Woman, Know Thyself: Producing and Using Phrenological Knowledge in 19th-Century America." *Centaurus* 55, no. 2 (May 2013): 104–30.

Blanchard, Margaret A. "The American Urge to Censor: Freedom of Expression Versus the Desire to Sanitize Society—From Anthony Comstock to 2 Live Crew." *William and Mary Law Review* 33, no. 3 (1992): 768–82.

Brandt, Allan M. *No Magic Bullet: A Social History of Venereal Disease in the United States since 1880.* New York: Oxford University Press, 1987.

Brodie, Janet Farrell. *Contraception and Abortion in Nineteenth Century America.* Ithaca, NY: Cornell University Press, 1994.

Brooks, Peter. *Reading for the Plot: Design and Intention in Narrative.* New York: Vintage, 1985.

Brown, Brené. *Braving the Wilderness: The Quest for True Belonging and the Courage to Stand Alone.* New York: Random House, 2017.

Brown, Brené. *Daring Greatly: How the Courage to Be Vulnerable Transforms the Way We Live, Love, Parent, and Lead*. New York: Avery, 2012.
Browner, Stephanie. *Profound Science and Elegant Literature: Imagining Doctors in Nineteenth-Century America*. Philadelphia: University of Pennsylvania Press, 2005.
Butler, Judith. *Bodies That Matter: On the Discursive Limits of "Sex."* London and New York: Routledge, 1993.
Butler, Judith. *Excitable Speech: A Politics of the Performative*. New York and London: Routledge, 1997.
Butler, Judith. *Gender Trouble: Feminism and the Subversion of Identity*. New York and London: Routledge, [1990] 2006.
Butler, Judith. "Imitation and Gender Insubordination." In *The Lesbian and Gay Studies Reader*, edited by Henry Abelove, Michèle Aina Barale, and David M. Halperin, 307–20. New York and London: Routledge, 1993.
Capo, Beth Widmaeier. *Textual Contraception: Birth Control and Modern American Fiction*. Columbus: The Ohio State University Press, 2007.
Carby, Hazel. *Reconstructing Womanhood: The Emergence of the Afro-American Woman Novelist*. Oxford: Oxford University Press, 1987.
Cayleff, Susan E. *Nature's Path: A History of Naturopathic Healing in America*. Baltimore: John Hopkins University Press, 2016.
Cayleff, Susan E. *Wash and Be Healed: The Water-Cure Movement and Women's Health*. Philadelphia: Temple University Press, 1985.
Charon, Rita. *Narrative Medicine: Honoring the Stories of Illness*. Oxford and New York: Oxford University Press, 2006.
Chauncey, George. *Gay New York: Gender, Urban Culture, and the Making of the Gay Male World, 1890–1940*. New York: Basic Books, 1994.
Chen, Mel Y. *Animacies: Biopolitics, Racial Mattering, and Queer Affect*. Durham, NC and London: Duke University Press, 2012.
Chrisler, Joan C. "A Reproductive Justice Approach to Women's Health." *Analyses of Social Issues and Public Policy* 14, no. 1 (2014): 205–9.
Coffield, K. D., C. Phillips, M. Brady, M. W. Roberts, R. P. Strauss, and J. T. Wright. "The Psychosocial Impact of Developmental Dental Defects in People with Hereditary Amelogenesis Imperfecta." *JADA* 136, no. 5 (2005): 620–30.
Colbert, Soyica Diggs. *The African American Theatrical Body: Reception, Performance, and the Stage*. Cambridge: Cambridge University Press, 2011.
Craig, Layne Parish. *When Sex Changed: Birth Control Politics and Literature Between the Wars*. New Brunswick, NJ: Rutgers, 2013.
Cuddy, Lois A. and Claire M. Roche. *Evolution and Eugenics in American Literature and Culture, 1880–1940*. Lewisburg, PA: Bucknell University Press, 2003.

Cvetkovich, Ann. *An Archive of Feelings: Trauma, Sexuality, and Lesbian Public Cultures*. Durham, NC and London: Duke University Press, 2003.

Daly-Galeano, Marlowe. "Louisa May Alcott's Unruly Medical Women." *Arizona Quarterly* 74, no 4 (2018): 61–86.

Davis, Cathlin M. "An Easy and Well-Ordered Way to Learn: Schooling at Home in Louisa May Alcott's *Eight Cousins* and *Jack and Jill*." *Children's Literature in Education* 42 (2011): 340–53.

Davis, Cynthia J. *Bodily and Narrative Forms: The Influence of Medicine on American Literature, 1845–1915*. Stanford: Stanford University Press, 2000.

D'Emilio, John and Estelle B. Freedman. *Intimate Matters: A History of Sexuality in America*. Chicago: The University of Chicago Press, 2012.

Dyckfehderau, Ruth. "Moral Pap and Male Mothers: The Political Subtexts of Louisa May Alcott's *Eight Cousins or, The Aunt-Hill*." *Legacy* 16, no. 2 (1999): 154–67.

Elbert, Sarah. *A Hunger for Home: Louisa May Alcott and Little Women*. Philadelphia: Temple University Press, 1984.

Ellis, Cristin. *Antebellum Posthuman: Race and Materiality in the Mid-Nineteenth Century*. New York: Fordham University Press, 2018.

Evans, Lynne. "'You See, Children Were the Raison d'Etre': The Reproductive Futurism of Charlotte Perkins Gilman's *Herland*." *Canadian Review of American Studies* 44, no. 2 (2014): 1–18.

Fausto-Sterling, Anne. *Sexing the Body: Gender Politics and the Construction of Sexuality*. New York: Basic Books, 2000.

Ferns, Chris. *Narrating Utopia: Ideology, Gender, Form in Utopian Literature*. Liverpool: Liverpool University Press, 1999.

Fielder, Bridgitte. *Relative Races: Genealogies of Interracial Kinship in Nineteenth-Century America*. Durham, NC and London: Duke University Press, 2020.

Foucault, Michel. *The History of Sexuality, Volume I: An Introduction*, translated by Robert Hurley. New York: Vintage Books, [1978] 1990.

Foucault, Michel. *Power/Knowledge: Selected Interviews and Other Writings, 1972–1977*, edited and translated by Colin Gordon. New York: Pantheon, 1980.

Foucault, Michel. *Society Must Be Defended: Lectures at the Collège de France 1975–1976*, edited by Mauro Bertani and Alessandro Fontana, translated by David Macey. New York: Picador, 2003.

Fox, Ann M. "A Different Integration: Race and Disability in Early-Twentieth-Century African American Drama by Women." *Legacy* 30, no. 1 (2013): 151–71.

Franks, Matt. "Breeding Aliens, Breeding AIDS: Male Pregnancy, Disability, and Viral Materialism in 'Bloodchild.'" In *The Matter of Disability: Materiality, Biopolitics, Crip Affect*, edited by David T. Mitchell,

Susan Antebi, and Sharon L. Snyder, 182–203. Ann Arbor: University of Michigan Press, 2019.

Frisken, Amanda. "Obscenity, Free Speech, and 'Sporting News' in 1870s America." *Journal of American Studies* 42, no. 3 (2008): 537–77.

Furst, Lillian R. *Between Doctors and Patients: The Changing Balance of Power*. Charlottesville and London: University Press of Virginia, 1998.

Goldenberg, Myrna Gallant. *Annie Nathan Meyer: Barnard Godmother and Gotham Gadfly*. Dissertation, University of Maryland—College Park, 1987.

Gordon, Linda. *The Moral Property of Women: A History of Birth Control Politics in America*. Chicago: University of Illinois Press, 2002.

Gordon, Lynn D. "Annie Nathan Meyer and Barnard College: Mission and Identity in Women's Higher Education, 1889–1950." *History of Education Quarterly* 26, no. 4 (1986): 503–22.

Gough, Val. "'In the Twinkling of an Eye': Gilman's Utopian Imagination." In *A Very Different Story: Studies on the Fiction of Charlotte Perkins Gilman*, edited by Val Gough and Jill Rudd, 129–43. Liverpool: Liverpool University Press, 1998.

Gray, Christine R. "*Mara*, Angelina Weld Grimké's Other Play and the Problems of Recovering Texts." In *Black Women Playwrights: Visions on the American Stage*, edited by Carol P. Marsh-Lockett, 69–85. New Brunswick, NJ: Routledge, 1999.

Gregg, Melissa and Gregory J. Seigworth, ed. Introduction to *The Affect Theory Reader*. Durham, NC and London: Duke University Press 2010.

Grosz, Elizabeth. *Volatile Bodies: Toward a Corporeal Feminism*. Bloomington: Indiana University Press, 1994.

Halberstam, Judith (Jack). *The Queer Art of Failure*. Durham, NC and London: Duke University Press, 2011.

Haller, John S. and Robin M. Haller. *The Physician and Sexuality in Victorian America*. New York: W. W. Norton and Company, Inc., 1974.

Hames-Garcia, Michael. "How Real Is Race?" In *Material Feminisms*, edited by Stacy Alaimo and Susan Hekman, 308–39. Bloomington: Indiana University Press, 2008.

Hamlin, Kimberly A. *From Eve to Evolution: Darwin, Science, and Women's Rights in Gilded Age America*. Chicago: University of Chicago Press, 2014.

Haraway, Donna. *The Companion Species Manifesto: Dogs, People, and Significant Otherness*. Chicago: Prickly Paradigm Press, 2003.

Haraway, Donna. *Simians, Cyborgs, and Women: The Reinvention of Nature*. New York: Routledge, 1991.

Haraway, Donna. *When Species Meet*. Minneapolis: University of Minnesota Press, 2007.

Harris, Sharon. "Rebecca Harding Davis' *Kitty's Choice* and the Disabled Woman Physician." *American Literary Realism* 44, no. 1 (2011): 23–45.

Hawksley, Lucinda. *Bitten by Witch Fever: Wallpaper and Arsenic in the Victorian Home*. New York: Thames & Hudson Ltd./The National Archives, 2016.

Hester, Michelle. "An Examination of the Relationship Between Race and Gender in an Early Twentieth-Century Drama: A Study of Angelina Weld Grimké's *Rachel*." *The Journal of Negro History* 79, no. 2 (1994): 248–56.

Horowitz, Helen Lefkowitz. *Rereading Sex: Battles over Sexual Knowledge and Suppression in Nineteenth-Century America*. New York: Vintage Books, 2002.

Horowitz, Helen Lefkowitz. *Wild Unrest: The Making of "The Yellow Wallpaper."* Oxford: Oxford University Press, 2010.

Horvitz, Deborah M. *Literary Trauma: Sadism, Memory, and Sexual Violence in American Women's Fiction*. Albany: State University of New York Press, 2000.

Jackson, Zakiyyah Iman. "Animal: New Directions in the Theorization of Race and Posthumanism." *Feminist Studies* 39, no. 3 (2013): 669–85.

James, Pearl. *The New Death: American Modernism and World War I*. University of Virginia Press, 2013.

Jordan, Winthrop D. "Historical Origins of the One-Drop Rule in the United States." *Journal of Critical Mixed Race Studies* 1, no. 1 (2014): 98–132. <https://escholarship.org/uc/item/91g761b3>.

Kafer, Alison. *Feminist, Queer, Crip*. Bloomington and Indianapolis: Indiana University Press, 2013.

Kaplan, Carla. "Before There Was Karen, There Was Miss Anne." Biographers International Organization. <https://biographersinternational.org/before-there-was-karen-there-was-miss-anne/>.

Kaplan, Carla. *Miss Anne in Harlem: The White Women of the Black Renaissance*. New York: Harper Collins, 2013.

Kline, Wendy. *Bodies of Knowledge: Sexuality, Reproduction, and Women's Health in the Second Wave*. Chicago: University of Chicago Press, 2010.

Kline, Wendy. *Building a Better Race: Gender, Sexuality, and Eugenics from the Turn of the Century to the Baby Boom*. Berkeley: University of California Press, 2001.

Koerber, Amy. *From Hysteria to Hormones: A Rhetorical History*. University Park: Pennsylvania State University Press, 2018.

Kuhn, Annette. *Cinema, Censorship, and Sexuality, 1909–1925*. New York: Routledge, 1988.

Kupetz, Joshua. "Disability Ecology and the Rematerialization of Literary Disability Studies." In *The Matter of Disability: Materiality, Biopolitics, Crip Affect*, edited by David T. Mitchell, Susan Antebi, and Sharon L. Snyder, 48–66. Ann Arbor: University of Michigan Press, 2019.

Ladenson, Elisabeth. *Dirt for Art's Sake: Books on Trial from "Madame Bovary" to "Lolita."* Ithaca and London: Cornell University Press, 2007.
Laqueur, Thomas. *Making Sex: Body and Gender from the Greeks to Freud.* Cambridge, MA: Harvard University Press, 1990.
Levitas, Ruth. *The Concept of Utopia.* Oxford: Peter Lang, 1990.
Longmore, Paul. "'Heaven's Special Children': The Making of Poster Children." In *The Disability Studies Reader*, fourth edition, edited by Lennard J. Davis, 34–41. New York: Routledge, 2013.
MacKell, Jan. *Brothels, Bordellos, and Bad Girls: Prostitution in Colorado, 1860–1930.* Albuquerque: University of New Mexico Press, 2004.
Mandel, Naomi. *Against the Unspeakable: Complicity, the Holocaust, and Slavery in America.* Charlottesville and London: University of Virginia Press, 2006.
Martell, Colleen. "Speaking Bodies: Listening for Mary Gove Nichols (1810–84)." *Feminist Formations* 27, no. 2 (2015): 146–64.
Martin, Emily. *Flexible Bodies: Tracking Immunity in American Culture—From the Days of Polio to the Age of AIDS.* Boston: Beacon Press, 1994.
McGregor, Deborah Kuhn. *From Midwives to Medicine: The Birth of American Gynecology.* New Brunswick, NJ: Rutgers University Press, 1998.
McRuer, Robert. *Crip Theory: Cultural Signs of Queerness and Disability.* New York and London: New York University Press, 2006.
Meier, Joyce. "The Refusal of Motherhood in African American Women's Theater." *MELUS* 25, no. 3/4 (2000): 117–39.
Mesch, Rachel. "A New Man for the New Woman? Men, Marriage, and Feminism in the Belle Epoque." *Historical Reflections* 38, no. 3 (2012): 85–106.
Mitchell, David and Sharon Snyder. *Narrative Prosthesis: Disability and the Dependencies of Discourse.* Ann Arbor: The University of Michigan Press, 2000.
Mitchell, David T., Susan Antebi, and Sharon L. Snyder. Introduction to *The Matter of Disability: Materiality, Biopolitics, Crip Affect.* Edited by David T. Mitchell, Susan Antebi, and Sharon L. Snyder. Ann Arbor: University of Michigan Press, 2019.
Mitchell, Koritha. *From Slave Cabins to the White House: Homemade Citizenship in African American Culture.* Urbana: University of Illinois Press, 2020.
Mitchell, Koritha. Introduction to *Iola Leroy, or Shadows Uplifted* by Frances Ellen Watkins Harper, edited by Koritha Mitchell. Ontario: Broadview Press, 2018.
Mitchell, Koritha. *Living with Lynching: African American Lynching Plays, Performance, and Citizenship, 1890–1930.* Urbana: University of Illinois Press, 2011.

Moran, Jeffrey P. *Teaching Sex: The Shaping of Adolescence in the Twentieth Century.* Cambridge, MA: Harvard University Press, 2000.

Morantz-Sanchez, Regina. *Sympathy and Science: Women Physicians in American Medicine.* Oxford: Oxford University Press, 2000.

Morris, Tim. "Professional Ethics and Professional Erotics in Elizabeth Stuart Phelps's *Doctor Zay*." *Studies in American Fiction* 21 (1993): 141–52.

Murphy, Michelle. *Seizing the Means of Reproduction: Entanglements of Feminism, Health, and Technoscience.* Durham, NC: Duke University Press, 2012.

Nash, Linda. *Inescapable Ecologies: A History of Environment, Disease, and Knowledge.* Berkeley and Los Angeles: University of California Press, 2006.

Nelson, Jennifer. *Women of Color and the Reproductive Rights Movement.* New York: New York University Press, 2003.

Otis, Laura. *Banned Emotions: How Metaphors Can Shape What People Feel.* Oxford: Oxford University Press, 2019.

Owens, Deirdre Cooper. *Medical Bondage: Race, Gender, and the Origins of American Gynecology.* Athens: University of Georgia Press, 2017.

Patterson, Martha H. *Beyond the Gibson Girl: Reimagining the American New Woman, 1895–1915.* Urbana and Chicago: University of Illinois Press, 2008.

Perkins, Kathy A. and Judith L. Stephens. Introduction to *Strange Fruit: Plays on Lynching by American Women.* Edited by Kathy A. Perkins and Judith L. Stephens. Bloomington: Indiana University Press, 1998.

Pernick, Martin S. *The Black Stork: Eugenics and the Death of "Defective" Babies in American Medicine and Motion Pictures Since 1915.* New York and Oxford: Oxford University Press, 1996.

Pfaelzer, Jean. *Parlor Radical: Rebecca Harding Davis and the Origins of American Social Realism.* Pittsburgh: University of Pittsburgh Press, 1996.

Pickens, Therí Alyce. *Black Madness::Mad Blackness.* Durham, NC and London: Duke University Press, 2019.

Puglionesi, Alicia. "'Your Whole Effort Has Been to Create Desire': Reproducing Knowledge and Evading Censorship in the Nineteenth-Century Subscription Press." *Bulletin of the History of Medicine* 89, no. 3 (2015): 463–90.

Ray, Sarah Jaquette. *The Ecological Other: Environmental Exclusion in American Culture.* Tucson: The University of Arizona Press, 2013.

Rich, Charlotte J. *Transcending the New Woman: Multiethnic Narratives in the Progressive Era.* Columbia: University of Missouri Press, 2009.

Richardson, Angelique. *Love and Eugenics in the Late Nineteenth Century: Rational Reproduction and the New Woman.* Oxford: Oxford University Press, 2003.

Robbins, Hollis. Introduction to *Iola Leroy, or Shadows Uplifted* by Frances Ellen Watkins Harper, edited by Henry Louis Gates Jr. London: Penguin Books, 2010.
Roemer, Kenneth. *Utopian Audiences: How Readers Locate Nowhere*. Boston: University of Massachusetts Press, 2003.
Rothstein, William G. *American Physicians in the Nineteenth Century: From Sects to Science*. Baltimore: The John Hopkins University Press, 1972.
Rusert, Britt. *Fugitive Science: Empiricism and Freedom in Early African American Culture*. New York: New York University Press, 2017.
Samuels, Ellen. *Fantasies of Identification: Disability, Gender, Race*. New York: New York University Press, 2014.
Sargent, Lyman Tower. "The Three Faces of Utopianism Revisited." *Utopian Studies 5*, no. 1 (1994): 1–37.
Schaefer, Eric. *"Bold! Daring! Shocking! True!": A History of Exploitation Films, 1919–1959*. Durham, NC: Duke University Press, 1999.
Schiebinger, Londa. *Nature's Body: Gender in the Making of Modern Science*. New Brunswick, NJ: Rutgers University Press, 2010.
Schull, Andrew. *Hysteria: The Disturbing History*. New York: Oxford University Press, 2009.
Schuller, Kyla. *The Biopolitics of Feeling: Race, Sex, and Science in the Nineteenth Century*. Durham, NC and London: Duke University Press, 2018.
Schuller, Kyla. *The Trouble with White Women: A Counterhistory of Feminism*. New York: Bold Type Books, 2021.
Seibers, Tobin. "Disability and the Theory of Complex Embodiment: For Identity Politics in a New Register." In *The Disability Studies Reader*, fifth edition, edited by Lennard J. Davis, 313–32. New York and London: Routledge, 2017.
Seibers, Tobin. "Disability Experience on Trial." In *Material Feminisms*, edited by Stacy Alaimo and Susan Hekman, 291–307. Bloomington: Indiana University Press, 2009.
Seibers, Tobin. "Returning the Social to the Social Model." In *The Matter of Disability: Materiality, Biopolitics, Crip Affect*, edited by David T. Mitchell, Susan Antebi, and Sharon L. Snyder, 39–47. Ann Arbor: University of Michigan Press, 2019.
Seitler, Dana. *Atavistic Tendencies: The Culture of Science in American Modernity*. Minneapolis: University of Minnesota Press, 2008.
Seitler, Dana. Introduction to *The Crux* by Charlotte Perkins Gilman. Durham, NC and London: Duke University Press, 2003.
Semonche, John E. *Censoring Sex: A Historical Journey through American Media*. Lanham: Rowman & Littlefield, 2007.
Smith-Rosenberg, Carroll. *Disorderly Conduct: Visions of Gender in Victorian America*. New York and Oxford: Oxford University Press, 1985.

Spongberg, Mary. *Feminizing Venereal Disease: The Body of the Prostitute in Nineteenth-Century Medical Discourse.* New York: New York University Press, 1997.
Stern, Madeleine B. "Louisa Alcott's Feminist Letters." *Studies in the American Renaissance* (1978): 429–52.
Stetz, Margaret D. "The Late-Victorian 'New Man' and Neo-Victorian 'Neo-Man.'" *Victoriographies 5*, no. 2 (2015): 105–21.
Stone, Andrea. *Black Well-Being: Health and Selfhood in Antebellum Black Literature.* Gainesville: University of Florida Press, 2016.
Swenson, Kristin. *Medical Women and Victorian Fiction.* Columbia: University of Missouri Press, 2005.
Tavera, Stephanie Peebles. "Her Body, *Herland*: Reproductive Health and Dis/topian Satire." *Utopian Studies* 29, no. 1 (2018): 1–20.
Tetrault, Lisa. *The Myth of Seneca Falls: Memory and the Women's Suffrage Movement, 1848–1898.* Chapel Hill: University of North Carolina Press, 2014.
Thrailkill, Jane F. *Affecting Fictions: Mind, Body, and Emotion in American Literary Realism.* Cambridge, MA: Harvard University Press, 2007.
Thrailkill, Jane F. "Doctoring 'The Yellow Wallpaper,'" *English Literary History (ELH)* 69, no. 2 (2002): 525–66.
Thurner, Manuela. "'Better Citizens Without the Ballot': American Anti-Suffrage Women and Their Rationale During the Progressive Era." *Journal of Women's History 5*, no. 1 (1993): 33–60.
Wald, Priscilla. *Contagious: Cultures, Carriers, and the Outbreak Narrative.* Durham, NC and London: Duke University Press, 2008.
Washington, Harriet A. *Medical Apartheid: The Dark History of Medical Experimentation on Black Americans from Colonial Times to the Present.* New York: Penguin 2008.
Wegener, Frederick. "'A Line of Her Own': Henry James's 'Sturdy Little Doctress' and the Medical Woman as Literary Type in Gilded-Age America." *Texas Studies in Literature and Language* 39, no. 2 (1997): 139–80.
Wegener, Frederick. "The Literary Representation of Women Doctors in the United States, 1860–1920." *Literature Compass* 4, no. 3 (2007): 576–98.
Wegener, Frederick. "'What a Comfort a Woman Doctor Is!': Medical Women in the Life and Writing of Charlotte Perkins Gilman." In *Charlotte Perkins Gilman: Optimist Reformer*, edited by Jill Rudd and Val Gough, 45–73. Iowa City: University of Iowa Press, 1999.
Weinbaum, Alys Eve. *Wayward Reproductions: Genealogies of Race and Nation in Transatlantic Modern Thought.* Durham, NC: Duke University Press, 2004.
Weingarten, Karen. *Abortion in the American Imagination: Before Life and Choice, 1880–1940.* New Brunswick, NJ: Rutgers University Press, 2014.

Werbel, Amy. *Lust on Trial: Censorship and the Rise of American Obscenity in the Age of Anthony Comstock*. New York: Columbia University Press, 2018.

Wheeler, Lorna Raven. "The Queer Collaboration: Angelina Weld Grimké and the Birth Control Movement." In *Critical Insights: LGBTQ Literature*, edited by Robert C. Evans, 179–92. Amenia, NY: Grey House Publishing, 2015.

Whorton, James C. *Crusaders for Fitness: The History of American Health Reformers*. Princeton, NJ: Princeton University Press, 1982.

Wolfe, Cary. *Before the Law: Humans and Other Animals in a Biopolitical Frame*. Chicago and London: The University of Chicago Press, 2013.

Wood, Janice. "Prescription for a Periodical: Medicine, Sex, and Obscenity in the Nineteenth Century, As Told in 'Dr. Foote's Health Monthly.'" *American Periodicals* 18, no. 1 (2008): 26–44.

Wynter, Sylvia. "Unsettling the Coloniality of Being/Power/Truth/Freedom: Towards the Human, After Man, It's Overrepresentation—An Argument." *The New Centennial Review* 3, no. 3 (2003): 257–337.

Yao, Xtine. *Disaffected: The Cultural Politics of Unfeeling in Nineteenth-Century America*. Durham, NC and London: Duke University Press, 2021.

Ziegler, Mary. "Eugenic Feminism: Mental Hygiene, the Women's Movement, and the Campaign for Eugenic Legal Reform, 1900–1935." *Harvard Journal of Law & Gender* 31, no. 1 (2008): 211–35.

Zschoche, Sue. "Dr. Clarke Revisited: Science, True Womanhood, and Female Collegiate Education." *History of Education Quarterly* 29, no. 4 (1989): 545–69.

INDEX

abortion, access to, 4, 7–9, 16, 26n, 181, 184, 186
Adams, Katherine, 59n
affect
    narrative, 6, 71–6, 90–3, 166
    queer, 144
affect theory, 8, 9, 26n, 94–5n, 168–9; see also narrative affect
affective
    attachments, 9
    economies, 10
    fear, 141–77
    fictions, 14–21
Age of Hysteria, 31, 58n
agential realism, 9–10, 70–1, 92, 108, 124
Ahmed, Sara, 10
Alaimo, Stacy, 43, 48, 63–4n
Alcott, Louisa May
    closed-system theory, 48–9
    Eight Cousins, or The Aunt-Hill, 29–32, 47–8, 50–3, 55–7, 57–9n, 61n, 77, 143
    feminism, 59n, 65n
    flowers, 176n
    Hospital Sketches, 32, 140n
    "My Contraband", 112–13
    outdoors as space for healing, 64n
    shame, 19
Alcott, William
    The Young Wife, 59n
    The Young Woman's Book of Health, 52
Allen, Judith, 172n, 173n
Altschuler, Sari, 3, 15, 39–40
amalgamation, 103–5, 111, 112, 118–20, 132n, 139–40n
"Amazonian coarseness", 50–1
amelogenesis imperfecta, 91, 101n
American Academy of Environmental Health (AAEH), 50
American Public Health Association (APHA), 49
American School of Evolution, 36
American Social Hygiene Association (ASHA), 171n, 172n
American Society for Sanitary and Moral Prophylaxis (ASSMP), 152

INDEX

Anderson, Margaret, 20, 46
animacy, 34–6, 44–5, 47, 105
animal subjectivity, 115
animality, 119–20, 130, 133n
  queer, 118–20
Antebi, Susan, *The Matter of Disability: Materiality, Biopolitics, Crip Affect*, 11
Anthony, Susan B., 113
anti-amalgamation, 122–4, 128–9, 132n, 133n, 138n
anti-lynching plays, 178–9, 193n, 194n
anti-miscegenation law, 119
anti-VD campaign, 88, 141–77, 170–1n, 193n
anti-VD campaign films, 141, 149, 163–5
Appiah, Kwame Anthony, 25n
Aristotle's Compleat Master-piece, 35
"arrested development", 15, 49
arsenic, 42–3
Atlanta Constitution, 111
The Atlantic, 25n
The Atlantic Monthly, 92
Atwood, Margaret, *The Handmaid's Tale*, 174n
Austin, J. L., *How to Do Things with Words*, 118–19

Baker, Newton, 145, 171n
Barad, Karen
  agential realism, 9–10, 63n, 70–1, 92, 124
  Hames-Garcia, Michael, 109–10
  "static entity", 42
  superposition, 108, 132n
  wave-particle duality, 125, 168
Barker-Benfield, Ben, 57n, 153
Barnum, P. T., 178
Beardsley, Monroe, "The Affective Fallacy", 71–2
Beer, Janet, 173–4n
"before the law", 102–40
  Black women, 22, 134n, 147
  Butler, Judith, 137–8n
  censorship, 17
Bennett, D. M., 45–6

Bigelow, Maurice, 193n
biocertification, 121
biological determinism, 2, 8–9, 30, 89
biopolitics, 6–14, 25n, 109–10, 131, 152–3, 179, 182
biopower, 6–7, 25n, 58n, 64n, 99n, 106–7, 138n
  agential matter, 36
  sentimental, 31
Bird, Robert Montgomery, *Sheppard Lee*, 15
birth control campaign, 4, 16–17, 172n, 174n, 180–2, 193n, 194n
The Birth Control Review, 181, 184
Black bodies, 178–9
Black female bodies, 74, 103–5, 112, 131
black female hypersexuality, 18, 112, 118–19, 134n, 191
Black female subjectivity, 102–40
"black humor", 118
black hypersexuality, 22, 37n, 144, 165
Black liberation, 7
Black madness, 114, 186–8
Black nursing, 115–17, 137n, 189
black rapists, 118–19, 182
black sexuality, 75
Black Souls, 178
The Black Stork (1915), 144, 147, 151, 163–5, 168, 171n
Blackness, 25n, 111–12, 122, 128, 130, 138n, 165–7
  and disability, 164
  embodied, 179–80
Blackwell, Elizabeth, 3
Blatchford, Judge Samuel, 45–6, 73
bodily markings, 121–4
Bohr, Niels, 108
book reviews, 68–71, 92–3, 94n
The Bookman, 68–9, 89, 93, 93n, 150
Brandt, Allan M., *No Magic Bullet: A Social History of Venereal Disease in the United States since 1880*, 162
Brieux, Eugene, *Damaged Goods*, 142, 148–50, 169–70n
Brooks, Peter, 100n

INDEX

Broun, Heywood, 17, 27n
Brown, Brené, 11–12, 17, 124, 139n
   Daring Greatly, 12
Brown, Charles Brockden, *Arthur Mervyn*, 15
Brown, Emily, 178
Browner, Stephanie, 47, 50
Buckley, J. M., 64n
Burrill, Mary Powell, 179
   Aftermath, 182
Butler, Judith, 69, 70–1, 75, 86
   Bodies That Matter, 35–6
   Excitable Speech: Politics of the Performative, 73–4, 93
   Gender Trouble: Feminism and the Subversion of Identity, 138n
   "Imitation and Gender Insubordination", 138n
   Precarious Life: The Powers of Mourning and Violence, 137–8n

The Call, "What Every Woman Ought to Know", 20
Camper, Petrus, 138n
Capo, Beth Widmaier, 16, 181
Carby, Hazel, 111–12
Cassell Publishing Company, 102
Castiglia, Christopher, 9
Cayleff, Susan, 52, 66n
censorship, 73–5, 96n, 102–6, 118–19, 138n, 141–2, 152, 180–1; *see also* Comstock law
Charcot, Jean-Martin, 58n, 60n
   Lectures on the Diseases of the Nervous System, 31
Charon, Rita
   empathy, 12–13, 40, 93, 131
   general versus particular cases of illness, 38
   identity without judgement, 99n
   intersubjectivity, 95–6n
   narrative in clinical medicine, 96n
   narrative medicine, 75–7, 84, 99n, 142–3, 163
   storytelling, 4, 127–8

Chauncy, George, 18
Chen, Mel Y., 10–11, 34–5, 43, 64n, 107, 118, 144
   Animacies: Biopolitics, Racial Mattering, and Queer Affect, 34–5, 95n
Chereau, Achille, 59n
Chicago, sex education, 145
Chicken Run (2000), 39, 55
Christian Recorder, 112
Christianity, 128–31
Civil Code Article 213, 89–90
Clarke, Dr. Edward H., 31–9
   Alcott, Louisa May, 47–9, 58n
   "arrested development", 15, 35, 49
   biological determinism, 89
   case studies, 60n
   closed-system theory, 30, 32–3, 99n
   female masculinity, 50–1
   New Woman, 79–80
   postpartum depression, 42
   Sex in Education, 1–2, 32–3, 35, 36–37
Clay, Edward William, "Practical Amalgamation" prints, 103–5, 118, 122, 132n
closed-system theory, 30, 32–3, 36–7, 48, 99n
Cockburn, Chief Justice Alexander, 46
Colbert, Soyica Diggs, 179
Cole, Rebecca J., 117, 132n
Commission on Training Camp Activities (CTCA), 145, 171n
Committee on Sex Hygiene, 145
Compain, Louise Marie, *L'un vers l'autre*, 89–90
companion species, 63n
The Competitor, 187
complex embodiment, 8, 16, 40, 62n, 166–8, 177n
complicity, 75, 126–7, 139n
Comstock, Anthony, 16–21, 43–8
   Alcott, Louisa May, 30
   censorship cases, 65n
   Morals Versus Art, 19

212

narrative, 71–3
obscenity cases, 102–5
reproductive control, 96n
Sanger, Margaret, 8, 180
shame, 162
suicide, 95n
Traps for the Young, 44–5, 64n
United States Post Office, 4
Comstock law, 16–21, 43–8
   anti-amalgamation, 123
   censorship cases, 65n
   impressibility, 73
   Knoedler, Edmund, 194n
   lynchings, 182
   obscenity cases, 24n, 102–5
   queer animality, 118–19
   Sanger, Margaret, 4
   SB8, 9
   sex education, 29, 145, 152
   sexuality, 64n
   shame, 12
   unspeakable, 74
   women writers of medical fiction, 3, 27n
   see also censorship
Comstockery, 19, 141
"conspiracy of silence", 141, 152
Coughlan, R., "Science Moves in on Viruses", 146
Coviello, Peter, 9
Craddock, Ida, 72
Craig, Jenny, 51
Craig, Layne Parish, 16, 184, 193n
crip affect, 6–14, 91–2, 145–55
   and race, 163–9
   see also disability
crip medicine, 29–67, 105
crip theory, 11, 65–6n
The Crisis, 182
Crow, Jim, 185, 187
Crumper, Rebecca Lee Davis, 117, 132n
Cvetkovich, Ann, 10

Daly-Galeano, Marlowe, 32, 59n, 140n
Damaged Goods (1914), 141–4, 147–51, 148, 149, 163–5

d'Annunzio, Gabriele, *The Triumph of Death*, 65n
danse du ventre, 103
Darwinism, 100, 113–14, 120
Davis, Cathlin M., 51
Davis, Cynthia J., 15, 19, 80, 89, 90, 92–3, 97n, 112, 134n, 139–40n
Davis, Paulina Wright, 112, 194n
Davis, Rebecca Harding, 29, 41–2, 48–9, 64n, 87
   Kitty's Choice: A Story of Berrytown, 31, 32, 52, 53–7, 57n, 68, 77
   Life in the Iron Mills, 32
   "The Wife's Story", 41–2
The Days' Doings, 118–19
de-animacy, 3, 105, 144
de-generation, 183–5, 189–91
D'Emilio, John, 158–9, 172n
Derrida, Jacques, "Before the Law", 137n
Dewey, John, 51
disability, 2–3, 8, 11
   and Blackness, 164
   con, 102
   ecology, 168
   see also crip affect; crip medicine; crip theory
disability narratives, affect in, 90–3
disabled
   embodiment, 167–8
   writers, 76–7
disaffection, 83
Dock, Lavinia, 87
Douglass, Frederick, 103
Douglass, Sarah Mapps, 112
Dyckfehderau, Ruth, 32, 50

"ecological body", 49
Ehrlich, Paul, 159
Elbert, Sarah, 58–9n
Ellis, Cristin, 7, 8, 9, 132–3n
   Antebellum Posthuman: Race and Materiality in the Mid-Nineteenth Century, 25n, 108

INDEX

emasculation, 78, 97n
emotion, 10–13, 40, 50, 53, 56, 71–5, 82–5, 91, 94–5n
empathy, 11–13, 40–1, 75–6, 83–4, 96n, 131, 163
English, Daylanne K., 184
environmental health, 29–67, 63–4n
erotic novels, 19–20
eugenic feminism, 135–6n, 155, 165, 174n, 177n
eugenic marriage, 100n, 113, 145, 147, 155, 165, 167
eugenics
   anti-VD campaign, 147
   birth control, 180, 182, 184
   Galton, Frances, 113–14
   Gilman, Charlotte Perkins, 100n, 135–6n, 155, 165–7, 173n, 176–7n, 193n
   "positive", 113–14
   sterilization, 172n
   Watkins Harper, Frances Ellen, 111
Evans, Lynne, 176–7n

Fanon, Franz, 120
"fantasies of identification", 107–8
The Fantastic Voyage (1966), 146
Fausto-Sterling, Anne, 60n, 121, 138n
fear campaigns, 155–63
female masculinity, 50–1, 54
feminism
   embodied, 113
   eugenics, 135–6n, 155, 165, 174n, 177n
femmes nouvelles, 89–90; see also New Woman
Ferns, Chris, 80
fertility, 174n
Fielder, Bridgitte, 7, 8, 111, 132n
   Relative Races: Genealogies of Interracial Kinship in Nineteenth-Century America, 122
Fifteenth Amendment, 118
Fitzgerald, F. Scott, *The Beautiful and the Damned*, 16
flowers, 61n, 176n

Foote, Edward Bliss, 20
The Forerunner, 88, 150
Foster, Hannah Webster, *The Coquette*, 147, 155–7
Foucault, Michel, 8, 25n, 58n, 138n, 152
   The History of Sexuality, Vol. 1, 64n, 99n
Fox, Ann M., 179
Freedman, Estelle B., 158–9, 172n
Freire, Pablo, *Pedagogy of the Oppressed*, 45
Frisken, Amanda, 18, 118–19

Galton, Frances, 100n, 113–14
Gibbs, Sir Phillip, 97n
   The New Man: A Portrait of the Latest Type, 78
Gilder, Jeanette, 89, 94n
Gilman, Charlotte Perkins
   anti-VD campaign, 147
   "Birth Control", 153–4
   The Black Stork (1915), 164–6
   Comstock law, 20
   "conspiracy of silence", 141–2
   The Crux, 87–8, 142–4, 149–50, 152–5, 165–8, 173n
   Damaged Goods (1914), 150–1
   environmental health, 48
   eugenic feminism, 176–7n
   eugenics, 113, 135–6n
   With Her in Ourland, 81
   Herland, 39, 80–1, 86, 135n, 165, 174n, 176–7n, 181, 193n
   Mag-Marjorie, 70, 73–4, 77, 85–91
   Moving the Mountain, 39, 153–4, 165, 173n, 181
   New Man, 70
   postpartum depression, 62–3n
   prostitutes, 172n
   sex education, 87–8, 173–4n
   "shadow feminism", 62n
   "The Vintage", 142–3, 151–2, 155, 159
   women writers of medical fiction, 4
   "The Yellow Wallpaper", 19, 30–1, 37–43, 53, 56–7, 86, 91, 102, 185

INDEX

Godey's Lady's Book and Magazine, 68
gonorrhea, 142–7, 154–5
Goodman, Daniel Carson, *Hagar Revelly*, 65n
Grady, Henry W., 111
Grand, Sarah, 97n
    "The New Aspects of the Woman Question", 79
Gray, Christine R., 188–91
Gregg, Melissa, 26n
Grimké, Angelina Weld, 179–82, 192–3
    "The Closing Door", 181, 183–4
    "Goldie", 181
    Mara, 179–81, 188–92
    Rachel, 179–88, 192, 194n, 195n
Grosz, Elizabeth, *Volatile Bodies: Toward a Corporeal Feminism*, 60n
gynecologic materialism, 57n
gynecology, 61n, 86–7, 102, 106, 116–17, 137n, 143, 153–4, 157, 175n, 176n

Haiselden, Harry J., 164, 165
Halberstam, Jack, 5, 39, 55, 62n
Haller, John S., 30
Haller, Robin M., 30
Hames-Garcia, Michael, 9–10, 133–4n
    "How Real Is Race?", 109–10
"happy ending", 89–90
Haraway, Donna, 7, 34, 35, 63n, 99n
Harper, Frances Ellen Watkins, 167
    Iola Leroy, or Shadows Uplifted, 75, 102, 106, 121–31
Harper's Weekly, "The Civilization of Blaine" cartoon, 118
Harris, Sharon, 53–4
Hawksley, Lucinda, 42–3
Heilmann, Anne, 173–4n
Hester, Michelle, 184, 195n
Heywood, Ezra, *Cupid's Yokes*, 20, 45–6
Hicklin test, 45–6
Holmes, Oliver Wendell, *Elsie Venner*, 15
homeopathy, 52, 100n
homosexuality, 18
Horowitz, Helen Lefkowitz, 44, 61–4n, 96n, 132n

Horvitz, Deborah M., 127
Howells, William Dean, 80, 81, 89
    Doctor Breen's Practice, 15, 92–3, 100n
Hughes, Langston, "Cora Unashamed", 16
Hull, Gloria T., 184
hydrotherapy, 53–4, 66n, 87
hypodescent, 121–5, 133n
hysteria, 29–67
    Age of Hysteria, 31
    Charcot, Jean-Martin, 60n
    Clarke, Dr. Edward H., 1–2
    Comstock, Anthony, 105
    Gilman, Charlotte Perkins, 85–6
    history of, 58n
    impressibility, 36–7
    male physicians, 61n
    materiality, 30
    rest cure, 102
    suffragists, 62n
    vulnerabliity, 99n
    women writers of medical fiction, 48–9

Ibsen, Henrik, *Ghosts*, 150
"illegal" immigrants, 129–30
The Immortal (1970–71), 146
Immunology Today, 146
impressibility, 30, 36–7, 46, 64n, 113–14, 131, 135n
    language of, 7
injurious speech, 73–5, 95n

Jackson, Zakiyyah Iman, 120, 133n
Jacobs, Harriet, *Incidents in the Life of a Slave Girl*, 114–15, 147
James, Henry, 72
    The Bostonians, 15
James, P. D., *The Children of Men*, 174n
Jewett, Sarah Orne, 15
    A Country Doctor, 52, 94n
Johnson, Georgia Douglas, 179
    Safe, 182–4, 186
Jordan, Winthrop D., 121, 128–9
Joyce, James, *Ulysses*, 20, 46, 65n

INDEX

Kafer, Alison, 11, 43, 48–9, 56, 63–4n, 66n, 79, 91, 168
   Feminist, Queer, Crip, 33–4
Kaplan, Carla, 168–9, 192–3, 196n
Kenton, Edna, 68–9, 89, 93, 93n, 150
Key, Ellen, 87
kinetic medicine, 102–40
kinship, 7–9, 63n, 110–12, 120–8, 130, 144
Kline, Wendy, 194n
Knoedler, Edmund, 102, 194n
Koerber, Amy, 31, 58n, 60n
Krafft-Ebbing, Eichard von, 100–1n
Kuhn, Annette, 149
Kupetz, Joshua, 168

Ladenson, Elisabeth, 65n
Lamarck, Jean-Bapitiste, 36, 47, 49
Lane, Mary E. Bradley, *Mizora*, 174n
language
   of impressibility, 7
   and materiality, 35–7
Larson, Nella, *Quicksand*, 186
Leech, Margaret, 17, 27n
Levitas, Ruth, 98n
Lewis, C. S., *The Screwtape Letters*, 45
liberalism, 7–8, 14
liberation, 8, 9–10, 108
Life magazine, 19
   "Science Moves in on Viruses", 146
Linnaeus, Carl, 61n, 176n
Lippincott's magazine, 29, 57n
The Little Review, 20, 46, 65n
Longmore, Paul, 177n
lynchings, 178–9; *see also* anti-lynching plays

MacKell, Jan, *Brothels, Bordellos, and Bad Girls: Prostitution in Colorado, 1860–1930*, 172–3n
McGregor, Deborah Kuhn, 159
McRuer, Robert, 11, 65–6n
Mandel, Naomi, 136n, 139n
   Against the Unspeakable: Complicity, the Holocaust, and Slavery in America, 74–5, 126–7
Mannish Lesbian, 100–1n
marriage, 89–90, 160–2
   eugenics, 100n, 113, 145, 147, 155, 165, 167
Martell, Colleen, 28n
Martin, Emily, 162–3
   "Historical Overview", 145–6
The Masses, 18
Materia Medica, 87, 99–100n
material entanglements, 108–9, 122–3
Material Feminisms, 109–10
materialisms, new, 62n, 108–9, 177n
materiality, 7, 36–7
   of language, 30, 35–7
maternalists, 173–4n
Maudsley, Dr. Henry, 61n
"meantime", 179
measurement, 120–1, 123–4, 138n
medical knowledge, 96n
"medical materialism", 29–30
Medical Review of Reviews, 169–70n
Meier, Joyce, 182, 186–7
Mesch, Rachel, 89–90
metaphor, 73–4
Meyer, Alfred, 156–7
Meyer, Annie Nathan, 2–3, 20, 142, 150, 164, 174–6n, 179–82
   Black Souls, 169, 180–1, 190, 192–3
   Helen Brent, M. D., 1, 13–14, 27n, 61n, 68–9, 77, 89, 93, 93n, 94n, 102, 142–3, 150, 155–63, 168–9, 174–5n
   It's Been Fun, 156, 175–6n
Mitchell, David T., 41, 90–1
   The Matter of Disability: Materiality, Biopolitics, Crip Affect, 11, 92
   Narrative Prothesis: Disability and the Dependencies of Discourse, 76–7
Mitchell, Koritha, 112–13, 116, 179, 182, 194n

Mitchell, S. Weir, 31–42, 47, 58n, 85–6, 88, 99n, 102, 112
   Fat and Blood, 37
   Narrative Prothesis: Disability and the Dependencies of Discourse, 96n
   Wear and Tear, or Hints for the Overworked, 37, 61n
Möbius strip, 60n
Moran, Jeffrey P., 145
Morantz-Sanchez, Regina, 85, 99n, 101n, 158
More, Thomas, *Utopia*, 55, 80
Morris, Tim, 97–8n
Morrison, Toni, *Beloved*, 186
Morrow, Dr. Prince, 87–8, 151–3, 155, 171n, 172n
   Social Diseases and Marriage, 153, 172n
Morton, Dr. Samuel George, *Crania Americana*, 120–1
Morton, Samuel, 15, 112
Mount Sinai Hospital, 157
Muller, Samuel, 121–2
Mutual Film Corporation, 148

Naquet laws, 89
narrative affect, 6, 71–6
   in disability narratives, 90–3
narrative medicine, 12–13, 68–101, 95–6n, 99n, 127–8, 143, 180
narrative nursing, 128–31, 140n
narrative prothesis, 68–101, 96n, 105–6
Nash, Linda, 49
National Association for the Advancement of Colored People (NAACP), 187–8
National Police Gazette, 118–19
neurathenia, 30
The New England Magazine, 102
New England Woman's Suffrage Association, 32
New Man, 70–2, 76–91, 93, 97n, 105–6
New Woman, 32, 77–80, 82–4, 88–91, 93, 97n, 100–1n, 105–6
New Woman doctor, 27n, 70, 81, 90

New York Recorder, 103
Nichols, Mary Gove, 55, 87, 112, 194n
   Mary Lyndon, 28n
Norplant Depo-Provera Trials, 144
nursing narratives, 128–31, 140n

obscenity cases, 24n, 102–6, 118–19
one-drop rule, 121–2
"one-sex system", 57n
Opportunity, 182
Otis, Laura, 94–5n
   Banned Emotions: How Metaphors Can Shape What People Feel, 72
outbreak narrative, 155–63
outdoor education, 48–52
"over-sexed" bodies, 153–4
Owens, Deirdre Cooper, 116–17, 134n

palimpsest, 10, 107, 123
"panmixia", 73, 112, 139–40n
performativity, 70–1, 86, 118, 120
Pernick, Martin S., 144, 149, 151, 164, 171n
Peterson, Christopher, 132–3n
Pfaelzer, Jean, 32, 55–6
Phelps, Elizabeth Stuart, 82, 87
   Doctor Zay, 15, 52, 70, 72, 74, 77–85, 88–92, 97n–100n
Pickens, Therí Alyce, 114–15, 187
"Pixarvolt" films, 39
posthumanism, 7, 8, 108–9, 119–20, 132–3n
postpartum depression, 19, 38–42, 62–3n, 185
Powers, Richard, *Gain*, 168
Practical Amalgamation series
   "The Wedding", 104
(p)rescription, definition, 4–6
prostitution
   Comstock law, 44
   MacKell, Jan, 172–3n
   Morrow, Dr. Prince, 172n
   sex hygiene films, 147–56
   syphilis epidemic, 142, 146–7
Puglionesi, Alicia, 20, 44, 96n

INDEX

queer affect, 144
queer animality, 118–20
queer culture, 18
queerness, 98n

race, definition, 2–3
"race health", 146–7, 180
race science, 120–8, 133n, 135n
race-making, 7, 15, 122–3
racism, 103
Random House, 65n
Ray, Sarah Jaquette, 53
Reader's Digest, 146
Regina v. Hicklin, 46
"repressive hypothesis", 64n, 152
reproductive justice, 178–96, 194n
reproductive knowledge, 16–17, 19–20
reproductive loss, 180
reproductive rights, 9, 16–18
reproductivity, 179–93
rest cure, 37, 47, 86, 88, 102
Restell, Madame, 72
Rich, Charlotte, 82
risk, 141–77
Ritchie, J. W., *The Primer of Sanitation and Physiology*, 146
Robbins, Hollis, 116, 134n
Robinson, Henry R., 103–5
Roemer, Kenneth, 98n
Rosen, Lew, 46
Rosen v. United States, 46
Rusert, Britt, 112
Rush, Dr. Benjamin, 138n
"R_xe-scription", 4–6

St. Nicholas: A Monthly Magazine for Boys and Girls, 29, 57n
Samuels, Ellen, 6–7, 107–8, 121, 164
Sanger, Margaret, 4, 8, 17, 19, 180, 184, 193n, 194n
    The Birth Control Review, 181
    "What Every Woman Ought to Know", 20
Sargent, Lyman Tower, 55

"The Three Faces of Utopianism Revisited", 98n
SB8, 9
"Heartbeat Bill", 26n
Schaefer, Eric, 149
Schiebinger, Londa, 61n, 138n, 176n
Schull, Andrew, 58n, 61n
Schuller, Kyla
    biological determinism, 30
    The Biopolitics of Feeling: Race, Sex, and Science in the Nineteenth Century, 2, 107, 113
    Lamarckian evolution, 36, 47, 49
    materialisms, 7, 109
    palimpsest, 8, 10, 123
    sentimental biopower, 31, 64n
    "(socio)biological (in)determinism", 57–8n, 133n
    "taxonomy of feeling", 94–5n
    The Trouble with White Women, 113
    unimpressibility, 135n
    Watkins Harper, Frances Ellen, 112, 114, 131
    white feminism, 196n
scientific disorder, 2, 57–8n
Search Lights for Health, 20, 44
seduction narrative, 145–56, 163–4
Seibers, Tobin, 8, 40, 167–8, 177n
    "Disability Experience on Trial", 177n
    "Returning the Social to the Social Model", 62n
Seigworth, Gregory J., 26n
Seitler, Dana, 165–6, 174n, 177n
self-pity, 72
Semonche, John E., 65n
sex education
    Comstock law, 96n
    eugenics, 100n
    Gilman, Charlotte Perkins, 87–8, 135n, 151–2, 155, 173–4n
    Meyer, Annie Nathan, 102, 158–9
    Sanger, Margaret, 193n
sex hygiene films, 141–7

US government sanctioned program, 171n, 172n
see also social hygiene education
sex hygiene films, 141–7
"shadow feminism", 6, 39, 62n
shame, 17, 19, 20, 72–3, 95n, 141, 147, 155–63, 168, 180
Shaw, George Bernard, 149, 164
Sims, J. Marion, 116–17, 135n, 137n, 157–8, 175n, 178, 193n, 194n
Sinclair, Upton, 142, 149, 164, 170n
slavery, 111–20
   anti-VD campaign, 164–5
   race science, 109
   and rape, 114–15, 117, 134n, 194n
   scale of, 140n
   Sims, J. Marion, 193n
   Watkins Harper, Frances Ellen, 75, 102, 106, 128, 130
Smith, William Benjamin, 112, 139–40n
Smith-Rosenberg, Carroll, 58n, 97n, 100–1n
Snyder, Sharon L., 41, 90–1, 96n
   The Matter of Disability: Materiality, Biopolitics, Crip Affect, 11, 92
   Narrative Prothesis: Disability and the Dependencies of Discourse, 76–7
social construction, 6–7, 108–10
Social Darwinism, 114
"social evil", 146–7
social hygiene education
   Alcott, Louisa May, 29–30, 47, 51–2
   Davis, Rebecca Harding, 55
   eugenics, 100n
   Gilman, Charlotte Perkins, 151–2
   Meyer, Annie Nathan, 156–7
   Morrow, Dr. Prince, 172n
   sex hygiene films, 141–7
   see also sex education
social purity movement, 158–9, 161, 175–6n
"(socio)biological (in)determinism", 2, 4–5, 57–8n
Stanton, Elizabeth Cady, 113

stereotypes, 15, 18, 81, 105–6, 111, 118, 139n, 177n, 179–80
sterilization, 153, 172n, 176–7n, 181
Stetz, Margaret D., 77–8
Stone, Andrea, 136n, 147
   Missouri v. Celia, a slave, 114–15
"stories with a purpose", 94n
storytelling, 4–6, 10, 12, 71, 95–6n, 96n, 99n, 127–8
suffrage, 113, 118, 175–6n
suicide, 19, 40, 72, 76, 95n, 184–6
Sumner, John, 18
superposition, 102–40, 132n, 144, 168
Swenson, Kristin, 81, 94n
   Medical Women and Victorian Fiction, 27n
syphilis epidemic, 3, 21, 102, 142–69, 193n
"syphilis of the innocent", 88, 151–2

Tavera, Stephanie Peebles, 135n, 165, 193n
   Legacy: A Journal of American Women Writers, 174–5n
"taxonomy of feeling", 94–5n
TedTalks, 11–12
Tenderloin, Number, Broadway, 46
theater
   live surgical, 178–9
   of lynching, 179–80
   medical, 178–96
third sex, 100–1n
Thomas, T. Gaillard, 157, 175n
Thraillkill, Jane F., 40
   Affecting Fictions: Mind, Body, and Emotion in American Literary Realism, 13, 71–2
Thurner, Manuela, 176n
Time, 146
Tinayre, Marcelle, *La rebelle*, 89–90
Tompkins, Jane, *Sensational Designs*, 13
toxicity, 42–3, 63–4n
trauma, 10, 75, 96n, 106–7, 126–8, 131, 179, 180, 185
   cultural, 84

Tuskegee Syphilis Study, 144, 165
Twain, Mark, 20, 44
"two-sex system", 57n

United States v. Bennett, 45–6
United States v. One Book Called "Ulysses", 46
"unruly women", 59n
unspeakable, 74–5, 163
US News, 146
US Supreme Court, 9
   Griswald v. Connecticut, 24n
"utopia", 55–6, 80–1, 98n, 153, 165, 173–5n

vulnerability, 73–4, 93, 99n, 115, 136n, 141–77

Wald, Priscilla, 144
Walker, A. B., "Let Anthony Comstock's Punishment Fit the Crime" political cartoon, 19
Ward, Dr. Lester, 87
Washington, Harriet A., 134n, 144, 165, 178, 193n
   Medical Apartheid: The Dark History of Medical Experimentation on Black Americans from Colonial Times to the Present, 163–4
Watkins Harper, Frances Ellen, 107, 136–7n
   Iola Leroy, or Shadows Uplifted, 111–20, 132–4n, 139–40n
   "We Are All Bound Up Together", 113
Weber, Moritz, 121

Wegener, Frederick, 3
Weingarten, Karen, 7–8, 16
Werbel, Amy, 18–19, 44, 72, 95n, 102–3, 118, 194n
Wheeler, Lorna Raven, 184
whiteness, 165–6
Whitman, Walt, 20, 44
Wimsatt, W. K., "The Affective Fallacy", 71–2
Wolfe, Cary, 115, 119–20, 136n
   Before the Law, 119–20, 137–8n
Woman's Journal, 65n
"a woman's right to know", 142–3, 152, 160–1
women doctors, 3, 101n
women writers of medical fiction, 20–1, 34, 46–7, 61n, 77, 102–3, 113
Women's Hospital, 157–8, 175n
Wood, Janice, 96n
Woodhull, Victoria, 17, 43
Woolf, Virginia, 72, 96n
Works Progress Administration (WPA), 116–17
World's Columbian Exposition, 103
Wright, Sir Almroth, *The Unexpurgated Case Against Woman Suffrage*, 62n
Wynter, Sylvia, 108, 120, 127, 133n

Yao, Xtine, 83, 90, 106, 112, 117, 132n
yellow fever epidemic, 3, 15, 143
YMCA Committee for the Suppression of Obscene Literature, 19
Young, Ella Flagg, 145

Ziegler, Mary, 135–6n, 172n, 174n

EU representative:
Easy Access System Europe
Mustamäe tee 50, 10621 Tallinn, Estonia
Gpsr.requests@easproject.com